THE RAJ AT TABLE
A Culinary History of the British in India

David Burton is a professional cookery writer living and working in New Zealand. He contributes to a range of magazines and newspapers about world cuisine. *The Raj at Table* was written as a result of exhaustive research which included two trips to India and many interviews.

The Raj at Table

—

A Culinary History of
the British in India

—

DAVID BURTON

faber and faber
LONDON · BOSTON

First published in Great Britain 1993
by Faber and Faber Limited 3 Queen Square London WC1N 3AU
This paperback edition first published in 1994

Printed by Clays Ltd, St Ives plc

A CIP record for this book is available from the British Library
ISBN 0–571–14390–3

2 4 6 8 10 9 7 5 3

Contents

Preface

——

Of all legacies of the Raj, none is more firmly or more happily rooted in British popular culture than curried food.

On every High Street in Britain today, tandoori restaurants, curry houses and Indian takeaways vie with the fish and chip shop and the burger bars. Perhaps there would still be a sprinkling of these eateries had the Raj never existed, but it is certain that today's Indian restaurateurs would never have been so uniformly successful but for the fact that their ancestors embarked upon the task, nearly 400 years ago, of educating the notoriously conservative palates of their English masters. Nowadays, jars of chutneys, pickles and curry powder are seen on every British supermarket shelf, a plethora of Indian cookbooks is available in English, and the specialist Indian food shops throughout the land sell every conceivable ingredient needed to cook Indian food, from tamarind to fresh curry leaves, asafoetida, chickpea flour, basmati rice, bitter melons and garam masala.

This is in sharp contrast to all other spheres of British life, where Indian influence has been minimal, especially in comparison with the British institutions which India herself has found so absorbing – the parliamentary system, the legal system, the bureaucracy, the gentlemen's clubs, the army and the railways. There was a cross-fertilization, but it was largely one way.

India, for example, may have given England polo, the most élitist of all games, but in return received her national sport, cricket. English remains the *lingua franca* in India today, and conversations in Indian languages are studded with English words. On the other hand, less than perhaps 1000 words from the Indian sub-continent have managed to transplant themselves into English, among them chutney, curry, kedgeree, mulliga-tawny, bangle, bungalow, dinghy, khaki, punch, pyjamas, shawl, swastika, thug, verandah and yoga.

Apart from the Brighton Pavilion and Sezincote House (a Mogul-style country mansion in Gloucestershire built in the early 1800s for Sir Thomas Cockerell), there are few examples of Indian-influenced architecture in Britain. In every corner of India, meanwhile, in the hill stations, the towns and the cities, the English visitor will find public buildings – a post office perhaps, or a railway station, council chamber or gentlemen's club – whose stern Victorian Gothic façade realls its equivalent in Huddersfield or Cheltenham.

The 'English' clubs are preserved as if time had stopped dead in 1947, with their billiard tables, wood panelling and stuffed trophies exactly as the sahibs left them. In Britain, the reminders of lost Empire amount to little more than a scattered jumble of keepsakes, in country houses and suburban villas, of sheathed kukris, elephant's foot wastepaper baskets, canes with knobs of beaten Rajasthani silver, trays of Benares brass, and moth-eaten tiger-skin rugs.

Only in the realm of food and cookery do we find the equation so neatly reversed.

In India, the lasting influence of British food has been so negligible it may be summarized as follows: biscuits (packed in solid corrugated cardboard, with brand names like Britannia), second-rate white soda bread, omelettes, and English breakfasts of porridge, boiled eggs, tea, toast and marmalade. Even the dining-room menus of the clubs, which for many years after Independence comprised nothing but English nursery fare, are today beginning to reflect the tastes of their Indian membership. By contrast, from the time the very first seventeenth-century traders sat down with Mogul princes to dine off delicately spiced meats and saffron rice, the story of India's influence on the British diet has been vast, colourful and fascinating.

Acknowledgements

———

A food historian could wish for no better mentor than a proficient librarian with a private passion for cookery.

For me, this was Mr George Jackson, late of Reader Services, the Oriental and India Office collections at the British Library, London. I thank George for the great personal interest he showed in this project, for guiding me through the richest lodes of an India Office cookery collection he himself described as a goldmine, and for unearthing a wealth of obscure and fragmented material I would never otherwise have found. Over time, our professional relationship evolved into friendship, and I thank George for elucidating, in the kitchen of his Notting Hill home, the mysteries of groundnut chop and other 'Afro-Anglo-Indian' delicacies, gleaned from his years in Malawi.

I would also like to thank the librarians at the School of Oriental and African Studies, London, and those at the Indian National Library, Calcutta, who were most helpful and patient. My entry to both libraries was facilitated by Professor W. Willmott of the Department of Sociology, University of Canterbury, Christchurch, New Zealand.

Sincere gratitude is due to Annette Hope, who appealed on my behalf to Raj survivors for information in her food column in *The Scotsman*, and to the many men and women all over the United Kingdom who responded. I especially thank Mrs Eileen Campbell for her detailed answers to my questionnaire, and Lady Mary Hay, MBE, for providing an extensive typescript of culinary memoirs and recipes.

The most hilariously pungent and telling anecdotes of this book were related to me by family friends, a former memsahib and her retired India regimental officer husband, who, for reasons which will be obvious, wish to remain anonymous. I thank them for enlivening the book so wonderfully. I also thank Mr G. P. Stewart of Nelson, New Zealand, for sharing with me his recollections of the food of the Raj; Mrs Enid Lorimer, also of Nelson, for showing me the collections of her late husband; Mr and Mrs E. F. Smith, proprietors of the Fairlawn Hotel, Calcutta, for recounting their memories of the Raj; and the Maharajah of Cooch Behar, for sharing his childhood food memories over a brandy-pani at the Darjeeling Planters Club.

Mr Harish Mukhtar, Superintendent of the West Bengal Tea Development Corporation, showed great kindness in taking me on tours of his tea gardens and factories, outlining the history and development of the Darjeeling tea industry, and arranging access to the library and records of the Darjeeling Gymkhana Club.

On my second research tour of India, Major and Mrs J. H. Wadia, Secretary, The Club, Mahabaleshwar, provided me with rare historical material and much firsthand information. I thank Capt. Lalit Dhawan for his hospitality at the Cricket Club of India, also Lt. Col. (Retd.) V. B. S. Manian, Secretary of the Secunderabad Club and the Secretary of the Royal Bombay Yacht Club, for granting me temporary membership, accommodation, and access to their club libraries and records.

I also thank Caroline Ball for her astute and creative editing, in reducing my unwieldy manuscript to publishable form.

Several extracts from Mrs Isobel Abbott's *Indian Interval* are reprinted with the permission of Barrie & Jenkins Ltd.

Every effort has been made to trace copyright holders (particularly Elizabeth Crawford Wilkin, or her heirs, for permission to quote from *Dekho! The India That Was*) but the author and publisher would be interested to hear from any copyright holder inadvertently overlooked.

Illustrations were kindly supplied by The Mary Evans Picture Library (Chapters 4, 5, 7, 8 and 12) and The India Office at the British Library (Chapters 2, 3, 6, 10, 11 and 14).

Note on Weights and Measures

———

Most of the recipes in this book have been transcribed as they originally appeared. Adapting them to conform with modern cookery-book style would have robbed them of much of their charm: 'a heaped soup spoon of plums', '2 tolahs of channa dhall' or 'line a chatty with buttered plantain leaves' would have lost much in translation. This does not mean the recipes are unworkable. I have tried very many of them in the course of writing this book, with successful and palatable results. A guide to the weights and measures used in Indian bazaars is given below, and it is worth remembering that accuracy was not a prime consideration in a kitchen where spice measures varied with the size of the cook's hand, and the heat of the stove was dependent on the cook's mate's energy in fanning the flames! You may be startled by the large amounts of oil, salt and chillies sometimes called for; just reduce these to whatever seems a reasonable amount.

Throughout the book there are also recipes which have been rendered into modern idiom. These are no less 'authentic', but were either sent to me by men and women who lived in India at the end of the Raj era, or have been updated from older recipes to take into account today's standard weights and measures, food processors and thermostatically controlled ovens. Measurements in these recipes are given in Imperial and metric equivalents; for conversion to cups, see below.

Indian Bazaar Weights

The smallest unit of bazaar weight, used for extremely costly spices such as saffron, was the *masha*. This was equivalent to about ⅛ of a teaspoon, or 19 grains avoirdupois.

Far more common was the *tolah*, a unit still widely used in India today. This originated with the silver rupee of British India, weighing 3 drachms or 180 grains avoirdupois (about 12 g). The coin was accepted as a weight, placed on one tray of the bazaar merchants' hanging scales. In general, 2½ *tolahs* were taken as equal to a British ounce, even though the true conversion was nearer to 2⅓ *tolahs*.

80 *tolahs* made up a *seer*, equal to 1 kg (or 2.2 lb). A *seer* also contained 16 *chittacks*, a unit taken as equal to 2 oz or 60 g.

Conversion to standard US/Australian 8 oz/250 ml cups

LIQUID MEASURES

$\frac{1}{4}$ pt =   5 fl oz (150 ml)   = $\frac{2}{3}$ cup
$\frac{1}{3}$ pt =   8 fl oz (250 ml)   = 1 cup
$\frac{1}{2}$ pt = 10 fl oz (300 ml)   = 1$\frac{1}{4}$ cups
$\frac{3}{4}$ pt = 15 fl oz (450 ml)   = 2 cups
1   pt = 20 fl oz (600 ml)   = 2$\frac{1}{2}$ cups
1$\frac{1}{4}$ pt = 25 fl oz (700 ml)   = 3 cups
1$\frac{1}{2}$ pt = 30 fl oz (900 ml)   = 3$\frac{3}{4}$ cups
2   pt = 40 fl oz (1.2 l)   = 5 cups

SOLID/DRY MEASURES

8 oz (250 g) butter or ghee = 1 cup
8 oz (250 g) flour   = 2 cups
8 oz (250 g) rice or sugar   = 1 cup

Tablespoons

Although the standard tablespoon is different in the United Kingdom, the United States and Australia/New Zealand, it may safely be assumed that *your* tablespoon is the right size. (The standard teaspoon is 5 ml in all countries.)

Coconut milk

The ubiquitous coconut features in many recipes, and 'take the first (or second) milk' is a frequent instruction. This 'milk' is not the watery liquid found inside a coconut, but is extracted from the flesh, first milk being thicker than second. The easiest solution is to use powdered or tinned coconut milk (make sure it is unsweetened), available from many Asian shops. Alternatively, you can make your own by steeping grated flesh (or desiccated coconut) in approximately the same amount of hot water. When cool, strain, squeezing well. Varying the proportions of coconut to water will give you thicker or thinner milk as required.

To
Rama-Swami
(a.k.a. Ramasamy)

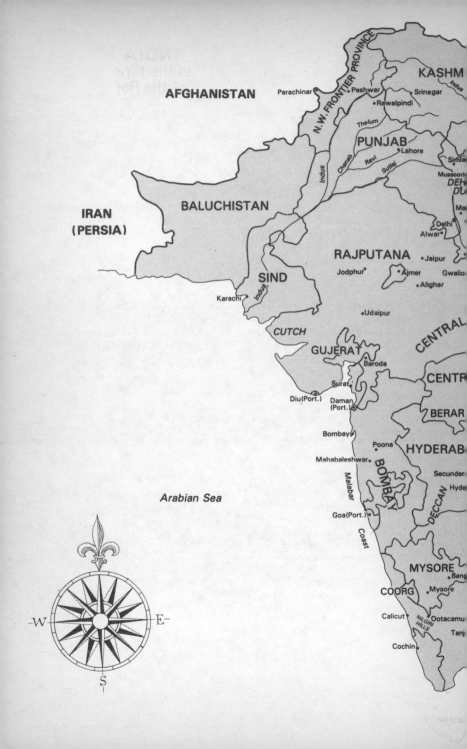

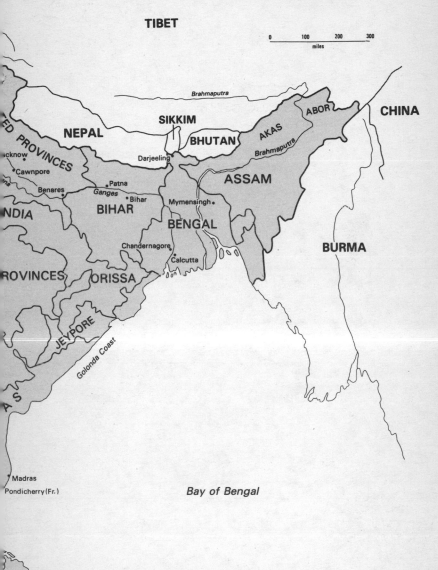

INDIA
at the time
of the Raj

TIBET

CHINA

0   100   200   300
miles

NEPAL

SIKKIM

BHUTAN

ABOR

AKAS

Brahmaputra

ASSAM

Darjeeling

UNITED PROVINCES

cknow

Cawnpore

Benares

Patna

Ganges

Bihar

BIHAR

Mymensingh

NDIA

BENGAL

BURMA

ROVINCES

ORISSA

Chandernagore

Calcutta

JEYPORE

Golonda Coast

AS

Madras

Pondicherry (Fr.)

Bay of Bengal

Trincomalee

Kandy   CEYLON

Colombo

I
Introduction
———

The whiff of spice lured Britain to India.

In 1599 a group of London merchants, flushed both by an emergent spirit of capitalism and by the English victory over the Spanish Armada eleven years earlier, formed the East India Company in the hope, among other things, of driving down the cost of pepper. This had trebled as Portugal attempted to fight off the Dutch challenge to its control of the spice trade, partly from South India but more importantly from the so-called Spice Islands, Java and the Moluccas.

A fleet of armed East India Company ships bearing optimistic names such as *Clove, Peppercorn* and *Trade's Increase* was put to sea, but very quickly ran into Dutch opposition in South-East Asia. This culminated in the beheading of ten company employees on trumped-up charges of conspiracy at Amboyna in the Moluccas in 1623, after which the company decided to retreat to their second choice, India. Here the vast landmass was felt to offer camouflage against attacks on Company trading posts.

Britain's first ship had arrived at Surat, near Bombay, in 1608, but despite a courteous reception from the Emperor Jahangir, the Company could not obtain a trading concession; it was believed the Portuguese were exerting pressure behind the scenes. Four years later, the British had, after holding Indian ships to ransom and thrashing four Portuguese men o'war in a show of sea power, forced Jahangir to reconsider, and in 1612 the first British 'factory' was established at Surat.

This 'factory', and others which followed, were in fact trading posts, collecting indigo dye from Agra and cotton cloth from Gujarat. Portugal continued to control the pepper-growing region inland from the Malabar coast, and only after harassing Portuguese shipping, culminating in the Treaty of Madrid in 1630, did the British receive access to Goa for the loading of spices. In 1640 some land was leased at Madras, while over on the west coast, Bombay was handed over to the Company in 1668, in exchange for a substantial loan to King Charles II. His wife, Catherine of Braganza, had brought the ownership of the seaport six years earlier as part of her dowry.

Finally, there was Calcutta. After years of violent skirmishes, the Mogul emperor Aurangzeb agreed in 1690 to let the Company establish a settlement on the banks of the Hooghly River in Bengal, near a village the locals named Kalikata in deference to their fearsome goddess of death. The name was anglicized into Calcutta, and the settlement very soon gained a reputation as a haven for the unscrupulous and rapacious. In Mogul court circles, it was referred to as 'hell well stocked with bread'.

The death of Aurangzeb in 1707 and the decline of Mogul power which followed paved the way for the expansion in the power of the East India Company. In the meantime, however, the Company had to contend with the French, who in 1746 attacked and took Madras. It was given back again two years later by the French government in return for concessions in North America, but fighting between the French and the British continued elsewhere in southern India, until the French were finally driven out of India following the conquest of Pondicherry in 1761

Much of the East India Company's expansion in India during the eighteenth century was the work of Robert Clive, the swashbuckling general whose defeat of the Nawab of Bengal at the battle of Plassey in 1757 broke the Mogul power in India and laid the foundation of the British Raj.

Having installed a puppet Nawab in Bengal, the Company obtained from the Mogul emperor Shah Alam the licence to collect his imperial revenues there. As long as the Emperor received his dues, the British were allowed to profit from the countryside in any way they liked. Within a dozen years of Plassey, profit margins of 25 per cent were regarded as merely moderate, with the result that the English merchants living in Bengal became fabulously wealthy. These were the nabobs, envied yet despised at home as being rather coarse and ostentatious, and in outward ways quite indianized by the mistresses many of them had adopted.

'Ordinarily we have dopeage and rice, kegeree and pickled mangoes,' wrote one of these nabobs, Peter Mundy. As well as living on Indian food, they used debased vernacular expressions, wore baggy cotton 'Moorman' trousers and banyan coats about the house, smoked hookahs and chewed *pan* and betel nut as an aid to digestion. Most of the men who served as fellow subalterns with Robert Clive, for instance, had their own betel-sets and spittoons.

The first generation of British officials studied Indian classics and Persian, the literary language. They were very much the visitors, too few in number, and too vulnerable to do anything about the aspects of Indian life of which they were secretly critical. In the early nineteenth century, however, indianized habits became yearly more rare in Calcutta. Clothes began to follow the London fashion, and Indian food, while it was still offered in punch houses and taverns as an alternative to plain English fare, was no longer the norm. True, curries were still being offered at dinner parties, but this was more to appease the old hands and eccentrics.

These changes of habit reflected a growing attitude of racial superiority among the British. In 1798, a new governor-general, Lord Wellesley, had nothing but contempt for Indians, and the social atmosphere changed accordingly. Indian mistresses were thrown out as more English women arrived in the British settlements and family life began – isolated islands of England in a sea of India. The arrival of missionaries in the early nineteenth century turned opinion against the 'barbarous' and 'pagan' religions of India, and as the numbers of British residents increased, so did their self-sufficiency as a community and their isolation from the Indians. Such adherence to 'home standards' continued right up until Independence, but was, of course, impossible to enforce completely. Inevitably there was much adapting to local conditions, particularly with regard to food.

It should by no means be assumed, however, that the first British settlers had considered the highly spiced cuisine of India so very outlandish or strange. In 1612, English cooking had itself barely emerged from the Middle Ages, and was still heavy with cumin, caraway, ginger, pepper, cinnamon, cloves and nutmeg. Indeed, spices had for the first time become affordable to all but the poor in England, due to the breaking of the Arab monopoly of the spice trade by the Portuguese a century earlier. So the 'dumpoked' (*dampukht*) fowl that the English merchants were served at their first factory in Surat, stewed in butter and stuffed with spices, almonds and raisins, may have been a recipe that came from the Mogul emperor Akbar's kitchen, but it nevertheless echoed the list of ingredients for an English chicken pie given by Gervase Markham in *The English Hus-wife* in 1615: chicken, currants, raisins, cinnamon, mace, sugar and salt.

In England forks were still not considered proper eating utensils for a gentleman at this time, and the English maintained the medieval custom of scooping food to their mouths with bread sops which they held in their hand – an identical practice to the Indians, both Muslim and Hindu.

The similarities of custom extended even to the spices eaten after a meal as an aid to digestion – in India *pan*, in Britain the voidee, were both ceremonies of handing around spices on elaborate gold or silver trays, or in boxes with compartments for different spices.

Thus, when the gentlemen of the Surat factory were fêted by their Muslim friends, they were probably not merely being polite when they pronounced the pilaus and biriyanis delicious.

These banquets were of such enormous length that coffee was served between courses while the guests' stomachs were given a rest, but even these paled in comparison with a feast given by the Mogul emperor in honour of Thomas Roe, who in 1608 had secured the original permission for the East India Company to begin trading in India. Sir Thomas's secretary, Edward Terry, sets the scene in *A Voyage to East India*:

The Asaph Chan entertained my Lord Ambassador in a very spacious and a beautiful tent . . . kept full of perfume. The floor of the tent was first covered all over with very rich and large carpets . . . and these were covered again with pure white and fine Callico cloths, and all these were covered with very many dishes of silver, but for the greater part of those silver dishes they were not larger than our largest trencher-plates, the brims of them all gilt.

We sat in the large room as it were in a triangle: the Ambassador on Asaph Chan's right hand a good distance from him, and myself below . . . and every one of us had his several mess. The Ambassador had more dishes by ten and I less by ten, than our entertainer had, yet, for my part I had fifty dishes.

They were all set before us at once, and little paths left betwixt them, that our entertainer's servants might come and reach them to us one after another and so they did so that I tasted of all set before me, and of most did but taste, though all of them tasted very well.

Now, of the provision itself, for our large dishes, they were filled with rice dressed. And this rice was presented to us, some of it white, in its own proper colour, some of it yellow, with saffron, and some of it was made green, and some of it was put in purple colour . . . And with rice thus ordered, several of our dishes were furnished; and very many more of them with flesh of several kinds, and with hens and other sorts of fowl cut in pieces, as before observed in their

Indian Cookery. To these we had many jellie and Culices; Rice ground to flour and then boyled and after sweetened with sugar, candy and rosewater to be eaten cold. The flower of rice mingled with sweet almonds, made as small as they could, and with some of the most fleshy parts hens, stewed with it and after, the flesh beaten to pieces, that it could not be discerned, all made sweet with rose-water and sugar candy, and scented with ambergreece which was another of our dishes, and a most lucious one, with the Portuguls call 'Manger Real', food for a king.

Even an everyday meal at the Surat factory was a grand affair. Lunch was then the main meal of the day, breakfast having consisted of little more than 'burnt wine' – wine which had been heated by dropping a red-hot ingot of gold in it. The factors, as the merchants were called, dined in a communal hall, from plates and cups made of pure silver. Both before and after lunch, a servant took around a large silver jug and basin for washing hands.

Padre Ovington, a chaplain who evidently saw no reason to give up the pleasures of the flesh, tells us with great enthusiasm that Indian, Portuguese and English cooks were employed to 'please the curiosity of every palate': everyday dishes included rice pilau, 'cabob' (a goulash-like curry), dumpoke, and plenty of chutneys and relishes, such as 'mango achar and sony sauce'.

Another favourite of those early days was Burdwan stew, a mixture of vegetables, fish, meat and fowl rather like the Spanish *olla podrida*. It took a great deal of time to prepare and, according to Dr Riddell, who wrote the *Indian Domestic Economy and Receipt Book* (1850), was good only if cooked in a silver saucepan:

BURDWUN STEW

Take a roasted or boiled fowl; cut it into pieces, and put them into a silver stewpan; put in two ladlesful of soup, with two dozen anchovies, a glass of white wine, some melted butter, some boiled or roasted onions, pickled oysters, and cayenne pepper; stir and let it warm through, and add a little lemon juice.

When this is prepared on purpose, the fowl or chicken is only half roasted or boiled; if boiled, the water or broth is used to make it instead of the soup.

Fish may be used, and essence of anchovy instead of the fish.

On Sundays and holidays the meal was even more large and splendid with deer and antelopes, peacocks, hares and partridges, Persian pis-tachios, plums, apricots and cherries. All of this was washed down with plenty of Persian Shiraz wine, Spanish sack, English beer and arrack (distilled palm sap) punch.

Albert de Mandelslo, a German nobleman who visited Surat in 1638, tells us that at dinner there were about 'fifteen or sixteen dishes of meat, besides dessert', although meat was sometimes in short supply. While the senior merchants never went without, the juniors had sometimes to content themselves with simple saffron rice and there were compulsory fasts for everybody on Ash Wednesday and Good Friday. The first President even set an example and fasted every Friday. Not that, the Surat Factory records nervously explained, 'our Fasts are as the Romanists', but by Church of England standards they were distinctly ascetic nevertheless. There were communal prayers, confinement to one's room and only a single meagre meal after nightfall.

It was inconceivable that a Muslim ruler should allow the British merchants to produce pork, and when Captain Downton tried to establish an abattoir for cattle, local Hindus bribed the Mogul governor to quash the scheme, so the Surat factors, like most of the British residents who were to settle in areas outside the major cities of India, had to be satisfied with chicken and mutton, supplemented with the occasional piece of game.

After a gargantuan lunch there would be an afternoon siesta, and work would begin again at four, only to finish two hours later for prayers and then supper. This meal was more informal, and on balmy nights the table was often laid out in the garden by the water, where the factors would 'spend an hour or two with a cold collation and a bottle of wine'.

These early accounts of Indian food make no mention of it being hot. The reason is simple: chillies were still too new to the Indian subcontinent to have become widely accepted into the cuisine. Today it seems impossible to imagine Indian food cooked without chillies, yet there is little doubt that they originated in Latin America, and were unknown in India before the Portuguese arrived to establish trading posts in Cochin and Calicut in 1501. There is no Sanskrit name for the chilli pepper and it seems peppercorns were the only 'hot' ingredient in Indian cooking prior to the Portuguese, who are thought to have brought the chilli from the West Indies. By 1542, three separate varieties of chilli were growing in India, mainly on the west coast and especially in Goa. Chillis first became well known in Bombay under the name of *Gowai mirchi* (Goan pepper). According to Clusius in his *Exoticorum* (1605), the chilli pepper was also cultivated in India under the name of Pernambuco pepper.

Other sixteenth-century Portuguese introductions included pineapple, papaya, cashew nut, and tomato, all of which later had a huge impact on the Indian diet.

The British in Calcutta ate huge amounts of every sort of meat, even pork and beef, both roast and curried: 'We were very frequently told in

England, you know, that the heat in Bengal destroyed the appetite,' wrote Eliza Fay in 1780.

I must own that I never saw any proof of that: on the contrary, I cannot help thinking that I never saw an equal quantity of victuals consumed. We dine at two o'clock in the very heat of the day . . . I will give you our own bill of fare . . . a soup, a roast fowl, curry and rice, a mutton pie, a fore-quarter of lamb, a rice pudding, tarts, very good cheese, fresh churned butter, excellent Madeira (that is expensive but the eatables are very cheap).

Stomach disorders, inevitably, were common, but everyone blamed the climate rather than the unsuitability of their diet. The Governor, Phillip Francis, wrote in 1775: 'I am tormented with the bile and obliged to live on mutton chop and water. The Devil is in the climate I think.' One writer noted that six of his friends had all had a severe attack of dysentery, and were blaming the climate. He, however, was unsurprised at their suffering, since after a 'light' tiffin of soup, several kinds of curried meat and generous quantities of beer and sherry, his friends had played cricket for three hours in the heat of the day before repairing to the table for a four-hour dinner. During the hot weather the Calcutta newspapers would carry much-needed warnings not to over-indulge in food and drink – in June 1780 one quoted the case of 'the surgeon of an Indiaman, who fell dead after eating a hearty dinner of beef, the thermometer being 98°'. It was estimated that one third of all hospital cases arose from liver complaints.

The new overland route to India, fully functioning by 1838, and then the opening of the Suez Canal in 1869, considerably speeded up the transit of both goods and ideas from Europe, including the Victorian fashion for French cuisine. The improvement in communications also brought the 'fishing fleet' – young unmarried English women who came out to India for a few months in the cold weather, ostensibly to stay with relatives or friends.

Although the memsahib has been often and perhaps wrongly blamed for introducing a disdain for things Indian, there can be little doubt that she fought strongly against Indian food. A memsahib herself, Eleanor Bobb says that highly spiced food often upset her poor digestion and through ignorance she regarded Indian food as hot and unpalatable. It also gave her a sense of superiority to despise the food of the natives.

The Englishman who had come out long before her had not had a sophisticated palate and had been more or less content to eat anything his Indian cook set before him. In time, he actually got to enjoy highly spiced food. By the late Victorian era, however, a new generation imbued with the notion of the White Man's Burden began to look upon such 'native preparations' as inferior and culturally backward, and French food was now considered the last word in good taste.

In 1878 Colonel Kenney-Herbert, the most entertaining of all Anglo-Indian cookery writers, was declaring in his *Culinary Jottings for Madras*:

Our dinners of today would indeed astonish our Anglo-Indian forefathers. With a taste for light wines, and a far more moderate indulgence in stimulating drinks, has been germinated a desire for delicate and artistic cookery. Quality has superseded quantity, and the molten curries and florid oriental compositions of the olden time – so fearfully and wonderfully made – have been gradually banished from our dinner tables; for although a well-considered curry, or mulligatani – capital things in their way – are still very frequently given at breakfast or at luncheon, they no longer occupy a position in the dinner menu of establishments conducted according to the new regime . . . men of moderate means have become hypercritical in the matter of their food, and demand a class of cooking which was not even attempted in the houses of the richest twenty years ago . . . dinners of sixteen or twenty, thoughtfully composed, are *de rigueur*; our menu cards discourse of dainty fare in its native French.

Colonel Kenney Herbert spent thirty-two years as a cavalry officer in southern India, in somewhat spartan conditions at some antiquated and rundown barracks in the garrison town of Secunderabad near Hyderabad, with extended periods in Bangalore, and later at Madras. This was where much of what later became *Culinary Jottings for Madras* was written, as a series of articles for the *Madras Mail*, under the pen name of Wyvern.

Around the turn of the century he returned to England and embarked on a full-time retirement career as a cookery writer, publishing articles on food, household management and fine dining in the nineteenth century, as well as writing five further books: *Fifty Breakfasts, Fifty Luncheons, Fifty Dinners, Vegetarian and Simple Diet* and *Commonsense Cookery*. The last concided with his founding of the Commonsense Cookery Association in London, with a cookery school attached to its premises in Sloane Street.

As the name of his association suggests, the Colonel was opposed to the worst excesses of Edwardian cookery, with its over-ornamentation, dependence on ready-made sauces and flavourings, and use of fancy colourings. In his advocacy of simplicity in ingredients, cooking and dishing up, he strikes a remarkably modern note.

Colonel Kenney-Herbert was a voice in the wilderness, however, as this overblown fare was precisely what was demanded of the Indian cook of the era. Faced with this task, without proper ingredients or any real tuition, and using primitive charcoal stoves with rudimentary implements, in a hot humid climate (which made the task of pastry making, for instance, almost impossible), it is little wonder that what the Indian cook produced fell somewhat short of classic French cuisine.

The many entrées, savouries and other new courses that appeared in the late Victorian and Edwardian eras were usually bad imitations of French cuisine disguised with a great deal of gaudy decoration, for which the Indian cook had a particular weakness. Especially popular was presenting food in anything but its original form, such as mashed potatoes in the shape of a bird or a motor car with little lights.

This type of cooking persisted right up until the last days of the Raj, and can still be found to some extent on the non-vegetarian menus of the 'British Clubs' of India today. Elizabeth Crawford Wilkin has a hilarious account of one such meal in the 1930s. (The British sahibs and memsahibs, especially in Bengal, came to be called *qui hai*, after the Urdu expression they constantly used for summoning a servant.)

Mrs Comet-Dane and the Brigadier were the first of the Qui-Hais to invite us to dine with them.

The Comet-Danes were the senior Qui-Hais of the station, the Brigadier having retired some years before, at which time they decided to live on in India rather than return to an England with which they had long since lost touch.

Their narrow driveway had been designed for carriages, so we were obliged to leave our motor and Ramaswami at the main gate. A ragged chokidar (watchman) holding a butthi (oil lantern) was stationed there. In Hindustani (for no good Qui-Hai would dream of employing an English-speaking servant) he warned us to guard against all things that crawl, and led us at a mournful pace to his master's bungalow, where we were welcomed by our hosts. Mrs Comet-Dane was resplendent in an ancient and voluminous black satin gown. A broad strap of the same material was looped over her left wrist, the other end of which was sewn to the hem of her train. The Brigadier, a rather frail but still handsome old gentleman, was tall and thin with white wavy hair which he wore longer than the present day fashion. His high turned-up collar was secured by a well-tied black silk stock.

There were eight other guests, six of them men, and when the last had arrived cocktails were served — mixed vermouth with an excess of Italian. For some curious reason the rims of the glasses had been dampened and subsequently dipped in bright red granulated sugar, a portion of which was immediately transferred to our faces.

When we had completed this sanguinary transformation we were led to the dining room where we were confronted by a long table in the centre of which was a fantastic arrangement of coloured rice. Thousands of small grains, dyed the most flagrant hues conceivable, were laid on the white cloth in the pattern of a flower basket, from which sprang in ricey splendour exotic blue roses, green zinnias, black corn flowers and pink golden rod.

When I could tear my reluctant eyes from this startling masterpiece, I observed at the place of each guest a small dish containing a raw egg removed from its shell. I was consumed with curiosity to know its purport and glanced furtively at Philip, who harbours an intense aversion to an uncooked egg. As the meal progressed I learned that it was to be turned into one's hot soup. I congratulated my husband on his poker face as he gallantly fell into line. When the fish arrived each piece appeared as a brown and arid island, segregated from its sister by a red and turbulent sea. We shortly discovered this body of water to be mashed potatoes dyed in beet juice!

By the time I had eaten purple carrots and red brussels sprouts I felt prepared for any eventuality, but the arrival of the iced pudding left me shaken and exhausted of surprise. It was served on a tray in what appeared to be a large blue Wedgwood china bowl of the most delicate texture and exquisite colouring. To my alarm, Mrs Comet-Dane took a fork and spoon and, raising them simultaneously a few inches into the air, brought them smartly down into the sides of the bowl breaking it into several pieces. That it was made of spun sugar had not occurred to me!

When the coffee was brought I was inured against anything that might present itself and was not surprised to see that, intead of being contained in a pot or percolator, it was spread on a wooden tray! The coffee beans were laid in a little pile; near them were a few cloves, twelve lumps of sugar, a glass of Kümmel, one of brandy, one of Benedictine, and one filled with the juice of half an orange. Our Qui-Hais had apparently forgotten, or perhaps ignored, the fact that three of their guests were total abstainers from alcohol. Mrs Comet-Dane, without consulting the tastes of anyone, tossed all these ingredients together with a quantity of water into a chafing dish which stood over a spirit lamp, and we were given no option to drinking the resulting mixture.

Elizabeth Crawford Wilkin was the last of a long line of authors who wrote so evocatively of their food experiences in India. Perhaps understandably, most tended to be women, such as Eliza Fay, a dressmaker and wife of a not particularly successful lawyer, who reached Calcutta in 1780, or Fanny Parkes, the incessantly curious wife of a Collector in the interior who took the trouble to become fluent in Hindi.

A generation later came Flora Annie Steel. Arriving in 1867, she proceeded to carve out a career as an architect, educationist and a writer, on top of being a wife and mother. At the age of twenty-nine, she had designed the town hall for a small place in the Punjab, and when she and her husband moved, she was presented with a brooch inlaid with jewels, every one of which had been taken from brooches belonging to local Punjabi wives. Everywhere she went, she opened schools for bazaar children, totally secular even though she herself was a devout Christian. Her efforts were eventually recognized by the Government, who appointed her Inspector for Female Schools for the whole region of modern Pakistan between Peshawar and the Punjab.

Her books included novels, an autobiography and an ambitious history of India, but the work for which she is best remembered is *The Complete Indian Housekeeper and Cook*, which earned her the reputation of the Mrs Beeton of British India. Written after twenty-two years of running households in India, it was enormously successful, running to ten editions.

The men who wrote about food generally only did so in passing. They include William Hickey, the Irish lawyer, gossip and man about town, whose massive nine-volume memoirs were compiled by Edward Spencer, and an army engineer, George Franklin Atkinson, whose *Curry and Rice on Forty Plates* paints such a vivid portrait of a fictional English station in the *mofussil*. There were, however, notable exceptions, such as Colonel Kenney-Herbert and the devoutly Christian Mr G. H. Cook, proprietor of a lime works near Agra, who around 1904 published *The English-Indian Cookery Book*.

Another Indian Army man with a life-long interest in food was Sir Francis Colchester-Wemyss. In *The Pleasures of the Table*, he recalls being grounded in cooking in a hard school – Eton: 'If he [the author] blacked his fagmaster's toast, or set before him porridge insufficiently cooked, he probably received seven strokes with a wire toasting fork; while an egg hard-boiled, or scrambled eggs spoilt by over cooking, meant at least ten.' On another occasion, he was forced to smuggle an illicitly caught perch back to his room curled around inside his top hat!

Destined for a life in the army, Colchester-Wemyss was sent off to France at the age of seventeen, so as to acquire some material to enable him to pass into Sandhurst. While in Versailles he lived with an elderly retired schoolmistress, who taught him, besides a good deal of small dish cooking, how to make an omelette and coffee. After voyages around the world in HMS *Euphrates*, he arrived in India in about 1890 aboard the troopship *Malabar*. He spent several years in India, much of it in remote regions, and in 1894 he was given charge of three rest camps, about 150 miles apart, which he had to visit once a week.

His adventurous spirit took him all over the world – eating ostrich eggs in South Africa, fishing for trout in New Zealand, dining on *bêche de mer* soup in Australia, savouring avocado in Panama. Like his mentor

Colonel Kenney-Herbert, Sir Francis spent his retirement attempting to reform eating habits back home. To this end, he wrote *The Pleasures of the Table*. Published in 1931, its opening chapter is headed 'The Sadness of Ordinary English Cooking', while in his chapter on curries, he thunders that '98½ per cent of the curries one comes across are best avoided – so-called curry is generally hashed mutton with a proportion of vague half-raw curry powder in the moist part, served with sodden rice.'

It was due, indeed, to the zeal of Colchester-Wemyss, through his writings and his lectures at colleges and institutions, that the English public of the 1930s began to beware of curry powders adulterated with flour, and to discover the delights of imported mango chutneys, Bombay ducks and poppadums.

2

Life and Society

Eighteenth-century social life in England is remembered for Hogarth's Gin Lane, cockfights, bear-baiting, whoring, gambling and devotion to the pleasures of the table. In Calcutta, such extravagance and licence was being carefully imitated by a rising merchant class, the nabobs. Fabulously wealthy, but with few unmarried women and little organized entertainment available to them, it is little wonder that boredom frequently drove the nabobs to even greater heights of indulgence in food and drink. English newcomers to Bengal of that time were shocked by the grossness of even the women's appetites. Disgusted at seeing one of the prettiest girls in Calcutta eat two pounds of mutton chops at a sitting, the satirist 'Quiz' went on to write about officers who:

> March to barracks where with joy
> Their masticators they employ
> On curry, rice, and beef and goat
> Voraciously they cram each throat

At meals guests threw chickens across the table, a habit the women joined in with when sufficiently drunk on cherry brandy, although they threw only bread and pastry and thought this 'the refinement of wit and breeding'. William Hickey describes an incident at a party given by Daniel Barwell which turned this custom sour:

In this party I first saw the barbarous custom of pelleting each other, with little balls of bread made like pills, which was even practised by the fair sex. Some people could discharge them with such force as to cause considerable pain when struck in the face. Mr Daniel Barwell was such a proficient that he could at the distance of three or four yards snuff a candle, and that several times successively.

This strange trick, fitter for savages that polished society, produced many quarrels, and at last entirely ceased from the following occurrence: A Captain Morrison had repeatedly expressed his abhorrence of pelleting, and said that if any person struck him with one he should consider it intended as an insult and resent it accordingly. In a few minutes after he had so said he received a smart blow in the face from one which, although discharged from a hand below the table, he could trace by the motion of the arm from whence it came, and saw that the pelleter was a very recent acquaintance. He therefore, without the least hesitation, took up a dish that stood before him and contained a leg of mutton, which he discharged at the offender, and with such well-directed aim that it took place upon the head, knocking him off his chair and giving him a severe cut upon the temple. This produced a duel, in which the unfortunate pelleter was shot through the body, lay upon his bed for many months, and never perfectly recovered. This put a complete stop to the absurd practice.

The atmosphere in both Bombay and Madras, however, was quite different. Both these settlements remained backwaters, while out in the remote wastes of the *mofussil*, as the rural districts were collectively – and disparagingly – called, things trailed even further behind. As late as the 1860s the traveller J. Kinney, author of *Old Times in Assam* (1896), witnessed a bread pelleting incident at a breakfast to celebrate the opening of the Assam railway, while his description of dinner in Tezbrusaugar would easily have fitted a sleazy Calcutta punch house of the previous century:

Oh! that dinner; shall I ever forget it? A table that had once been varnished, – teak wood I should think as far as I could judge through the encrusted dirt of ages that coated it, – three or four odd plates (two of them soup-plates) of the violent blue, yellow and red pattern sometimes seen in kitchens, a yellow greasy mass – or mess – of curry in a slop bowl, and a gritty heap of half-husked rice in a dish; sundry very brassy spoons and forks floating around and penetrating all through other flavours, the (to me) disgusting odour of the huka which the mem-sahib (who sat at table with us) had indulged in a few final whiffs of just before dinner, to give her an appetite. The plate placed in front of me had apparently not been washed since it was made. The memories of a past decade of breakfasts and dinners hung solidly to its sides. In a weak moment I ventured to remark, – 'Mr Ribiera, would you mind asking your servant just to wipe this plate a little'. He laughed, – a great oily, jovial laugh: I must admit he is a genial sort, according to his lights. 'Ar-reh! man,' said he, 'you're very particular. You soon get used to this kind of khannah when you stop longer in Tezbrusaugar.' Then he turned to his khansamah – a Bengali coolie apparently – promoted from the lines I have since heard, on account of a family connection; and said something. Whereupon the man took my plate; looked at it sideways in the light of the oil-lamp to find out what I objected to; and finally, picking up a corner of his nether garment – dhoti I have heard it called – gave the plate a dry rub with that fearful weapon, and clumped it down before me with a grunt, as much as to say 'I hope you are satisfied now'.

The missionaries who inhabited these outlying areas were perhaps the most frugal of all. Many were too preoccupied with their work to be unduly bothered by what they ate, and there are accounts of their bread being green before a new batch came in. The nephew of a missionary named Swartz describes the fare at his house in Tanjore:

He rose at five, breakfasted at six or seven on a basin of tea made in an open jug, with hot water poured on it, and some bread cut into it. One half was for himself, the other for me. The meal lasted not five minutes. He dined on broth and curry very much as the natives. He never touched wine, except one glass on a Sunday.

The eminently more class-conscious clergymen of the Church of England who were posted to these remote stations, however, had a completely different attitude, neatly satirized by George Franklin Atkinson in his *Curry and Rice on Forty Plates* in the character of the Rev. Josiah Ginger:

He considers that the duties of the pastor may well be enlivened by the sports of the field; and that creeds and confectionary, doctrines and devilled kidneys, spirituality and sociability, may consistently run hand in hand, while hams and hermetically-sealed delicacies are not entirely irreconcilable with heavenly-mindedness. And we must confess it, that the combinations are effected with striking and satisfactory results, as we find that the salad of the Saturday, as manufactured by 'Our Padre' at mess, in no way clashes with the sermon of the Sunday.

For those who could afford it, tinned and dried European provisions provided a relief from the meagre monotony of the *mofussil* diet of chicken and rice, ship's biscuits, home-made porridge and gritty chapatis made from wheat ground on stones. Unless the Europeans banded together to form a mutton club (see page 144) very often the only meat available would be chicken – and even regular supplies of that were not available in up-country cantonments until the last decades of the eighteenth century. The only compensation was that chicken, and indeed most food, was generally much cheaper than in the cities.

A common custom at remote stations was to invite guests to come to a large dinner party 'camp fashion'. That is, they brought their own servants, plates, cutlery, glasses and sometimes even their own chairs. 'Ex-civilian' (an anonymous army officer) writes in *Life in the Mofussil* (1868):

It was amusing to see three pretty girls, daughters of an indigo planter of a remote part of the district, drinking champagne out of three pint pewters, which they had brought with them as safer than glass. They were clearly accustomed to 'camp fashion'. Nevertheless, the supper was probably more enjoyed than if it had been supplied in the best style by Gunter.

Camp-fashion arose because the length of stay at these remote settlements was uncertain, and people who moved around a lot did not want to be encumbered by possessions.

Naturally there was always the elderly bachelor who would have none of these makeshift arrangements, and insisted on sitting down to an immaculately laid table every night in a dinner jacket, even if he were on tour in a rough tent. Sir Francis Colchester-Wemyss tells of one such fellow, a Colonel Boughey, in an out-of-the-way spot called Hoshunga-bad in 1894:

He was a wonderful epicure and was blessed with a marvellous Genoese cook; every night of his life, whether in his bungalow or in camp in the district, he dressed in proper evening dress and sat down, nearly always by himself (his district was about the size of Wales, and there were not a dozen white men in it) to a dinner which would have been hard to beat in London or Paris. He was most hospitable, and I had a standing invitation to dine every time I visited my rest-camp at Hoshungabad. Colonel Boughey certainly did himself well – I remember, for instance, that caviar from the Caspian reached him once a week all through the cold weather.

Another such character, though earlier and more famous, was the Comte de Boigne. Born in 1751 at Chambéry, he was forced into exile at the age of seventeen after having killed a Piedmontese noble in a duel. At one time he was a lover of Catherine the Great of Russia, who tired of him after a while and sent him off to the Turkish war. He was captured at Tenedos and sold as a slave in Istanbul, later freed only to be recaptured by Arabs when his ship foundered off the coast of Palestine. Having charmed his captors sufficiently to get them to pay his passage to Alexandria, he proceeded to India. Scindia, the effective Regent of the Mogul Empire, made him head of some forces with which he scattered the Rajput armies and made Scindia the most powerful ruler in India. De Boigne lived at a remote spot called Alighar with his Persian princess wife, and entertained any passing Europeans in great style, including Mr Twining in 1799:

Dinner was served at four. It was much in the Indian style; pilaws and curries, variously prepared, in abundance; fish, poultry and kid. The dishes were spread over a large table fixed in the middle of the hall, and were, in fact, a banquet for a dozen persons, although there was no one to partake of it but the General and myself.

The hour of this meal is significant, for it represents the halfway point in a gradual transition of dinner from noon to the evening, a trend which began in the closing years of the eighteenth century and continued throughout the nineteenth. In 1798 Lord Wellesley reported that the dinner hour was 5 p.m., while by 1830 a Mrs Pringle tells us it was 6.30 p.m. In 1846 Mrs Clemons, an army major's wife, informs us that 7 o'clock is 'a very usual time', and by the 1930s the hour had crept up to 8.30 p.m. Lady Mary Hay, an army doctor's wife in the Sind in the 1930s, in a letter to me says the 8.30 p.m. dinner hour gave one time to bath and change after perhaps a game of tennis.

As late as the 1770s, breakfast in India had consisted only of tea and toast, but by the early nineteenth century it had become a huge meal of meat, fish and fowl in order to compensate for the later dinner hour. Tiffin, which in the early nineteenth century replaced the midday dinner and was described by Captain Thomas Williamson in his *East India Vade Mecum* as 'a little avant dinner', was taken at one or two o'clock, a time which remained unchanged right up until Independence. Supper, which had been substantial when the dinner was taken early, now became little more than a snack.

Predictably, the more reactionary *qui hais* steadfastly refused to fit in with the new arrangements, and one reads of a few old ladies of Calcutta who would take pride in having their dinner in the afternoon and receiving visitors in the evening, rather than between 11 a.m. and 2 p.m. as was the new custom. This persisted until the early 1900s, when the habit of calling between 4 p.m. and 6 p.m. came into existence.

Even more significant than the change in dinner hour was a change in the nature of the food itself. Throughout the nineteenth century, Indian food became increasingly rare at dinner, whether for entertaining or for the family, and was relegated instead to more informal breakfasts and lunches.

Plain roast and boiled meats, often in obscene amounts, became ever more common at early nineteenth-century dinner parties. Emma Roberts, whose *Scenes and Characteristics of Hindostan* appeared in 1835, points out that most Anglo-Indians had left England too young to have lost their schoolboy relish for plain hearty fare, and that more sophisticated newcomers were usually too timid to fight the local custom for 'tables groaning beneath the weight of the feast'. Nevertheless, she continued, the Indians were excellent cooks and 'might easily be taught the most delicate arts of cuisine', if only Anglo-Indians would give up the notion that they could not do anything beyond their pilaus.

For these, or some other equally absurd reasons, made dishes form a very small portion of the entertainment given to a large party, which is usually composed of, in the first instance, an overgrown turkey (the fatter the better) in the centre, which is the place of honour; an enormous ham for its vis-a-vis; at the top of the table appears a sirloin or round of beef; at the bottom a saddle of mutton; legs of the same, boiled and roasted, figure down the sides, together with fowls, three in a dish, geese, ducks, tongues, humps, pigeon-pies, curry and rice of course, mutton-chops and chicken-cutlets. Fish is of little account, except for breakfast, and can only maintain its post as a side-dish . . . There are no entremets, no removes; the whole course is put on the table at once, and when the guests are seated, the soup is brought in.

The army, with its innate conservatism, resisted any attempts to introduce 'fancy' cooking into the mess. Sir Francis Colchester-Wemyss recalled that very early in his career, as the junior of the three officers forming the mess committee of his battalion, he set out with great enthusiasm to improve his *khansamah*'s repertoire, by translating recipes from Audot's book, *La Cuisinière de la campagne et de la ville* into Hindi, long before he was proficient in the language. 'It was a worse than thankless task, because almost inevitably the first try was a failure, and then the mess president would curse me and my misbegotten zeal, and ordain that such a bloody mess was never again to appear.'

The regimental mess was a nineteenth-century development; originally the East India Company's regiments had none, as each company was granted only 120 rupees for the mess, and each officer had to provide his own chair, crockery and cutlery. In some regiments the individual officer had had to look after his own catering arrangements completely, but it eventually became the custom for each officer in turn to host the others at dinner, with the invitation usually extending to the following day's breakfast and tiffin also. The messing system was established by General Orders of 8 May 1808, and in the early days a *banian* was contracted to provide meals at a fixed rate per head.

The food served at mess dinners was generally fairly indifferent in quality but very elaborate in its service. The officers would assemble in their dress jackets and skin-tight trousers, and march in order of rank into the mess, in which were kept the hallowed regimental colours and the silver plate.

Invariably the meal began with what was called 'first toast' – a sardine or perhaps half a hard-boiled egg on a piece of leathery toast, followed by tinned fish or perhaps a pilau. The main course would be a roast, accompanied by Yorkshire pudding if it were beef, or perhaps an Irish stew or beef olives. Puddings were in the heavy British tradition of bread and butter puddings, steamed puddings, rice or sago puddings, or stewed fruit. The meal ended with another small savoury, known as the 'second toast', a custom only followed nowadays on club or formal menus.

On guest nights the regimental silver, often quite historic and valuable, would be laid out and wine would be drunk. An everyday meal would be accompanied by water, but at the end the port (or madeira and/or marsala) would be passed around the table. Nobody could light up their cigars or cheroots until the senior officer had done so, nor leave the table before he did.

For the British other ranks the fare was notoriously meagre. In the days of the East India Company army, the men at Madras had to pay for their own provisions while in garrison. In the field, the company paid for an unvaried daily ration of mutton, biscuit and rice, of which Clive himself took a cut for some years, eventually making £40,000 out of it.

Conditions were little better for the regular British and Indian armies, despite Sidney Blanchard's claim in *Yesterday and To-Day in India* (1867) that 'the condition of the British soldier in India has immensely improved . . . his food rendered more wholesome by variety and better cookery; his drink regulated by sanitary considerations.' Even in the twentieth century, it was a frequent complaint among the ranks that they were forced to spend all their money supplementing their diet to stave off malnutrition. There was always a stream of camp followers eager to fill the demand, and hawkers would parade around the barrack rooms selling ham, butter, milk, eggs, cakes and sweets. The stews and rice puddings fed to troops on train journeys were often of such low quality and so tainted with smoke that they were hardly eaten, and given away to beggars and dogs.

In the nineteenth century, curry for breakfast was common. 'You will be soon used to the curry,' Mrs Clemons cheerfully assured the prospective army wife, 'which, when it is not made too hot, is a most wholesome dish, and on a march is eaten for breakfast, as you cannot get bread.' This was also an East Indiaman tradition, and one which later spread to the the merchant navy, where a curry, different for each morning of the week, would be served between the porridge and the bacon and eggs.

For the troops in India, curry had been dropped as a breakfast item by the 1930s, in favour of the more usual porridge, fried liver, steak and onion, and sausages (perhaps Poona sausages, whose recipe included ginger and cayenne). Curry would still be served once or twice a week for lunch, however, and indeed regimental curry lunches are still a feature of mess life today.

In the interwar years, when Indians became accepted into the higher echelons both of the defence services and the Administration, a certain mingling of cultures, and thereby of foods, took place. The final acceptance of the food and other aspects of Indian culture took place during the Second World War, with the huge influx of British troops who had not time to acquire the traditional prejudices of the old colonials.

3

Hospitality

When a traveller by the name of Hampton was entertained in the 1870s by the proprietor of the largest indigo estate in lower Bengal,

hardly any luxury to be had in England was wanting, while the numerous native dishes, and the turbaned line of servants (each guest bringing his own) gave a most imposing look to the meal. Here he tasted, at breakfast, the real 'Nawabee Pillaw' – rice, butter, almonds, raisins, and spices, piled up in fascinating confusion over a tender joint of lamb or pair of well-fed chickens. Cutlets, done to a turn, of the splendid Biktee and Ruhoo fish, invoked him by their crispy brownness to eat them. For the first time in his life did he find wild ducks so common that a savoury stew was made of their breasts only, sliced fine in a gravy the secret of which the old Khansamah (butler) would not divulge for untold gold. Here the plump quail and still plumper little ortolan afforded gentle amusement after the graver labours of the table, while the piquant Bombay duck (a kind of dried fish) gave zest to the vintages of Lafite or La Rose.

Such a grand feast was dubbed a *burra khanah*. They were usually celebrations to record an important domestic event, such as a birthday, christening or wedding anniversary.

The cold season was the time for dinner parties. They were given in the hot weather as well, but generally ended early and were looked on as unavoidable afflictions. From November to March, however, everyone made up for the discomfort of the hot months. Government House balls, the Viceroy's private parties and all the great official receptions took the first rank, then came the military and private balls, each vying with the other in providing the finest music and most lavish suppers.

The only way a newcomer might expect dinner invitations was to observe the curious Anglo-Indian custom of going around the whole settlement to drop his visiting card in the little black box set outside each bungalow for the purpose.

Emerald Cunard once received a letter from Lord Curzon, which contained an invitation to dinner but also a second note which must have been slipped into the envelope by mistake, as it was obviously intended for another woman. It began: 'My beautiful white swan. I long to press you to my heart . . .'

While some British in India were doubtless able to regard giving dinners as a simple pleasure to be enjoyed for its own sake, in a society which placed so much stress on hierarchy and protocol, the dinner party more often turned into an awesome ritual, offered out of duty and frequently considered something of an ordeal. It was the perfect opportunity for a display of the all-important order of precedence: before entering the dining room, a procession would form, at the head of which would be the host and the most senior lady present. Her husband would accompany the mistress of the house, and the other guests followed in order of seniority. Each guest's seat would be indicated with a place-card. At dinner, the senior lady would sit at the right hand side of the host, and the hostess would have the senior man on her right. For ladies, the etiquette was to talk first to the man on the right and then the man on the left, and to open conversations but never to close them.

An essential handbook for any hostess was *The Warrant of Precedence*, ten pages of closely printed information which enabled her to work out where, for instance, an Inspector of Smoke Nuisances should be seated in relation to a Junior Settlement Officer.

Early in the nineteenth century there was a spate of bitter debate as to precedence. Two or three questions had to be sent home for final adjudication, and the wives of some senior Indian Civil Service officials were mortified to learn that they were not entitled to take the place of the wife of a younger brother of an English noble.

Right up until Independence the order of seating continued to be observed even at quite informal parties, and anybody who flouted it could be certain of a sharp rebuke. A former memsahib told me that at one of the first dinner parties she went to, dinner was announced and she walked gaily in with her host, the Colonel. Later, when she was in one of the bedrooms powdering her nose, one of the older women remarked: 'I realize you have not been in this country very long, but will you remember for future reference that single women do not go into dinner before married ladies.'

At her very first dinner party the memsahib had been saved embarrassment by her bearer: 'I told him to put out my blue linen frock. Later, however, I discovered he had not put it out at all. I asked him why, and he replied that my hostess that evening would be wearing her second-best evening dress, and so he had put out my second-best evening dress as well. The servants knew everything that was going on!'

The last word on the order of precedence belongs to the Governor who, at a formal dinner at Government House, found himself flanked on both sides by the wives of recently knighted husbands, each of whom considered herself superior to the other. Finally, the wife seated on his left could bear the indignity no longer. 'I suppose in a place of this size it is difficult to know sometimes just how to place people at table,' she commented.

'Not at all,' His Excellency suavely retorted. 'You see, the people who matter don't mind, and the people who mind don't matter!'

Some, such as the fictional magistrate in George Atkinson's *Curry and Rice on Forty Plates*, had a subtle ulterior motive for giving dinner parties:

In social life Chutney entertains extensively; and uncommonly pleasant parties he gives, which the extra-intelligent declare are given for the general patronizing effect which they are designed to produce, and for a more effectual exhibition of the silver plate.

Atkinson's book was subtitled 'The ingredients of social life at "Our Station" in India', and in a later chapter he draws a cruel but undoubtedly accurate picture of the desperation of some of these social gatherings:

There, now, an invitation to dinner! – to a 'Burrah Khanah', literally a grand feed; one of the periodical explosions for which the Byles are celebrated, as it gratifies simultaneously the animal appetites of the guests and the sociable propensities of Mrs Byle, who prefers these wholesale entertainments, these general amalgamation spreads, as productive of a great amount of effect.

Byle, as you are aware, is a gunner, and commands the Cow Battery. A jolly fellow is Byle; a terrific sportsman, always prowling about the ravines after tigers, and sitting up all night, perched upon crazy structures of bamboo, lying in wait for leopards, bears, hyenas, and such-like small game. Mrs Byle is a splendid rider, and ready for any fun, thinks nothing of her five-and-twenty miles before breakfast, and would go into action with the guns as soon as take her evening canter.

Delightful people the Byles! But the truth must be told: these grand spreads are cruelly ponderous, and indigestible to the feelings – those awful periods between the heats – that stifling room, with the incense of savoury meats (which lie in hecatombs on the table) hanging about like a London fog, which the punkah fails to disperse.

But stay; the company have assembled – there they are, ranged in a semicircle with a formidable degree of precision . . . awaiting the advent of dinner with silent expectancy.

Byle has sallied forth, for the fifteenth time at least, to expedite the movements of the table attendants, and fearful threats of summary vengeance are floated into our ears . . .

But the dinner is at last, fairly set going; the host and hostess occupy their respective centres of the table, while the top and bottom, with their appalling concomitant consequences of turkey and ham to carve, are studiously shunned, and become the refuge for the Griff [junior newcomer to India], who in this sphere of action imbibes his earliest lessons in carving.

But the time would fail me to tell of how the feast progresses; indefatigable are the slaves in catering for their master's wants, and eager in the pursuit of the choicest dishes, and vigorous in their contests for the cool champagne – which limpid beverage has had the charm of rousing dull echoes; for now the conversation flows apace. Chumach, the Griff, dissects the turkey, but consigns a pound and a half of the stuffing into the velvet lap of the adjoining Mrs Koofter; the flounce of the punkah becomes partly disengaged, and, after flapping about remorselessly like an unreefed sail in a gale of wind, succeeds in whisking off the protecting wire-gauze top of the lamp, and launching it on the apex of Miss Goley's head, occasioning the blowing-out of the lamp, and the consequent oleaginous effluvium that proceeds from the expiring wick, to the general discomposure of the nasal organs. Then the punkah has to be stopped to undergo reparation; and frantic and awful is the heat that is engendered thereby.

Then, after an interregnum of considerable duration, the second course is produced, succeeded by a pause more fearful than before.

The sweets have vanished, and at last the dessert, indicative of a concluding climax; the decanters are circulated, and the fair hostess telegraphs to the 'Burra Beebee' [senior lady] the signal for departure, and a move (in the right direction) is made.

Then the gentlemen are doomed to a further session, which terminates in the production of coffee, when the gong tells its tale of midnight. The piano is heard in the adjoining room; some faint voice warbles a doleful strain, the 'Burra Beebee' rises, and a general dispersion ensues.

In the *mofussil* there was a tradition that the senior lady 'dined the station' once a year at least, inviting every senior official in her husband's district. Emma Roberts paints a rather dismal picture of these occasions.

These station-dinners, as they are called, . . . are the dullest things imaginable when composed of some eight or ten individuals, who have nothing on earth to say to each other when they meet . . .

There is nothing so fatiguing as ennui; at nightfall, it would have been much more agreeable to prepare for bed than to sit upon the chubootur, or terrace, in expectation of guests, from whose conversational powers little pleasure could be anticipated; and frequent repetition had diminished the amusement at first derived from the absurdity of making a formal and state affair of a meeting between persons located in the same wilderness, and whose happiness might so much have been increased by a more rational method of spending their time. At the hour prescribed . . . these votaries of fashion began to arrive; carriage after carriage drove up to the door, until the whole council of ten were fairly set down from their respective vehicles; the ladies dressed in ball attire, and the men uncomfortable in the prospect of being obliged to sit with their feet under instead of on the table, without due allowance of cigars . . . The dinner of course was dull, the conversation confined to those commonplace topics which may well be agreeable to a family party, but which offer lenten entertainment to a formal circle. After a few hours, wasted in vain attempts to amuse people who belong to the most difficult class in the world, a sort of universal joy takes place at the separation; the guests are glad to go, the hosts are glad to see them depart; they have been defrauded of a comfortable sleep; they rejoice that a disagreeable duty had been performed, and that a considerable period will elapse before they shall think themselves called upon to perform it again.

Conversation at these station dinners only became animated when a passing stranger happened to be present. Otherwise it might degenerate into pure cattiness, as a former memsahib recalls:

I used to get up at 5 a.m. and go riding with the Brigadier. This all went well until I was at a dinner party and a young unmarried captain said 'Oh, you ride do you?' and asked me to join him. Whereupon one of the ladies present interjected 'You needn't bother asking Miss B——, she only rides with married men.'

The grandest dinners of all took place at Government House in Calcutta. A couple's place in Anglo-Indian society would be betrayed from the very moment they arrived, whether by landau, brougham, victoria, or by a rather shabby hired carriage known as a *ticca*, whose driver sat on top of a bundle of hay used to feed the horses.

The ladies of the Private Entrée, who sat on the Governor's right at dinner, entered the grounds through a different gate, and always in landaus. They were ushered into the vice-regal presence an hour earlier, possibly to slower music, and it was advisable not to tread on the vast trains of their dresses – or their haughty feelings.

One's visiting card would be passed down a line from one ADC to another until it was read out, and, with interminable bows and curtsies, one would be led into the great marble banqueting hall, capable of holding a hundred diners with ease, and with such a high ceiling that for an important banquet whole palms might be brought inside for decoration.

There were not, however, always sufficient silver forks to go around, and those at the side tables might have to make do with humble steel cutlery. In preparing for large dinner parties it was a long-standing custom in British India for the servants to make up any shortfalls in silver and crockery by borrowing from neighbouring houses, usually without bothering to ask permission of the master or mistress beforehand. A former memsahib recounted to me that once, when she was quite new to India, she was at a dinner party where there were some green Wedgwood plates.

'They're just like your Wedgwood plates,' she said innocently to her sister.

'Shut up you fool, they are!' her sister replied out of the corner of her mouth.

'Actually,' she recalls, 'we entertained in a very tight circle. You met your dinner plates at every party and didn't bat an eyelid.'

Unlike private dinner parties, it was not the custom to bring one's own servants to a Government House dinner. There were more than enough on hand already, all garbed in white muslin vests and trousers, with scarlet cummerbunds, and turbans surmounted with silver crests.

Lavish service remained a feature of Government House dinners until the last days of the Raj. Lady Mary Hay recalls in a letter a special occasion in Delhi, dining at Viceroy's House in the time of the Mountbattens: 'It was a very splendid affair and such a change after wartime restrictions. There were a hundred guests, brilliant lighting, a servant behind each chair.'

Everything on the table was unabashedly solid and substantial, a state of affairs mirrored in Government House dinners in the Madras Presidency of the early nineteenth century. An unknown young woman (quoted in *The East India Sketch-book*, 1832) wrote home:

The first thing that amazes you is the hecatombs with which the table is covered. He must, indeed, be 'a man given to appetite', who retains the least inclination to devour, after the display made on the uncovering of the dishes. Soup – fish – sirloins and rounds of beef – saddles of mutton, – ham and turkey, the everlasting delight of Indian epicures, – fowls of all kinds, – stews, – curries, – all steams at once under one's nostrils, until human nature is reduced to the last gasp. Imagine the barbarism of no division of courses, – no well-graduated succession softening the transition between soup and sweet-meats . . .

The habit of placing all the dishes on the table at once was an imitation of Indian custom, and one which suited many as it enabled them to see all at once what there was for dinner, and to eat what most took their fancy. Diners might have their plates changed five or six times as they ate a little from each dish, always reserving the curry for last. However, by the 1860s this style had given way to service as we know it today, with one course following another in succession. This was service *à la russe*, and in this the Anglo-Indians were merely following the fashion in Britain.

At the same time, there was a distinct trend to lighter fare. Until the middle of the nineteenth century, the only concessions made to refinement on the menu had been the exclusion of heavy joints, and the substitution of a loin for a saddle of mutton. In 1835 Emma Roberts had complained that it took 'the courage of an Amazon' for a hostess to attempt any innovation in dinner party fare, such as reducing the number of dishes or the size of the joints, as this 'would infallibly be imputed to the meanest motives.'

By the 1860s, however, only the elderly and old-fashioned were still serving heavy almond soups, great saddles of mutton and boiled fowls at dinner parties. Their place was taken by dainty dishes in the new fashionable French style. Menus were now written out entirely in French, causing more than a few headaches for domestic translators. Cookbooks provided glossaries of French terms, so that *dail*, the distinctive Indian curds, now became 'gros lait', and 'Podolongcai au jus' proved to be Indian 'snake vegetable' or gourd in brown gravy.

Despite the fact that the wealthy were able to provide imported champagne, caviar and pâté de foie gras, or tinned truffles to put in the sauce périgueux which Colonel Kenney-Herbert suggested for the local seer fish, one wonders just how successfully this French cuisine was transplanted.

If the very idea of French food cooked by Indians for the British seems preposterous enough, consider how the heat of the tropics worked against it. The beef which would have gone into Colonel Kenney-Herbert's filets de boeuf au crème d'anchois, for instance, would have been killed that very morning to prevent it going off, and would have been as tough as leather as a consequence. The aspic for his quenelles de perdrix (partridges), might well have refused to set, while one can only guess at the outcome of a potage à la julienne made as the Colonel suggests, from a tablet of imported 'French preserved julienne' vegetables.

A great many memsahibs must have tried to impose such sophistication on their cook without success, and then left him to fall back on the usual hotchpotch menu of clear soup, fried fish, mutton cutlets with tomato sauce from a bottle, roast chicken, caramel custard or perhaps fruit salad, and sardines on toast. This was a far cry from the seventeenth century when the Indian cook had been given full reign to produce the gorgeous Mogul dishes he knew so well, but then the Victorians were inclined to be contemptuous of all things Indian, including the food.

With the advent of tinned foods, refrigeration and improved communications, dinner giving in India became easier in the twentieth century, although other things – fewer servants, rising expenses – made social life more difficult. Generally speaking, however, it was an aspect of the Raj that did not alter greatly, except in degrees of lavishness and outward show, during the entire time the British were in India.

It was usual, even if only family were present, to dress for dinner. In a hot sticky climate it made sense to change one's clothes at the end of the day, and the evening wear was always laid out by the bearer.

In the eighteenth century a gentleman could go to a formal dinner comfortably dressed in jacket, waistcoat and trousers made of white or buff-coloured cotton. In the early nineteenth century, however, he was expected to arrive for dinner in a formal black coat. Then a faintly ridiculous ritual would be enacted, where the host or hostess would invite him to swap his heavy black coat for a lighter one. This he would politely accept, and he would then go out to the verandah where his bearer would be waiting with the lighter jacket, having been instructed to bring it along in anticipation of this very invitation.

Later in the century things became even more formal, with men having to dress in complete black woollen dinner suits as they did in Britain in the depth of winter. Even white cotton trousers became the exception rather than the rule. As C. P. A. Oman, author of *Eastwards, or Realities of Indian Life* commented in 1864, some men in Calcutta became used to this and did not seem to feel the heat, but 'to see, however, some stout Colonel from the north-west provinces, or a robust individual fresh from home under the ordeal is painfully ridiculous.' Right up to the First World War men would appear at dinner parties in boiled white shirts, white waistcoats, black or white ties, and tail coats or dinner jackets.

Table decorations exuded a similar formality. The snowy white tablecloth would be laid with enough gleaming silver cutlery to accommodate five or six courses, and the napkins would be folded into fancy shapes, such as peacocks, and placed in the wine glasses. In the centre of the table massive floral arrangements would be flanked by bowls of ice and little dishes of nuts and other nibbles.

Overhead fluttered the *punkah*, an elephantine fan of wood, canvas and plaster, every movement of which sent a shower of dust into the food and scattered the guests' name-cards about the table. On a particularly hot night the guests might also have their servants cool them with huge hand-held fans made of a perfumed grass called kuscos.

In June, as the hot weather was about to break into the monsoon, came the insects, when even the Viceroy had to put up with unbidden guests to his table. Attracted by the lights, they flew into the room in countless numbers and fell into the plates at dinner. At times they reached virtual plague proportions, as a letter from Madras in 1838 shows:

The black bugs are not so horrible as the green ones, but bad enough, and in immense swarms. One very calm night the house was so full of them that the dinner table was literally covered with them. We were obliged to have all the servants fanning us with separate fans besides the punkah, and one man to walk round the table with a spoon and napkin to take them off our shoulders. Except Mr S——, who contrived to be hungry, we gave up all idea of eating our dinner; we could not stay in the house, but sat all evening on the steps of the verandah, playing the guitar. (Quoted in *The Sahibs: the life and ways of the British in India*, by Hilton Brown, 1948.)

There was one variety of black horned beetle which was so strong that when placed under a wine glass, it could push it across the table!

At the end of the meal, after the savoury, the finger bowls would be brought out, and all sorts of chocolates, pralines, nuts and pickled ginger were handed round. Then the ladies would retire, leaving the men to their port or madeira. In the early days the bearers would now produce the hookahs and set them behind their master's chair, bringing the 'snake' around and placing the mouthpiece in the master's hand. A loud hubble-bubbling followed and the scent of perfume-spiked tobacco would fill the air. In the nineteenth century the hookah came to be considered almost disreputable and its place after dinner was taken by cigars and cheroots.

At balls, just as at dinners, there was strict observance of precedence, with ladies being led out to the opening dance in descending order of the rank of their husbands. However, stiff formalities tended to diminish as the evening progressed, and at nineteenth-century balls the dancing frequently continued until dawn. For this reason it was quite normal for the dancers to sustain themselves with two suppers, one at midnight and the other at about 3 in the morning. The anonymous author of *The East India Sketch-book* describes one particularly debauched ball in the 1830s, at which there were not two but three suppers:

In the 'very witching time of night' supper was announced and there was a rush in the direction of the tent.

The tables were covered – were groaning beneath the slaughtered hecatombs. It was a feast fit for Homer's heroes . . . Soup of all kinds – mulligatawney, and vermicelli, and turtle; huge turkeys and huger hams; barons of beef; saddles of mutton; geese, and all manner of tame fowl; legs of pickled pork, and pease pudding – these were the delicacies that tempted the appetites of Indian epicures. Two or three ultra-fashionists, just imported from cold and icy Europe, stared, and turned a little pale as they inhaled the stream arising from the various 'savouries' – swallowed a jelly, and a biscuit, and a glass of wine; but the rest of the party addressed themselves valiantly to the work of devastation. They drank beer in huge tumblers, men and women; they ate of the beef, and the mutton, and the pork, and the turkeys and the fowls, and they closed with real Mussulmauni curries . . .

In process of time, dancing recommenced, and the scrambling and laughing and vociferating were more emphatic than before. And they whirled in Spanish dance, until some became giddy, and others stumbled, and others fell. Then there was a second supper – of grills and stews, and lukewarms, and colds, of which the majority of the ladies partook, and dancing was resumed – reels and country-dances, until by the aid of frequent refreshings of negus [a hot drink of spiced port and lemon], the greater part of the loftier sex were in a condition which admonished their gentler partners, not only of the propriety, but of the absolute necessity of a retreat.

When they were fairly deposited in their various vehicles – tonjons or palanquins – a scene of uproarious revelry commenced . . . Bursts of the coarsest laughter repaid jests as coarse, toasts and tempests of applause, songs and thundering knocks upon the table, led the way to a third supper, before the termination of which, glasses, bottles, dishes, and viands were flying about in all directions. One by one the guests walked off, or were carried . . .

Weddings were another occasion to devour almighty spreads of beef, mutton, pork and turkey:

> Then followed the dessert. The marriage cake
> Pre-eminent uprears its snowy head,
> In Alpine dignity; and jellies shake
> Their yellow bosoms; and rich gingerbread
> Is seen, in humbler guise, its cause to plead;
> Nor does the raspberry, or the pure cream ice,
> Of being recommended stand in need;
> Puddings and tarts, and home preserves and pies,
> Made by the bride's fair hand, complete the rich supplies!
>   (From *Tom Raw, the Griffin*, by Sir Charles D'Oyly, 1846.)

Rather more demure were the tea dances which followed in Edwardian times. These were held at the club in the late afternoon, and always broke up in time for people to return home for dinner.

Christmas was the time for Indian merchants and contractors to call on their Christian employers and clients with garlands of flowers and *dalis*. The latter were baskets decorated with flowers and containing fruit such as apples, bananas, papayas, pomelos, tangerines, dates and nuts. Atop these would be a store-bought Christmas cake decorated with gaudy icing, Christmas crackers, and boxes of chocolates and Indian sweets, tied with a ribbon. In the early days gifts of jewellery were included, but by the twentieth century these were considered tantamount to bribery, and government officials, in particular, were not allowed to accept anything made of silver or gold.

For their part, the British would reward their domestic servants in small ways. Mary Fitzgibbon wrote in her diary of Christmas at Chutunhully in 1866:

A good size pig was killed for the domestic servants and portions given to them for the evening meal. I cooked a pork chop, with new potatoes of my own planting and a few French beans: in addition I made a plum pudding with brandy sauce so that we had something of an English Christmas dinner.

For nostalgic reasons turkey was always favoured, but where it was not available a peacock might be substituted, given long cooking and continually basted with bacon fat or butter to counteract its natural dryness. In certain parts of India it was not permitted to eat pea-fowl, however, out of respect for Hindus, who consider the bird sacred.

In Calcutta a Christmas dinner towards the end of the nineteenth century might also include ham and tinned salmon brought out from England, quail, ortolans, roast beef, saddle of mutton, perhaps some prawn curry, mango fish (which came into season in the river Hooghly around Christmas), and curries and pilaus of chicken.

The making of mince pies and Christmas cake was one kitchen task the memsahib often preferred to do herself, calling in her children to give the mixture a ritual stir.

The Dutch community in Sri Lanka had their own style of Christmas cake, incorporating the cardamon, cloves and cinnamon for which the island is famous:

SRI LANKAN CHRISTMAS CAKE

2 oz (50 g) candied peel, chopped
2 oz (50 g) glacé cherries, chopped
2 oz (50 g) dried papaya, chopped
2 oz (50 g) raisins
2 oz (50 g) currants
8 oz (250 g) sultanas
2 tbsp brandy
2 tbsp liquid honey
1½ tbsp rose water
1½ tbsp vanilla essence
few drops almond essence
4 oz (125 g) butter
8 oz (250 g) sugar

6 egg yolks
4 oz (125 g) semolina
4 oz (125 g) strawberry jam
4 oz (125 g) pineapple jam
4 oz (125 g) almonds, slivered
4 oz (125 g) raw cashew nuts, chopped
4 oz (125 g) crystallized ginger, chopped
½ tsp ground cardamom
1 tsp ground cinnamon
½ tsp ground nutmeg
½ tsp ground cloves
3 egg whites

Place all dried fruits in a bowl and pour over the brandy, honey, rose water, vanilla essence and almond essence. Leave for 24 hours.

Cream the butter and sugar together. Beat in the egg yolks and when the mixture is fluffy, fold in the semolina a little at a time. Next, fold in the pineapple and strawberry jams, then the soaked fruit, nuts, ginger and spices. Beat the egg whites until stiff and fold in just before turning the mixture into a 10 × 11 in (25 × 28 cm) cake tin lined with several thicknesses of paper (the uppermost layer greased with butter).

Bake at 150°C/300°F/Gas Mark 2 in a preheated oven for an hour, then lower the temperature to 120°C/250°F/Gas Mark ½, and leave for another hour. If the cake seems to be getting brown during cooking, cover it with aluminium foil.

Allow the cake to cool before turning it out of the tin.

The cake may be iced with almond icing if desired. Stored in an airtight tin, it will keep for several months. Traditionally, long thin slices of the cake are wrapped in coloured cellophane to resemble Christmas crackers.

On Christmas Eve the officers' mess or the club might have thrown open its doors and given a children's party. Long tables would be set out on the lawn, and gigantic Christmas crackers suspended from bamboo poles. When tea was over the crackers would be burst with sticks, sending down a shower of rice and little presents over the assembled children.

British social contact with Indians tended to be restricted to nobility.

As members of governing classes with a taste for hunting, feasting and drinking, the two races had much in common. Some of the more important Muslim and Hindu festivals throughout the year would be attended by British officers, as a mark of respect. Mrs Clemons describes the Muslim feast of Mohurrum:

The floor or ground is carpeted, and tables are arranged in different directions, containing sweetmeats and fruit, which are supplied in great abundance. Rose-water and attar are freely used by all.

The nautch was a popular entertainment given for the English by their local pet rajah or nawab. In *Curry and Rice on Forty Plates*, George Atkinson sets the scene:

And now, let us drop in to his palace for such an occasion. The guests arrive, and are installed in velvet-cushioned chairs, and otto of roses is handed round with dried fruits and sweetmeats. Then come the dancing-girls, gyrating on their heels, ogling and leering, and shaking their uplifted palms . . . indicative in the Eastern eye, of grace and dignity of motion. But 'Our Nuwab' invites us to supper; and there we find our tables groaning with the productions of Sticker and Doss's Europe shop, for which 'Our Nuwab' has given unlimited orders. But liberality and redundancy have been more considered than appropriateness of assortment. Lobsters and tart fruits commingle, while truffled sausages and truffled almonds share mutually the same dish. Nor is it for want of crockery, and dishes and plates, and vessels even of the most domestic character, grace the board, side by side with silver plate and glittering ormolu, to the unsmotherable amusement of the guests.

But the wines and beer have been properly cooled, and, considering they came from Sticker Doss's, are not so bad. We have great fun, and the laughter is prodigious; the Nuwab, who, as a strict Hindoo, sits complacently a looker-on, joining our mirth, but urging us to partake with greater courage; which, indeed, it needs, for the table slaves of his highness are not adepts at Christian cookery, and trifling irregularities greet the senses. The salad indicates the presence of cod-liver oil, and we have faint suspicions that 'Day and Martin' has been introduced as a sauce.

But the Nuwab is blissful unconsciousness of it all, and we drink his health the three times three, which gratifies him intensely. Then we adjourn to witness the fireworks, and a troop of fifty pariah-dogs let loose, each with a lighted squib at its tail, is pronounced to be great sport.

In pre-Victorian days, the menus on such occasions had made far fewer concessions to conservative English palates. In 1837 a woman wrote home from Madras:

A—— whispered to me that I must eat as much as I could to please the poor old Armagum, so I did my best, till I was almost choked with cayenne-pepper. The

Moorman pillaws were very good; but among the Hindoo messes I at last came to something so queer, slimy and oily, that I was obliged to stop.

A hundred years later the problem was the very opposite; by now the nawabs and rajahs were trying too hard to provide 'English fare'. Elizabeth Crawford Wilkin recalls in *Dekho! The India That Was* (1958):

The dinner, for all the good intention, was a towering failure. The soup was too peppery, the fish too salt. A none-too-tender peacock, which the cook had failed to stuff, was served with a jar of strawberry jam which did proxy for the absent cranberry sauce. Ordinary Indian maize represented a sweet-corn souffle, and an iced pudding which had refused to freeze made its watery appearance before a final indigestible savoury. Had our hospitable host but realised how much more we would have welcomed a good hot Indian curry, he would have spared himself trouble and us a very painful experience.

At Cawnpore the Nana Sahib's table arrangements caused the officers of the British garrison great mirth. One of the guests describes the confusion:

I sat down to a table twenty feet long (it had originally been the mess-table of a cavalry regiment) which was covered with a damask tablecloth of European manufacture, but instead of a dinner napkin there was a bedroom towel. The soup – for the steward had everything ready – was served up in a trifle-dish which had formed part of a dessert service belonging to the Ninth Lancers – at all events the arms of that regiment were upon it; but the plate into which I ladled it with a broken tea-cup was of the old willow pattern. The pilau which followed the soup was served upon a huge plated dish, but the plate from which I ate it was of the very commonest description. The knife was a bone-handled affair; the spoon and fork were of silver, and of Calcutta make. The plated side-dishes, containing vegetables, were odd ones; one was round, the other oval. The pudding was brought in upon a soup plate of blue and gold pattern, and the cheese was placed before me in a glass dish belonging to a dessert service. The cool claret I drank out of a richly-cut champagne glass, and the beer out of an American tumbler, of the very worst quality. (Quoted in *Bound to Exile*, by Michael Edwardes.)

Occasionally the choice of crockery might prove to be an outright blunder, as A. Fenton recounted in *Memoirs of a Cadet* (1839). The scene is a nawab's palace in Lucknow, early in the nineteenth century:

A great entertainment was ordered to be prepared for the European residents, altogether in the English fashion. The Kansaman General, anxious that everything should be in the highest style, repaired to the Europe shop in Lucknow, in order to make provision for the feast. Perceiving a large batch of certain earthenware vessels, which he considered to be a beautiful service of crockery, on account of the family likeness they bore to each other, he carried the whole stock to do honour to his master's board.

In due time, when the ladies and gentlemen were ushered into the supper-room, the most conspicious objects were these very vessels plentifully bestowed about the table, laden with jelly, blancmange, etc., etc.

It was impossible for even the gravest countenance to withhold a smile at the innocent error of the purveyor; but the mistake was complete and unequivocal.

The 'vessels' the *khansamah* had proudly displayed were the store's supply of chamberpots!

Picnics were introduced to India by the British in their first days at the Surat factory in the early seventeenth century. They were also popular in old Calcutta, although a sentry had to keep watch for brigands, and the men had to wear their swords en route. This did not seem to deter them, and once a pleasant spot under mango trees had been found, carpets were spread and on these bolsters and cushions laid. Over the whole party a giant mosquito net would be draped, tied from branch to branch from the tree. This kept out the flies and the wasps as well, although marauding monkeys might make an unwelcome appearance.

Once the ideas of the early nineteenth-century Romantic movement had spread to India, picnics were seen as an escape from the city to reflect on the beauty of nature. As the anonymous author of *Sleepy Sketches from Bombay* (1877) noted: 'Picnics are the best amusements, though they differ so much from picnics at home. The sky, except in the monsoon, is always clear, so a moonlit night can easily be predicted after the day's work is over.' There ought not to be more than twenty or thirty people, the writer advised, and they should all be friends. Moreover, there should be an advance guard to go and make preparations at Vehar Lake or some chosen spot . . .

After a long drive the lake is reached, and a dinner or supper found displayed, lighted by a hanging roof of Chinese coloured lanterns, whose light, mixed with the moonlight, makes the bottles, pies, and meats, and glasses, all look as though made of jelly, shaken by a wind. The influence of the moon, Chinese lanterns, and champagne has an excellent effect on conversation.

Sandwiches were the great standby: egg and mango chutney; sardine and cucumber; pounded chicken and tomato; egg, fillet of anchovy and watercress. The memsahib was advised to have them wrapped up in a large damp napkin for the journey, and on no account to allow the *khansamah* to use plantain leaves for the purpose, as they tainted the flavour of the bread. Champagne was the favourite drink, and in the

1930s some sophisticates were taking along ready-mixed cocktails in thermos flasks.

Constance E. Gordon's *Anglo-Indian Cuisine* (1913) gives an idea of the scale of such feasts.

Picnic Tea and Luncheon Basket for 12 persons

4 nice sized fish, soused; 1 good pigeon (or game) pie; 1 ox tongue pressed (or tinned); 2 lb cold ham; cold roast turkey; 6 lb cold beef (boiled, pressed or roast); 6 lettuces for salad; 1 tin apricots; 2 fruit tarts; 1 cake, good sized, plum; 1 cake, good-sized, plain; few jam puffs; 1 lb tin mixed chocolates; 1 doz dinner rolls; 6 half loaves; 1 tin cheese biscuits; cruet-stand filled and packed in box; 1 bottle mixed pickles; 1 bottle walnut pickles; 1 pot of French mustard; 1 bottle salad oil; salt; 1 bottle cream (boiled) for tarts, fruit etc.; 1 jar of butter; 1 bottle coffee essence; 1 lb cheese; 1 tin tea; 1 tin sugar; 1 bottle milk, boiled; matches; 1 spirit stove and kettle; 1 big bottle water; tea pot and cosy; 1 doz teacups, saucers, spoons; 1 bottle spirit of wine; 3 doz knives; 3 doz forks; 1 doz meat plates; 1 doz pudding plates; 1 doz cheese plates; 6 dishes; 2 glass bowls; 1 salad bowl; 1 doz spoons; 1 doz small tumblers; 1 doz table napkins; table cloth; 9 butler's towels; 30 lb ice; 1 pail in which to put some lumps of ice and your tinned fruit; tin opener; ice breaker.

Let the butler make a nice French Salad to go round with the Cold Meats.

4

Travellers' Fare

In British India everybody's work involved travel at some time or other, whether as a magistrate, forestry officer, box-wallah, missionary, or those in the police or army. Since government officials typically had jurisdiction over vast areas, many were obliged to spend a large part of the year on tour.

Before the days of proper roads, there were only three means of travel in India: by river, on horseback or in a palanquin carried by relays of bearers. Some sort of entourage was inevitable: tents and heavy trunks had to be carted on bullocks, while coolies were needed to carry baskets of food and crockery on their heads. Then there had to be a cook, a tent lascar (who pitched and took down the tent), as well as a horsekeeper and a grass cutter to dig up roots for the horse's feed, for there was no hay to be had in India. In Victorian times this was considered the absolute minimum: there was one collector who did not consider it unusual to tour with sixty house-servants and eighty porters, while Lord Auckland, on his grand tour of India as Governor-General from 1837 to 1840, moved with a camp as large as a city.

Lord Auckland's younger sister Emily accompanied him on this tour, and wrote in her diary for 11 December 1837:

The King of Oude sent his cook to accompany us for the next month, and yesterday, when our dinner was set out, his khansamah and kitmutgars arrived with a second dinner, which they put down by the side of the other, and the same at breakfast this morning. Some of the dishes are very good, though too strongly spiced and perfumed for English tastes. They make up some dishes with assafoetida! But we stick to the rice and pilaus and curries.

And on 9 November 1838, at Buddee:

When we stopped half-way between Sabathoo and this place . . . the dear old khansamah, with his long white beard, went passing about, in and out of the tents and the trees, and there were fires burning amongst the grass, and tea made in minutes; and then he came with half-a-dozen fresh eggs, which he must have laid himself, and a dish of rice, and in minutes we had an excellent breakfast. (From *Up the Country*, by Emily Eden, 1866.)

Touring was not always a chore; some went on camping expeditions for pleasure. This is the hero of *Curry and Rice on Forty Plates* extolling the joys of life under canvas:

Then are the table attendants actively alert; the sacrifice of the chicken has been accomplished; the savoury condiments for our curry have been amalgamated, and are seething in the pot; the everlasting omelette is about to be cooked, and the unfermented cakes prepared. Then we indulge in our bath, and at the door of our tent, placing ourselves in a suitable position, receive the welcome shower from the hand of the water-carrier. We reinvest our limbs in the lightest and the loosest of vestments, and then we breakfast. Fire is next vehemently called for, by which our fragrant cheroots are lit; we throw ourselves on to the cot of ease, and resign ourselves to the indulgence of the latest periodical, with occasional interpolations of the 'balmy'.

Thus we while away the lingering hour, till hunger and the slave warn us it is time for tiffin. The feast is spread, the pale ale glimmers in the glass; we find that the tent's high temperature, the morning walk, the mid-day slumber, have parched the throat, and that one bottle is of no avail – we try a second, and that scoundrel slave asserts we try a third. But we have had a famous dinner; the curry, flavoured with a spicy pungency, is good indeed – the pale ale most insinuating; – we once more call for fire, and then, like a good old patriarch in days of yore, we sit at the door of our tent and watch the flocks and herds, and much cattle, as they 'wind slowly o'er the lea' and pass our tent.

The most refined of travellers took a portable stove, in which their servants baked fresh bread, cakes and scones. In the hills, it had the added bonus of keeping the tent warm and drying clothes. A cruder form of oven could be concocted by placing a pot in a pit of hot embers and shovelling more embers over the lid – any form of rough camp bread was preferable to the only other alternative, the 'country biscuit' made of flour and water.

A portable meat safe could be improvised from an old umbrella with a bag of mosquito netting over it. Some travellers even took a cow with them, sending it on with a cowman to the next camp, so that it could have chewed its cud and produced fresh milk by the time they arrived. Nor was butter necessarily a problem: a jar of cream suspended from a camel would churn itself into butter during the course of a day's march.

Not everybody was so fussy about what they ate, however, as can be seen from the institution of the pepper-pot, directions for which were given in a manual called the *Anglo-Indian's Vade Mecum*, compiled by Edmund Hull:

First, get a medium-sized iron pot, lined with enamel. It ought to have a lid fastened by a hinge, and fitting tightly when closed. To prevent a tendency to burst when the pot is at the boil, there should be a little valve at the top of the lid, free to rise to the pressure of steam from below. So much for the pot; next for its contents. The evening before starting on a journey, put in a fowl, one or two pounds of mutton chops, some potatoes and onions – in fact any meat and any vegetables; add a due proportion of water, salt, pepper, and spices, and then allow all to boil slowly, or stew, for as long as is necessary. Now add a little Worcestershire or Harvey sauce, for piquancy, and the whole is ready. Take the pot with you, and on arriving at the halting station, heat it up again, and set it on the table. After dinner, let your servant kill and dress another fowl, add it, or some chops, steaks, a hare, jungle fowl, or anything else of the same kind that may be obtainable, a few hard-boiled eggs, vegetables, salt and pepper, and boil again; next day repeat the process *da capo*, and your pepper-pot will last the whole journey, giving a savoury meal whenever required.

Such fearsome concoctions were more commonly known as 'all blaze', and were still being cooked for bachelors out in camp in the 1930s. The all blaze could be improved by a foundation sauce of game stock and claret known as 'tickle gummy', which Flora Annie Steel claimed would 'keep good for a month'.

Provisions such as tea, coffee, flour, dried fruit, pasta, cheese, pickles, jams, nuts and bacon had to be taken on the journey; the only foods that a traveller could depend on being able to buy from Hindu villages were milk, pulses, fruit, chillies and vegetables. Generally the latter were 'country' vegetables such as aubergines, yams, gourds, *bhindi* (okra, known as ladies' fingers) and red spinach. Flora Annie Steel suggested stewing country carrots like beetroot with vinegar and oil, while country turnips, mashed and squeezed of their water, then mixed with milk and butter, she continued cheerfully, 'lose nearly all their paint-like taste'.

From Muslims the traveller might also buy eggs, fowls and kid meat, but nothing was guaranteed.

Villagers were often suspicious of strangers and might not understand the use of money. In Victorian times many a servant virtually pillaged what he needed in the name of his master. Much more sensitive was the approach of the wife of a survey officer, who sat in camp and received offerings of food from women in return for beads, combs and mirrors.

Tinned foods were a boon for the traveller, even if in the early days they had a distinctly metallic taint. The technique was developed in England about 1818, and tinned foods soon spread to India, where in the 1830s truffled hare pâté from the Périgord was available in Simla, and truffled woodcock in Mussourie (the foothills of the Himalayas).

Tinned Australian and other preserved lumps of meat [wrote Colonel Kenney-Herbert] are valuable additions to the store box of the jungle-wallah, but they require delicate handling, because they are almost always overdone. The really nutritious part of a tin of Australian meat is the gravy that surrounds it. Ramasamay knows this, so beware of unrighteous dealing, see the tin opened, and have every atom of the gravy strained off into a bowl. In cold weather, such as you have in the Deccan during December and January for instance, the gravy in these tins becomes jelly.

Messes like Messrs Crosse and Blackwell's 'ducks and green peas', 'Irish stew', 'ox cheek and vegetables' etc. should be avoided carefully, but if you find that your butler has sent such things to camp, you must pick the meat out of its surroundings, dress it up with some fresh chicken meat as a rissole, or a mince, and cook the gravy and vegetables with some fresh chicken broth as a sauce.

Food provisions had other handy uses: cayenne pepper could be poured down ant holes to deter the hated white ants, whole cloves could be used to moth-proof clothes, and vinegar could be used to treat scorpion stings.

Naturally there was occasionally an utter disaster with provisions, as Sir Francis Colchester-Wemyss recalls:

In 1897 I and a brother officer travelled to Mussourie and set off to walk through the hills to Simla, where we were bound for the Viceroy's Fourth of June dinner. (I had damaged my riding muscle and walking was supposed to be good for it.) There came a day when my khidmutgar, rather than cross the gorge of the Tons River dangling in a loop under a very ancient rope, bolted back with all our very modest supplies except a bag of onions, and we had to live on those and the fifth-class rice used by the coolies who carried for us for ten days – the only exception being when, one happy day, we found an old man catching small fish in a stream with a casting-net. We bought all he caught – about a dozen, weighing about three pounds – and I can remember nearly every mouthful of the two meals they provided, the menu being boiled, thin, bony fish, boiled rice, boiled onions, without even pepper and salt. I think that must be the worst menu that I have thoroughly enjoyed.

When a large fish was caught out in camp, an old India hand knew to have it caked completely in mud and then baked in the fire, a method which kept in all the moisture and flavour.

Before the advent of the railway, regimental marches were a feature of army life all over India. In peacetime, the high command tried to restrict the movement of troops to the cold weather, but since a regiment had to stay put until it was relieved by another which might be late arriving, some marches were unavoidably delayed until the hot season.

To avoid the heat of the day, the march would take place at night, with the officers on horseback and their wives in palanquins. A shepherd would drive a flock of sheep before him, and hens would cluck from their cages which were strapped, along with cooking pots and frying pans, to light wooden bedsteads known as charpoys, which would be carried by four bearers. The crockery would be carried on the heads of bearers, but as they were prone to falls, so much might be smashed that by the end of a march a family of five might be reduced to one tumbler and a cup and saucer between them.

After a morning's rest, there would be a slight stir in the camp at about half past one, as the butlers set off for the local bazaar to buy food, and the cooks began making fires. The sisters, wives and mothers of the sepoys (Indian soldiers in the British Army) would also begin to cluster about in little groups.

After a bath, the European officers would have their main meal of the day at about three o'clock in the afternoon, washing down curries and roasts with cold claret and Hodson's pale ale.

Immediately after this meal an advance party of servants and cooks would be sent off to the next camping spot, where they would set up tents and prepare breakfast for the soldiers when they arrived the next morning.

Around five o'clock the sepoy soldiers began preparing the meals. A member of the Rajput warrior caste might cook for an inferior caste, but not vice versa. After bathing, the Rajput would make a fire and then draw a circle around it, which the European officers and those of inferior castes knew not to enter. If they did, the ground would immediately become polluted and would have to be purified with water. Worse still, if they happened to touch his eating or cooking vessels, these would have to be smashed on the spot. The sepoys then set about kneading chapatis, clapping them into shape between their hands, and cooking them on an earthenware vessel upturned on the fire. They would also have a little brass pot in which they cooked meat or vegetables. If the sepoy were from Bengal or the south, there would more likely be rice instead of chapatis. Then, around seven o'clock, the camp would pack up and set off once more.

Every third day it was necessary to call a halt, to refresh both men and beasts. Wherever possible, these halts were planned to take place near a European settlement, so that food supplies could be replenished. On this day the wives dined at the officers' mess, and if the station were a particularly sociable one, a ball and supper might be arranged for the regiment. Emma Roberts tells of an ill-fated dinner given by the officers of one regiment for those of another they met on the road:

Preparations were made upon a grand scale; the presiding *khansamah* did his best, produced his choicest stores of European luxuries, and committed great slaughter amongst the sheep and poultry. The roasts, boils, grills and stews, were of the most approved quality, and as usual, in quantity superabundant.

Just as dinner was taking up lo! a sudden and most tremendous hurricane swept over the plain, burying fires, pots, pans, and eatables in one wide waste of sand. The distraction of the servants at this unexpected catastrophe is not to be described; vehement in their gesticulations, some beat their breasts, others tore their hair, while the more collected secured the joints, sole wrecks of a splendid dinner. The sand had penetrated everywhere, inundating the soup-kettles, and enveloping the grills; the only resource was to pare off the outsides of the ham and the legs of mutton, and these mutilated relics were placed upon the board by the crest-fallen khansamah, who, having got over the first burst of his despair, gravely informed the hungry guests, gazing upon the empty space before them, that 'it was the will of heaven that they should go without their dinner'.

In the 1840s travel became very much more comfortable with the building of a network of travellers' bungalows throughout India. Known as *dak* bungalows, they were plainly furnished single-storeyed houses, usually surrounded by a verandah, unpretentious but sufficiently solid for many to have survived and still be in use today. Prior to the *dak* bungalow, there had been a limited number of huts known as *choultries*, but these were cheerless, uninhabited, echoing to no sounds but the howl of jackals and the hum of mosquitoes, and the traveller usually either had to rely on the hospitality of friends, or sleep in a tent or even his palanquin.

Indian butlers were installed to run the *dak* bungalows and offer meals. Known variously as peons, sepoys or mussalchees, they were paid only a token salary by the government, and were expected to make their profit as 'licensed victuallers'. While some enterprising butlers did indeed lay in stores of beer, brandy and tinned meats, and sell them at vast profit to travellers, at most *dak* bungalows the fare was dreadful.

After a breakfast of tea in big, thick cups poured from a chipped teapot, and buttered toast upon a willow-pattern plate which did not match anything, the traveller could look forward to lunch of the inevitable curry and rice or roast chicken and chapatis, followed by a dinner where the courses consisted of leg of mutton left over from an earlier repast, served upon cracked plates with metal reservoirs of hot water under them, and embellished by tinned peas of anaemic olive pallor. Caramel custard was served *ad nauseam* and the highlight of the whole meal might well be the fresh fruit (bought from a hawker at the bungalow door) which rounded it off.

In between meals, there was nothing to do; George Atkinson graphically evokes the longueurs of *dak* days in *Rice and Curry on Forty Plates*:

The hours lag long and wearily; the punkah, of limited dimensions, with a deranged flounce and with unsymmetrical ropes, waggles with a quaint and threatening aspect, and affords but little mitigation of the burning heat. We have a tattie at the door, and the slave keeps it well saturated; but its ambiguous form admits the fiery blast. We lie recumbent on the cot, which has the authorised and popular number of legs, of which the chairs cannot said to boast; we have dozed; we have read the regulations that hang upon the walls forty times at least till we know them by heart; we have drunk tepid beer, and warm soda-water has allayed our thirst; we have recorded our names in the book of fate and of the Bungalow; when, at last, upon a grateful ear the sounds of the relieving palankeen-bearers announce that the sun has set and that the hour of departure is at hand.

Where a bungalow butler did make an effort with the catering, he might be rewarded with testimonials from satisfied travellers, such as that given by a Mr Cadet Brown:

> So I will praise Peter wherever I go,
> And always speak well of his Dak bungalow;
> If I always gets food just as good as he gives
> In time I shall get jolly fat – if I lives!

Up to the early nineteenth century, the budgerow was the main form of transport along the large river systems of northern India. These were lumbering, keelless barges, clumsy but secure, which were either rowed or sailed. At the aft were a sitting room and a bedroom, with a flat wooden roof on which the passenger sat during the day. Sometimes the cooking might also be done on this roof, but more often a smaller cook-boat followed on behind. Because of its size, the cook-boat was used to go to the river bank to buy fish and other supplies from the villages. However, it was advisable to keep supplies of food, charcoal and cooking utensils on board the budgerow, for the cook-boat might lag far behind, especially when there was shopping to do.

While the damp atmosphere of the river might turn the bread for breakfast a little mouldy, there was always the alternative of freshly baked chapatis, local milk could be churned into butter, water for tea could be boiled over a charcoal fire on deck, and fresh and dried fish, eggs and rice provided omelettes and kedgeree. To ensure supplies of fresh poultry and milk, live chickens and milking goats might be taken along on the journey.

At mealtimes, the cook-boat would be lashed alongside the budgerow to make the service easier. During the rainy season, it was advisable to have the main meal of the day in the afternoon, for at night, after the candles were lit, troops of insects would swarm in from neighbouring swamps, attracted by the light, often making it preferable to sit in darkness.

With the opening up of the Ganges to commercial passenger boats in the early nineteenth century, the indiscriminate hospitality that British residents had formerly showered on European river travellers began to die out. However, as late as the 1840s, gifts of fresh fruit and vegetables might still be sent to 'the gentleman in the budgerow' at remote riverside stations, even if he were a total stranger.

In the course of the nineteenth century the budgerows gave way to steamers. Some of these, such as the steamer which went from Calcutta up through the Sunderbunds (the river jungle of the Ganges delta) to Assam, were luxuriously appointed. The dining tables in the saloon was covered in starched white cloth, the china and silver marked with the steam company's crest, there was a huge carved sideboard, and the chairs and settees had linen covers. When Lord Auckland took a steamer through the Sunderbunds in 1837, his party was looked after by 140 Indian servants and two French chefs. The menu of a steamer on the Brahmaputra River in the 1860s was rather less salubrious, however, relying on tinned fish and unpalatable snacks, with fresh bread, milk or vegetables a very rare treat.

Eventually the railways were to prove the death of the steamers, though their food was no better. 'The most objectionable feature in connection with the Indian railways is the extreme defectiveness of the refreshment arrangements,' stormed Edmund Hull in his *The European in India* in 1871. 'These are for the most part decidedly bad – in the face, as must however be acknowledged, of great difficulties. The number of travellers likely to frequent the refreshment rooms is small, and many of them carry what provision is required for the road with them.'

A well-organized Edwardian rail traveller would take a wooden box partially packed with ice, on top of which would be a metal tray containing food. This would gradually sink further down into the box as the ice melted, keeping the food cool for two days.

By the 1920s every big station had three dining rooms on the platform – European, Hindu and Muslim. Anybody with any sense avoided the European restaurant, except perhaps to buy a luke-warm soda or beer, for the food was as horrendous as it was over-priced. The Muslim dining rooms were quite a different story, however, and the delicious aromas of kebabs and pilaus which wafted from them proved a temptation for many a European traveller, provided they could turn a blind eye to the kitchen conditions out the back.

Early Indian railway carriages had no corridors, so where the train had a restaurant car, the passengers had to wait until the train stopped at a station before they could walk along the platform to it. There they would be greeted with much salaaming by a barefooted and white-uniformed waiter, with a felt cummerbund around his waist and the railway company insignia pinned to his turban, who would proceed to serve them the inevitable chicken curry with soggy rice, and it was not until the train reached the next station that the diners would be able to get back to their compartment. *Chota hazri* ('little breakfast') would, however, be delivered on a tray to the passengers in their compartments, usually at about 6 a.m. It consisted of tea and a piece of fruit such as a banana or an orange.

Later, when air conditioned carriages with corridors were introduced, the meals would be brought into the compartments on trays by bearers, as they still are on Indian trains today.

5
Servants

By any standards, the retinues of servants kept by the British in India were enormous. In the eighteenth century it was not unusual for a nabob of Madras or Calcutta to keep a hundred or more servants, including a baton bearer or silver pole carrier, whose sole job was to march in front of the master's palanquin, and a servant especially to fill his hookah. Even William Hickey, who was not a wealthy man by Calcutta standards, employed sixty-three servants, including eight to wait at his table, two cooks, two bakers, two to cool his drinks, three to tend to his garden, a coachman and four grooms, a hairdresser and nine valets.

That so many servants could be maintained was due to the low wages that were paid, but it also stemmed from a British obsession with matching the grandeur of the Mogul princes. Captain Williamson, in his *East India Vade Mecum*, published in 1810, lists the servants in existence at that time:

banian, or money agent and banker
sircar, or immediate agent for the receipts and payments and cash-keeper
daroga, or *gumashta*, or factor, or superintendent

munshi, or translator and language teacher
jamar, or chief of the retinue
chobdar, or silver pole bearer
suntabardar, or silver baton bearer
khansamah, or chief table attendant

karani, or clerk in the office

khitmutgar, or table waiter

massalchi, or flambeau bearer

hookabardar, or preparer of the hookah

bhisti, or water bearer

bawarchi, or cook

darzi, or tailor

dhobi, or washerman

mahaut, or elephant driver, who had always one or more coolies, called mates, to assist

sarwan, or camel driver

syce, or groom

chaubak asswar, or horse breaker

mali, or gardener

compadore, or purveyor, under the khansamah

harkara, or messenger

peon, nearly the same as the *harkara*

daftari, or office keeper

hajjam, or *nai*, or nappy, or barber

farash, or furniture-keeper

mehter, or sweeper; a female for the same duties being termed mehterani

duria, or dog-keeper to feed, groom and walk the dogs

kalassi, or camp-equipment keeper

bheriya, or shepherd

chaukidar, or watchman

durwan, or gate-keeper, or porter

kahar, or palanquin bearer

coachman, or postilion

ayah, or female attendant in charge of children

dhai, or female attendant on a baby.

During the nineteenth and twentieth centuries the retinues of servants declined steadily as technological advances rendered many of these positions redundant: the carriage displaced the palanquin and its bearers, the ice box the *aubdar* or water cooler, the electric fan the *punkah-wallah*, and running water the *bhisti* or water-carrier.

More importantly, however, the decline was due to the employers' shrinking incomes and rising costs. In the 1930s a staff of seven would have cost the employer about 200 rupees a month, a sum which would have paid the salaries of four times that number of servants in the 1880s. In the meantime, the value of the rupee had declined from about 2s to 1s 6d (10p to 7½p), while salaries had remained more or less static.

In some cases, the duties of several former servants were contracted into one. For instance, in the early nineteenth century the *khitmutgar* (waiter) took over the duties of the *aubdar* (water-cooler) and hookah-bearer, while the sweeper also became the dog-keeper. The Indian servants themselves placed strict limits on this, however, since they had their tasks as clearly demarcated as any trade union. The *khansamah* might do the shopping but refuse to carry it home, while the cook who prepared the food would have nothing to do with the washing-up afterwards, politely but firmly replying to any such requests with 'that is not my custom'. Much of this demarcation was due to caste restrictions. A high-caste Hindu *khitmutgar*, for instance, would not demean himself with cooking, while everybody but the lowly sweeper would refuse to handle dogs, dead animals or even the master's leather footwear.

Attitudes towards servants varied greatly, ranging from kindly paternalism to frank distrust and racism. In her *Culinary Art Sparklets*, which appeared in 1904, Beatrice Vieyra calmly informs us that 'carefulness and honesty are two qualities rarely met with in servants however honest they appear to be', while Dr Riddell's *Indian Domestic Economy and Receipt Book* claimed that besides 'cunning and double-dealing', the main vice of Indian servants was 'an intolerable habit of lying'. In the 1888 edition of Mrs Beeton we read:

Indian servants are good, many of them, but they cannot be trusted implicitly, and will cheat if they have a chance, and it is absolutely necessary to look after the cook (khansaman), who will probably be the marketer.

It has to be said that some servants were indeed outright swindlers. One of these was Lord Curzon's cook, who returned 596 chickens as having been consumed within a single month, when the true figure (as confirmed by the tradesman who had the contract) was 290. It was true, too, that most Indian servants purloined small quantities of such supplies as tea, sugar, milk, paper, half-burnt candles, and leftover meat, but in this they were no worse than their counterparts in England.

Then there was the *dastur*. This was the butler's bonus, and meant simply that he collected a profit of one anna in the rupee, or one sixteenth, of every purchase in the market. More than any other, it was this servants' practice which scandalized the moralistic Victorian newcomer to India, but the old hand recognized it as an established custom and took a pragmatic view: 'This is certain' wrote Sidney Blanchard in 1867, 'your Indian servant, if he plunders you a little himself, will not allow anybody else to do so.'

It was believed that permitting the *khansamah* to gain a small profit on his bazaar accounts enabled him to support his family in a way he could not manage on his bare wages, and thus he would remain happy and faithful to his employer. Besides which, if the memsahib decided to take the matter into her own hands and do her own shopping, she could be sure of paying twenty-five per cent more on everything at the bazaar. Similarly, the *ayah* could expect a small payment from a hawker if the memsahib bought anything from him, and the horsekeeper would receive a present from the farrier each time he did the horses' shoes.

At the beginning of each month the butler brought in an account of the household expenditure, and a list of wages due to himself and the servants under him. In the case of the cook, a daily cash account was checked for food purchased by the cook from money advanced weekly. Where the memsahib thought that the *dastur* was extortionate, she might politely tell the butler or cook she thought he had made a little mistake and ask him to do his sums again, or she might simply make an arbitrary deduction.

In seeing that the memsahib's orders were carried out, wrote Flora Annie Steel, the secret lay in making rules and keeping to them: 'The Indian servant is a child in everything save age, and should be treated as a child; that is to say, kindly, but with the greatest firmness.' She suggested fining the servants sums raging from one pice for forgetfulness, to a full rupee for lying.

To show what absolute children Indian servants are, the same author has for years adopted castor oil as an ultimatum in all obstinate cases, on the ground that there must be some physical cause for inability to learn or to remember. This is considered a great joke, and exposes the offender to much ridicule from his fellow servants; so much so, that the words 'Mem Sahib tum ko zuroor kiaster ile pila dena hoga' (The Mem Sahib will have to give you castor oil), is often heard in the mouths of the upper servants when new-comers give trouble.

There was a positive and caring side to this paternal attitude towards servants, as outlined in a letter from Lady Mary Hay, who lived in India from 1928 until 1947:

Our principal servants were with us for many years and moved around India to many places far from their homes. All their families came too and lived in servants' quarters within our various compounds.

One felt responsible for all those people and paid almost daily visits to their quarters to discuss with the women the problems of the many children's health and to see that those of a suitable age were going to school.

There was a very paternal relationship between the conscientious memsahib who stayed in India long enough to understand the problems, and it was a pleasure to be greeted with affection and trust by these simple people.

Most servants were either Hindu or Muslim, but in Bombay there was a large number of Portuguese Goans, Parsis and Eurasians. In Madras Indian Christians took the place of the Parsis of Bombay, while in Calcutta there was a mixture of every race and creed, since those moving to the seat of government from elsewhere in India would take their servants with them.

Sidney Blanchard describes in *Yesterday and To-Day in India* the variety at a Calcutta dinner party where, according to Anglo-Indian custom, every guest brought their own servants:

The tall man bearing the pudding is a Calcutta man – a Mohammedan, of course, as the Hindoos of Bengal, though they will occasionally deviate into drinking our wine and even eating such an abomination as our ham, decline most positively to serve us at our tables. Behind him, bearing the two bottles of champagne which he has just taken out of the ice, is his little boy, who is being bred up to the parental profession, and looks as Mohammedan little boys are apt to do, preternaturally sharp for his years. The old man who bears the wine sauce with such a profound sense of responsibility cannot be a Mohammedan, or he would most assuredly wear a beard at his age. I take him to be a Bombay Hindoo of an accommodating caste, like the Madras man opposite. In both Bombay and Madras the restrictions of caste do not nearly so much interfere with domestic service as in Bengal.

In the early days of Calcutta there were a few European servants, but they were expensive, as they required a house and servants of their own. They were also apt to leave at short notice and set up their own business, and had the additional disadvantage (from the employer's point of view) of being able to understand dinner conversations and thus become potential scandalmongers. European women servants were likely to leave and get married no sooner had they stepped off the boat.

The greatest prejudice was reserved for English-speaking Indian Christians. 'At the risk of scandalizing a number of really good people,' wrote the anonymous author of *The Englishwoman in India*, 'I must give as the result of my Indian experience the following piece of advice: as much as possible, secure for your servants a set of unmitigated heathens. Converts are usually arrant humbugs; Catholics are little better; indeed, the domestics who have robbed and cheated us during our sojourn in India, have with one exception been Christians, and I have resolved never to engage another knowing him to be "master's-caste".'

It was claimed that Christian converts, having been disowned by their relatives and thus cut off from traditional caste restraints and social ties, turned to dishonesty and alcohol. A common attitude was that they would consider their European masters under an obligation to provide for them. Such arguments were no doubt simplistic, but on a purely pragmatic level, there may well have been truth in the assertion that a Christian *khansamah* might be boycotted in the bazaar and that the family food supply would suffer as a result.

In the eighteenth century the servants were frequently slaves brought in from Mauritius, known as *coffres* or *caffers* (the forerunner, perhaps, of the derogatory South African expression 'kaffir'). They were also taken to Bombay from the Malabar Coast south of the city. These slaves were often given their freedom but that they were frequently ill-treated is obvious from the many newspaper advertisements and posters giving notice of escaped slaves. The East India Company did not prohibit the slave trade until 1789.

Such master–slave attitudes were echoed in the treatment of paid servants: in the late seventeenth century Elihu Yale, founder of the famous American university, had had his butler hanged on a trumped-up charge of piracy, simply because he had left without giving proper notice. And in 1832 we read an entry in an army officer's journal of a march where the cook had lagged three hours behind: 'Thrashed him soundly, and felt warm and comfortable with the exercise.' Even as late as 1868 Florence Marryat thought it was a great joke that 'a certain lady Tartar in Bangalore' had thrown some boiling-hot batter pudding in the eye of a *khansamah* because she considered it sub-standard. If a short-tempered employer did not make a habit of physically assaulting his servants, he would undoubtedly address them at times as 'you *soor*', 'you *gudha*', 'you *ooloo*' – you pig, you ass, you owl.

The number of servants increased with the seniority of the master. The police sergeant in his bungalow could live simply with a cook-bearer, helped by a sweeper-woman from the bazaar, but a senior civil servant or box-wallah would be expected to keep a full household. There was no way around this. The protocol was enforced by peer pressure, but was also of the Indians' own dictating, since the status of the servants increased with the master's seniority and nobody would be happy if one tried to compromise.

Hiring a servant tended to be hit or miss, since Anglo-Indian society was so mobile that a previous employer had usually left the district by the time a character reference could be followed up. This led to a dependence on written references, which may well have been borrowed, inherited, or written to order by the local money-lender or professional letter-writer. For a few annas the letter-writer would compose a modest testimony of the owner's culinary abilities, his honesty and loyalty. For a few annas more it became a glowing, poetic account of the flower that bloomed unseen. The bearer of the note was a master of industry, an artist of gastronomy. All the chits ended, regardless of the price paid, praying for the prospective employer's long life and prosperity.

Sometimes a discrepancy of dates betrayed borrowed references, but even where they were genuine, they might be of limited value since when an employer turned away a servant, he might well give a better character reference than the servant deserved, omitting the real reason for the sacking. At best, they were an indication of the length of service and the honesty this implied. Even so, the *Indian Domestic Economy and Receipt Book* advocated having servants' names registered with the local police so they could tell who were the old offenders.

A testimonial was a servant's most prized possession, although he might not understand its veiled ironies. That of a certain night-soil man, for example, stated that he had a most discreet cough and took a great interest in all that he carried out.

As head of the household staff, the *khansamah* or butler lorded over the other servants, who would alternatively bask in the glow of his approval or cringe in the shadow of his anger. In Madras he might be known as the *dubash*, while in other areas simply 'the bearer', but invariably he was a rigid disciplinarian, and a dusty table, a dropped knife or an overdone chop would provoke ferocious reprimands. Sometimes he was even known to beat the more menial servants, whom he was able to hire or dismiss at will.

Much of the *khansamah*'s work went unseen. Sometimes he did some of the more dainty cooking, such as making confectionery, pastry, jams and jellies. At other times he might appear to do nothing more than stand behind the master's chair at meals or bring him his mail on a silver salver, or perhaps wait on the table when there were guests, yet without him the household would fall to pieces. Besides seeing that inferior outdoors servants carried out orders properly, he supervised the table and also went to market to buy the day's provisions. Up until the mid-nineteenth century he had a full-time *compadore* or market man to carry the shopping home, and even after this a coolie had to be hired for this task, since it was considered beneath the *khansamah*'s dignity. With the dimunition of household retinues from the late nineteenth century onwards, he often assumed the duties of the master's valet or 'dressing-boy'.

Next in line to the *khansamah* was the cook, who very often was the highest-paid member of the staff. He was most commonly a Muslim but could also be a Hindu of a low caste. A high-caste Hindu servant would refuse to have anything to do with the kitchen, and some carried their principles so far as to refuse to touch a clean plate, since it had been defiled by a portion of a slaughtered animal.

Goan Christians were said to be the best cooks of all, if only because their religion permitted them to cook every sort of meat, including pork.

Some families had been butlers and cooks for generations, and thus recipes were handed down from father to son, and learned by heart. Despite such backgrounds, however, the British frequently underestimated their abilities. Isobel Abbott recalls her father-in-law arriving at her house with a cabbage in one hand and a ham bone in the other.

He thrust the bone and cabbage into my hands. 'I've come all this way because I want you to cook this for me. Nobody in this country can cook cabbage like they do in England, perhaps you can.'

These ingredients were subsequently handed on to her trusted Muslim cook.

Lunch was a happy meal. J. H. [the father-in-law] was pleased with all our work and especially pleased with the cabbage.

'Hum, this is what I've been trying to tell these Indian cooks to do – not serve it all wet and mashed up. Thank you, my dear. I knew only an Englishwoman could cook a cabbage.'

Some Englishwomen were totally dependent on their cooks, never having lifted a hand to a saucepan in their entire life. E. A. M. Franklin tells the following tale in her *Wife's Cookery Book* of 1906:

I know one poor young wife, whose servants all left her without warning, and in the morning she lit a fire, and boiled the water for tea, and with tea, bread and butter, they contrived to make a meal; it was seasoned with love and sweet contentment. The young husband had to go to his work; it troubled him to leave his girl-wife to cope with these difficulties, but she assured him she could manage . . . The husband returned home from work; he was weary and hungry, and a pleasant smile of satisfaction beamed on his face. There was a neatly set table, a soup tureen (one of the wedding gifts) at the head of the table; bread and other accessories and a covered dish, which he felt sure contained some appetising morsel. He opened the tureen and proceeded to help his little wife, whom he thought looked tired. He scooped up a pasty mass. Horror! What was it? Rice boiled almost to conjee. He uncovered the other dish.

'What is it, darling?' he asked dubiously, as he looked at the coarse, unappetising looking stuff contained therein.

'Chutney, Harry dear,' she answered, 'and I ground it all myself.'

Poor man, he did not wish to hurt his wife's feelings, so he essayed to eat. In vain, neither he nor the little wife could manage it. And so with laughter and some tears from the little girl-wife, the evening meal also consisted of bread and butter and tea. Could any good housekeeper conjecture as to what the chutney was made of? It consisted of all the ingredients usually put in a curry, coriander, turmeric, etc. Conceive the nauseating mess. The young wife's mother told the story, and was rather amused. It seemed to her such convincing proof of her daughter's girlish innocence.

On the other hand, some more hard-boiled memsahibs were full of unsolicited advice for their cooks:

Most likely you belong to a family of *khansamahs*, cooks and *khitmutghars*; so, of course, it is likely you know a good deal about your business, but it is also certain that you do not know everything. Now it is no disgrace not to know what you have been taught, but it is a disgrace not to try to learn.

So began Flora Annie Steel's advice to the cook, which was also available as a pamphlet, translated into Urdu. She also had advice for the especially haughty memsahib who wished to impart such improving instruction to the cook without actually getting her hands dirty:

If the mistress wishes to teach the cook a new dish, let her give the order for everything down to charcoal, to be ready at a given time, and the cook in attendance; and let her do nothing herself that the servants can do, if only for this reason, that the only way of teaching is to see things done, not to let others see you do them.

It should not be thought, however, that no memsahib ever did any cooking, as some of their personal diaries are full of references to making pastry, chutney, stewed fruit and cakes. Angela Spry even had the audacity to suggest that the cook be told how to prepare his own indigenous dishes:

I would strongly advise every memsahib to superintend the making of the daily curry. If she cannot spare the time to watch the whole process or prepare the same herself on an oil cooking stove, let her cook or khansamah show her all the necessary condiments, which should be brought to her neatly arranged and pounded on a plate.

Colonel Kenney-Herbert, on the other hand, had a much more humane approach to managing the cook:

After some years of observation, I have come to the conclusion that if you want to put nice little dinners upon your table, you must not only be able to take an infinite amount of trouble, but you must make a friend of your chef. Unless amicable relations exist between a cook and his mistress or master, the work will never be carried out satisfactorily.

. . . An artist who can actually compose a 'Vol au vent à la financière', a 'kramousky aux huîtres', or a 'suprême de volaille' deserves some consideration at our hands.

I place those who do not have patience first on the list of persons whom I deem incapable of managing their cooks. I do so advisedly, for of all failings inimical to the successful direction of a native servant a hasty temper is the most fatal. The moment you betray irritation and hastiness in your manner towards Ramasamy, he ceases to follow you: his brain becomes busy in the consultation of his personal safety, and not in the consideration of the plat you are endeavouring to discuss with him.

Once upon a time I knew very intimately the Mess President of a Regiment (not yet forgotten I fancy at Bangalore) who possessed to an eminent degree the qualities necessary for his difficult position. He was an acknowledged connoisseur in wines, excelled in the composition of a menu, and rejoiced in a bountiful development of the bump of management. Long association, however, with one of the best Messmen a Regiment ever had in England had spoilt my friend for the up-hill task of managing Ramasamy. The consequence was that the ordering of a dinner with him was generally productive of a very stormy morning. I remember one special day my friend's voice raised to its highest pitch; presently the door of the little room he occupied as an office flew open, and out rushed the cook followed by his preceptor violet in the face with wrath. The unhappy menial, in a state of hopeless mental aberration, had taken down that he was to boil the pâté de foie gras, and ice the asparagus!

Language could prove a barrier to ordering even the most basic of European provisions, as the author of *Life in the Mofussil* recalls:

Our khansamar or head table-servant, was supposed to know English, or at any rate the English names of the table necessaries; and on the morning after we had entered on possession of our house, he came to inform me that it was advisable to lay in a small stock of certain kitchen requisites. 'Would I be pleased to make a list, and get them from the European shops?'

Accordingly I took my pen, while he, standing with his hands clasped in the native attitude of deferential respect, commenced:

'Makrakurma.' 'What?' said I. 'Makrakurma,' he repeated.

'I had never heard of any English eatable of this name; but he assured me it was very common and absolutely necessary. 'Well,' said I, wishing to temporize, 'pass on to the next thing.' 'Burrumchellee,' he said. This was no better than the first item; but he insisted it was equally well known and equally necessary.

Eventually the hapless author had to pay a bazaar translator eight annas to learn that the two articles were simply macaroni and vermicelli!

Often the cook's repertoire of dishes bore rather peculiar names, strangely transmogrified from their original titles: 'one mutton of line beef for alamoor estoo' (à la mode stew); 'mutton for curry pups' (puffs); 'eggs for saps, snobs, tips and pups' (chops, snipes, tipsycake and puffs); 'mediation (medicine) for ducks' – and at the bottom of the butler's bill 'ghirand totell' (grand total) and 'howl balance' might confound the uninitiated memsahib.

William Hickey has a story of a cook's misinterpretation of orders:

An acquaintance of Mr Hyde's who was stationed at Rungpore sent him a bag of walnuts, then considered a rarity, as they grew nowhere within the province of Bengal except at Rungpore, and even there only one tree. Mr Hyde being particularly fond of that nut, conceived he had given very precise directions to his consumah [*khansamah*] about preserving them and sending a part to table daily as long as they lasted. He had a peculiar way of speaking without raising his head from the book he was reading or the paper he was writing on, and his voice being low it was difficult to understand what he had said unless to those accustomed to his delivery. Having desired the walnuts might be boiled in milk the outer skin taken off, and a plate of them put on the table with the dessert, he proceeded to order a mango pudding, a dish he also admired. The consumah heard something about boiling, peeling, milk, and pudding, and being aware how much his master disliked being obliged to repeat any orders relative to dinner, he without requiring any explanation chose to judge for himself by concluding the walnuts were to be made into a pudding. He accordingly so applied the whole quantity! Dinner being served, after the viands were done with, the dessert followed, when the consumah placed a most enormous pudding at the head of the table before Mr Hyde, who all astonishment exclaimed, 'What the dickens have we got here! I never beheld anything like this. Surely it must have been prepared for the whole garrison of Fort William. Pray, Mr Consumah, what in the devil's name is the meaning of this outrageous dish, and what may you be pleased to call it?' 'Walnut pudding, my lord,' answered the consumah, with his hands closed together, a position of respect when addressing a superior. 'Walnut pudding! Walnut pudding! What does the brute mean by walnut pudding?' angrily asked the Judge. To which the consumah replied, 'My Lord, order walnut to boil and peel, and milk, and pudding, so, my lord, I make pudding for my lord according order.' The Judge quite confounded and almost bursting with rage, which was not decreased by the whole party's laughing most immoderately, looked up in the consumah's face saying, 'You unaccountable beast, you brute without parallel!' Then alternately addressing his guests and the terrified consumah, he continued, 'A walnut pudding, gentlemen! the first, I believe, that ever was made! Oh, you cursed fool, you abominable stupid ass! Any gentlemen choose a bit of walnut pudding? Oh, curse you! A bit of walnut pudding sir? Damn you, you beast!' and thus he continued, upbraiding and ironically recommending the novel sort of pudding for some minutes, his guests being almost convulsed with laughter. One of them proposed tasting the extraordinary performance, which having done he pronounced it excellent, and that it was an admirable way of serving up walnuts though on rather too profuse a scale! The gentleman's facetious remarks entirely failed to restore the Judge's good humour; he remained much out of humour the rest of the day, nor could he with any patience hear a walnut spoken of for a long time after.

Each morning the cook would have a consultation with his employer about the daily menu, and whether any guests were expected. Then he would produce a pile of plates and the memsahib would unlock the storeroom and dish out on the plates all the ingredients needed for that day. Freshly killed chickens or fish would also be brought for inspection. Although many employers preferred to talk to the cook through the medium of the butler, it was not always a good idea, as the cook tended to resent the butler's interference, and Colonel Kenney-Herbert advised speaking to the cook himself in person, in his own patois.

The patois is easily acquired and you will soon find yourself interpreting the cherished mysteries of Francatelli or Gouffe in the pidgin English of Madras with marvellous fluency. You will even talk of 'putting that troople', 'mashing bones all,' 'minching', 'chimmering', &c., &c., without a blush.

Considering the very primitive kitchen and cooking pots, and the charcoal stoves which had to be fanned with one hand while the cook stirred the pots with the other, it is perhaps surprising that anything was ever sent out fit to eat. 'As it is,' wrote the author of *The Englishwoman in India*, 'a native cook will frequently put to shame the performances of an English one; soups, cutlets and made dishes in particular. Their abilities vary greatly, and so does their pay.'

An example of their dedication is related by Mrs Major Clemons, who once visited the cook-room to see why dinner was late coming to the table:

On putting my head within the door, I found everything dished and placed on the ground without covers, in regular order, as if on the table, and the butler and cook disputing in high terms. On my inquiring the reason of all this, they told me they always laid the dishes thus, to see which way they would look best when placed on table! Frequently disputes arise between the contending parties regarding the relative merits of fowl or stew for a side-dish.

When the cook was not cooking, he might be found stretched out on a string bed in the sun, while his unpaid apprentice or 'matey' peeled vegetables and ground spices, and the scullion scoured the saucepans with ashes, sand and cold water.

The scullion, known either as the *musolchi* or 'tannycatch', was often a woman, and besides washing dishes, she had to sweep the dining room and sometimes the verandahs, attend to lamps and clean the master's boots. She was supposed always to have hot water ready, and looked after poultry if only a few fowl were kept. Her status was very low and one would often hear her being sworn at during dinner parties. Mrs Clemons described her as 'generally a dirty, disagreeable-looking person' and Flora Annie Steel concurred with this view entirely: 'In most houses the scullion is an unknown quantity, a gruesome ghoul of spurious cleanliness, bearing, as his badge of office, a greasy swab of rag tied to a bit of bamboo.'

There were eight immutable laws of sculliondom, averred Mrs Steel:

1 Plates are plates, and include cups and saucers, teapots, side-dishes, and milk jugs.

2 Spoons are spoons, and include knives, forks, toastracks, &c.

3 Water is water, so long as it is fluid.

4 Cloths are cloths, so long as they hold together. After that they are used as swabs.

5 The floor is a floor, and nature made it as a table.

6 Variety is pleasing; therefore always intersperse your stoneware plates with china teacups.

7 At the same time, union is strength; so pile everything together, use one water and one cloth, and do not move from your station till everything is dried and spread carefully in the dust.

8 Only one side of a plate is used by the sahib logue; it is therefore purely unreasonable for them to cavil at the other side being dirty.

In time the scullion might hope to be promoted to *khitmutgar*, or table servant, known in Madras as the 'matey'. The *khitmutgar*'s main job was to wait at the table where, according to Emma Roberts, they would 'stir the tea for their masters, and would cut the meat upon their plates, if permitted to show their diligence by such minute attentions.' They had also to polish the silver, lay the table and dust the furniture. The latter task they took over from the *furrash*, or furniture-keeper, who had largely become redundant by the middle of the nineteenth century. Often there was an apprentice known as the 'under kit' who also did a bit of cooking and washing up. 'This servant is a curious mixture of virtues and vices,' wrote Flora Annie Steel.

As a rule, he is a quick, quiet waiter, and well up in all dining-room duties; but in the pantry and scullery his dirt and slovenliness are simply inconceivable to the new-comer in India.

The best of them will, if put to, give a final polish to your teacup with some portion of his own clothing; or place fresh-made mustard on top of the old to save the trouble of cleaning out the pot.

In laying the table, she continues to advise, the *khitmutgar*

should not devise ingenious patterns with the spare silver. He should not attempt to fold up the cloth unaided, and so reduce it to creases. He should not make a separate journey to the pantry for each separate article, but use a tray, like a reasonable human being . . . He should not clear away the table and lay it for the next meal whilst the family are still at table. He should not use the table napkins as kitchen cloths . . . Finally, he should not say the kettle is boiling when it is not. This is an inexcusable offence, but universal.

Dirt, illimitable, inconceivable dirt must be expected, until a generation of mistresses has rooted out the habits of immemorial years. Till then look at both sides of your plates, and turn up the spare cups ranged so neatly in order in the pantry. Probably one-half of them are dirty.

With knives, however, the problem was one of over-enthusiasm. According to one domestic manual, *The Englishwoman in India*:

It is hopeless to expect knives to last. Bath brick may be given out, and yet the boys will pound up a bit of broken china, as if for the express purpose of wearing them out as fast as possible; rubbing knives is one point of cleanliness into which every servant enters with his whole heart; he will grind at them by the hour together and in less than a year the makers' name will be obliterated.

In places where there was no running water a *bhisti* or water carrier was needed to carry water (in pots or a goatskin *mussack*) from the well for baths and kitchen use. He also helped water the garden, sprinkled the verandah with water during the heat of the afternoon, and heated the bath water. Sometimes the water had to be brought in from far way, on bullocks.

The most menial and yet the most essential of all household servants was the *mehter* or sweeper. Generally a low-caste Hindu, he swept in and around the house, fed and took care of any dogs or other unclean animals, and emptied toilets where no sanitation was laid on.

The *mali* or gardener was the most common outdoor servant. One of his most important duties was to provide fresh flowers for the table, for which he was often paid a bonus. How he managed to do this even where the 'garden' was no more than a dusty compound can be seen by a reference given by one employer which read: 'This [*mali*] has been with me fifteen years. I have had no garden, I have never lacked flowers, and he has never had a conviction.'

Those who kept animals would have to hire special servants for them: a *gowlee* to take cows, buffaloes and goats out to graze; another to care for poultry, and for horses, both a *syce* (groom) and a grass cutter. With the advent of the motor car, the coachwaun or coachman of old was replaced by a car driver who might also act as a mechanic.

There were also *chuprassies* (often paid for by the Government) to sit on the verandah and deliver messages. In the 1920s there were no rural telephones and so these *chuprassies* were still very much in use. Later, as the role of *durwan* or gatekeeper fell into disuse, the *chuprassies* took over the function of scrutinizing all visitors. They would know which ones would be expected to enter the house and which should wait on the verandah while master and memsahib were informed. In the north-western provinces during the nineteenth century they generally wore swords at their sides.

Lady Hay recalls that in Bundelkhand (central India) there was no electricity as late as the 1930s: 'In this place we had two extra employees – *punkah-wallahs* – to pull a *punkah* from outside the room day and night. The night ones could do it by fixing a rope to a foot and perform the movement while 99 per cent asleep.'

Some servants were only part-time and paid a small monthly retainer. These included the *dhirzee* or tailor, a barber to shave the master each morning and cut hair when required, and the *dhobi-wallah*, who waged war on the family's clothes. The washing technique, though murderous to delicate garments, was highly effective and remains unchanged throughout India to this day: the clothes are washed down by the water's edge, in cold water, by soaping and then slapping vigorously against a flat slab of stone.

An old India hand knew not to let the *dhobi* keep expensive women's clothes on a Sunday, since if he were unscrupulous he might hire them out to soldiers' wives and Indian women, and they could arrive back stained or torn. For wilful damage of this sort, *The Englishwoman in India* suggests that 'it is positively necessary to fine, however disagreeable it may be. There is no other remedy, unless the delinquent is sent up to the police and flogged.'

In a class of her own was the Indian wet nurse known as the *amah* or *ayah*, who brought up nearly every British infant in India. Unlike other servants, they were fed and clothed by the employer, and were highly paid, despite often having very humble backgrounds as coolies or grasscutters. An *ayah* could also be a lady's maid, and Portuguese-Goan or Madrasi mission-educated women were able to command a premium wage as they were able (besides assisting in dressing the lady of the house) to do her hair, wash laces and stockings, and work with a needle and thread.

In *The Englishwoman in India*, the instructions given for feeding the wet nurse read like those for a prized pedigree cow: 'Should her milk diminish slightly after several months' nursing, a basin of sago congee, given between her supper and dinner, will almost always produce a sufficient supply.' Another Anglo-Indian domestic manual warned that 'the greatest trouble arises in getting them to restrict themselves to proper food; they are prone to indulge, opium, tobacco, pawn, suparee, &c.; they are perfectly careless of any regularity as to their state of health, and require great watching.' A commonly expressed belief was that unless the employer was careful, the *amah* might slip a child a pill of opium to send it off to sleep.

At five or six months the infant would be given a thin congee, or gruel, made of sago or *rolong* (semolina), and from about the age of two the child would graduate to a fully solid diet of meat, broth, bread and puddings. This practice was greatly frowned upon by some such as Edmund Hull:

It has often struck me that Anglo-Indian children are ordinarily indulged with far too stimulating a diet. The youngest are given broths etc., almost before they are weaned, and those slightly older are constantly fed on meat etc., when in Europe farinacious food would only be considered suitable. Wine and beer too are not uncommonly given. Altogether, this would seem to be a very unnatural state of things.

A daily routine was rigidly adhered to. At daybreak the children would be given their *chota hazri* (little breakfast) of fruit juice and a banana or an orange – mangoes and grapes were denied the Victorian child as they were considered unwholesome. Breakfast proper would be eaten with the parents, perhaps out on the verandah.

After lessons or play, lunch, which was often the children's main meal, would be taken on their own low table in the nursery half of the dining room. Such was the Indian love of children that the servants tended to clamour round them at meal times, showering them with service even at the expense of the master and memsahib. Almost as soon as they could talk, Anglo-Indian children would be accustomed to having a willing *amah* or *khansamah* at their beck and call, which inevitably gave the young masters and mistresses a grossly inflated idea of their own importance.

Because of the disease prevalent in India, parents were very careful about their children's food, especially their milk. Often a special nursery cow was kept and the cow-keeper had to bring it around to the verandah where the *amah* was supposed to inspect his hands for cleanliness before watching him milk the cow, to ensure no water was mixed in with the milk. The milk then had to be boiled thoroughly, and when the children went off to tea parties they would be given their own bottles of milk (carefully wrapped in tissue paper) to take along, since no other mothers were trusted to boil the milk properly.

Children brought up in India soon acquired a taste for curry and rice, but medical authorities of the time, not to mention the parents themselves, disapproved of this and more often fed them plain nursery dishes such as Irish stew, croquettes of pounded chicken, milk puddings and perhaps more cooked and raw fruit than was eaten in Britain. A favourite children's pudding was steamed bananas served with melted ghee and sprinkled with sugar.

Of the peculiarly Anglo-Indian nursery dishes, the most famous was a mixture of rice and chicken or mutton called pish-pash, whose origins go well back into the nineteenth century. Mrs J. Bartley's *Indian Cookery 'General' for Young Housekeepers* (1901) describes it thus:

BABY'S PISH-PASH

Cut in inch pieces and wash quarter pound lean mutton, place it with a tea-cup of water to boil. Remove the scum and reduce the fire. Tie in a bit of clean coarse muslin, a dessert-spoon of washed fine rice, put this in the broth with quarter inch piece ginger, and a little salt. Keep the chatty well covered, and boil gently for an hour. Strain the broth into a cup, and place the rice in a saucer. A little of the mutton minced into shreds may be mixed with the rice and broth to feed baby with.

Of another typical dish, 'Dhobi' or Washerman's Pie, Henrietta Hervey wrote in *Anglo-Indian Cookery at Home* (1895) 'I am not prepared to state why this is so named, but I know it to be a favourite with us out there, especially where there are "young mouths" to fill.' Perhaps the sheet of mashed potato which covers this pie is reminiscent of the pristine white linen the *dhobi-wallah* managed to produce despite the bad soap and cold water he was forced to work with.

DHOBI PIE *serves 4–6*

6 lamb or mutton chops
pepper, salt and flour
1 onion, sliced (optional)
2 tbsp Worcester sauce

2 lb (1 kg) potatoes, peeled
2 oz (50 g) butter
2 eggs, beaten

Trim the chops of fat; for a more refined version, cut the meat off the bone and dice it into cubes. Season the meat with salt, pepper and flour and brown on both sides in a frying pan. Sauté the onion (if using) until transparent. Now put the meat and onion in a saucepan with water to barely cover, and simmer gently for about 20 minutes. Add the Worcester sauce. Transfer to a pie dish.

Meanwhile boil the potatoes until soft, drain them, and mash with the butter. When cool mix in the beaten eggs.

Lightly flour a board (to prevent sticking) and roll out the mashed potatoes to a thickness of about ¾ in (2 cm).

Slip this 'pastry' on to the pie dish which should be held close to the edge of the board and bake in a moderate oven (180°C/350°F/Gas Mark 4) for half an hour.

Another children's favourite was Dhal Baat, or dal and rice. Lady Mary Hay sent me this recipe.

DHAL BAAT *serves* 2

7 oz (200 g) lentils (red or green)	7 oz (200 g) rice (long-grained,
2 eggs	white or brown)

Put the lentils into a saucepan with 2 pt (1.2 l) of water. Slowly bring to the boil. Remove any scum which has come to the surface, almost cover with a lid and cook very slowly for at least an hour, stirring occasionally. When cooked, add salt to taste.

Cook the rice by the usual method.

Serve the rice with the dal spooned over it, and top each serving with a poached egg.

6

The Cookhouse and Store Cupboard

———

With the arrival of the English and the Portuguese in India, the kitchen was removed from the main house and set apart as a makeshift little mud brick hut, perhaps only twelve feet square; often it was situated as much as thirty yards away, for the sake of the sahib's comfort. Currents of heat and smoke from a crude woodstove would struggle to escape through the door and the loosely tiled roof, shrouding the shed in a blue haze.

'Look into that Oriental kitchen,' invited George Atkinson:

If your eyes are not instantly blinded with the smoke, and if your sight can penetrate into the darkness, enter that hovel, and witness the preparation of your dinner. The table and dresser, you observe, are Mother Earth.

The preparation of your dinner must therefore be performed in the earth's broad lap, like everything else in this Eastern land. As a matter of course you will have curry, the standing dish of the East. There are the slaves busy at its preparation. The chase for the fowls has terminated in a speedy capture. Already the feathers are being stripped, and the mixture of spicy condiments is in course of preparation. There, on his hams, is the attractive-looking assistant, grinding away at the savoury stuff which is soon to adorn that scraggy chicken, and to excite the palling appetite. There is the prime mover of the undertaking, trimming with a skilful hand the other domestic fowl, that has been immolated for cutlets . . . Thus, you perceive, simplicity is the prevailing feature in an Indian kitchen.

In time, however, and certainly in the towns, the Raj introduced a completely new style of kitchen to India, with upright stoves, and many built-in features such as shelves, benches, cupboards and sinks. The cook now worked at the bench to chop vegetables and meats, stooping to the floor only to use the giant stone mortar and pestle.

Some memsahibs preferred not to know what went on in the cookhouse. Mrs Clemons, writing in 1841, did not wholeheartedly advise it:

Few people think it necessary to visit the cook-room (by which name all kitchens are called), and as this is some distance from the house, none of the disagreeables of that department are ever seen; perhaps the sight of the place, and of the manner in which many a dainty dish is prepared, might affect the delicate stomachs of our countrywomen . . . It is not at all necessary, nor is it agreeable, at least to the good taste of the English, to pry with too great minuteness into the mysteries of making the different dishes for the table; it is quite sufficient to know by experience that they are excellent.

Such attitudes no doubt encouraged some rather questionable practices by the cooks, such as holding melba toast to the fire with their toes, stirring the rice pudding with their fingers, or using the master's socks to strain the soup or coffee. A popular story told of an exchange which went:

'Boy, how are the master's socks so dirty?'
'I take, I make e' strain coffee.'
'What, you dirty wretch, for coffee?'
'Yes, missis; but never take master's clean e' sock. Master done use, then I take.'

If the more conscientious memsahib could not bring herself to make a daily tour of inspection of the pantry, kitchen and scullery, she at least had the cooking utensils laid out on a mat on the verandah for inspection.

'Give out washing soda,' advised Colonel Kenney-Herbert, 'for you cannot keep things clean without it; and be very particular about the cloths that are used by the cook. There is a horrible taste which sometimes clings to soups, sauces, etc., which a friend of mine specifies as "dirty cloth taste". This is eloquent of neglect, and dirty habits in the kitchen.'

The interior of a well-kept cookhouse was whitewashed regularly. Since the Indian cook preferred to work from a squatting position, the 'benches' were wooden boards a foot or so from the ground. Very often the preparation might be done outdoors, in order to escape the oppressive heat of the kitchen.

The stove or *chula* was a mud brick platform with four or six (or as many as twelve) round plastered holes in front, which connected with grates on top. These holes held glowing charcoal and were kept at the right heat by the cook fanning furiously with a fan held in his spare hand. When complicated dishes were being prepared, the cook's assistant would do the fanning. Often all six fireplaces were in use at one time, for the typical Anglo-Indian dinner, even for a small family, consisted of six or eight dishes.

The cooking was done in handle-less tin-lined copper vessels known as *dekchies*, or in small round earthenware vessels called *chatties*. *Tavas* or *thoars* — large saucer-shaped griddles — were also used for frying. The *dekchies* had to be re-tinned once a month, while for hygiene's sake the *chatties* were smashed and replaced after two or three months' use. Towards the end of the nineteenth century enamel-lined pots gained favour, and later still aluminium vessels. By the First World War the latter could be obtained in almost any part of India.

A *tizal* or large earthenware pot on three legs was used for baking or roasting. Hot coals were placed both under the pot and on the lid, which was flat with a broad rim running around the edge to keep the coals from falling off. No doubt because the *tizal* was a 'native' implement, Flora Annie Steel insisted instead on an iron case with a door in front, set into bricks with a space above and below for charcoal. This surely amounted to much the same thing, but she was adamant:

The mere sight of a tizal with two crooked legs, the missing third supplied by a tottering pile of bricks, and three inches of dust and ashes inside to prevent utter cremation of the wretched cake, is enough to dishearten anyone. No one need be astonished if, in the frantic effort to get the lid full of burning coals off or on, the whole frail structure collapses, and khitmutgar, charcoal, ashes, cake and tins are mingled in hopeless confusion.

In Goa, as early as the seventeenth century, the Portuguese had introduced brick ovens in which they baked bread (*pao*), eaten with spicy chorizo sausage.

Water was kept in another large earthenware pot (or later, old kerosene tins) with a dipper, while washing up was done in a container like a sink but without taps or a drainage hole.

If a London chef had been put in an Indian kitchen

and there told to prepare a dinner, consisting of every delicacy in flesh, fish, and pudding, for twenty people, and by seven o'clock p.m., his first emotion would have a direct tendency to suicide . . . Nothing that he would call a spit, a grate, an oven, or any one convenience would meet his wildered eye; and he might as well go into the Highlands to look for knee-buckles, as there to search for a dripping-pan, or a roller; sieves, dredgers, cullenders and such like would be just a plentiful as blackberries are in Hyde Park, and even a dishclout would be difficult to procure. Yet the ingenious cook will, out of this nettle, pluck the flower, good dinner. (Quoted in *Bound to Exile*, by Michael Edwardes.)

This is an exaggeration, of course. The Indian cook was more than likely to possess a sieve, albeit one woven from bamboo rather than wire, and nor were refinements such as egg beaters, scales, pastry cutters, lemon squeezers, *bain maries*, larding needles and potato mashers completely unknown. It is true, however, that the Indian cook tended to oppose Western kitchen innovations or put them to uses the inventors would never have thought of, as Colonel Kenney-Herbert discovered once when he was staying with a friend in the Hills:

The water for my bath was brought, I noticed, in the outer vessel of a 'Warren's patent cooking pot'. 'Yes,' said my friend sorrowfully when I mentioned the occurrence, 'I could never prevail upon my fellows to use the thing in the kitchen, so they do what they like with it: the inner vessel makes a capital tom-tom for beating a sholah.'

Left entirely alone, with articles of his own selection around him, the native cook is, however, a singularly ingenious creature. All men who have been accustomed to a nomad life under canvas – far from the busy hum of cantonments – will I think, agree with me in this. Given a hole in the ground, and a couple of stones for her range, with a bundle of jungle sticks, a chatty or two, perhaps a dekshaw, and a fan, wherewithal to prepare a dinner, can you picture to yourself the face of Martha, 'the thorough good cook' of an English household?

An amusing expisode happened some five years ago which struck me at the time as illustrative to a degree of Ramasamy's opinion of the British system of cookery. I happened to be with a Regiment at Secunderabad which, for reasons connected with the antiquated barracks it occupied, was ordered into a standing camp. Our Colonel, an exceedingly young and fortunate officer, was a rampant officer of the new school. His brain was ever busy with new ideas: it was even reported he slept with 'Wolseley's soldier's pocket-book' and 'The rules for Signalling in connection with Outpost duty' under his pillow. The order to march into camp delighted him. After issuing his orders concerning the geometrical lines in which he wished the tents to be pitched, not even forgetting the whitewashing of the tent pegs, he turned his attention to the kitchens. Here was an opportunity for practically establishing a 'Wolseley's field kitchen'. Two Officers who had recently passed successfully through the Garrison course of instruction were accordingly sent for, and as a personal favour to the Commanding Officer, requested to go out to the camping ground, and lay out a series of broad-arrow kitchens for the Regiment. The work was done, and we marched into camp the next day. Whilst the men were busy at stables, the Colonel rode about inspecting everything; presently he came upon the neatly excavated kitchens, but, to his astonishment, found them deserted! Not a cook was to be seen! Orderlies flew to find out where on earth the men's breakfasts were being cooked, and in a few minutes the whole corps de cuisine was discovered squatting at work *more suo* in a dry nullah [stream bed] hard by. The Colonel furiously demanded why the proper kitchens had not been used, and 'all this abominable mess prevented?' Presently a cook of greater daring than his colleagues replied: 'What sar! that bad sense kitchen, sar, I beg your pardon: too much firewood taking: see sar this praper kitchen only.' In the face of so irresistible an argument, the Colonel (albeit beyond measure) was constrained to abandon his cherished project.

When presenting Ramasamy, therefore, with novel utensils, let us guard against his denouncing them 'bad sense'. We must patiently show him how to use them, proving, if we possibly can, by practical illustration the satisfactory results, saving of time, and so forth, to be gained by their means.

On the other hand, the Indian cook was likely to possess several implements which his Western counterpart would never have seen, such as a coconut scraper, a roller and stone for grinding spices, and various oar-shaped ladles for making halva.

The hot case was a peculiarly Anglo-Indian piece of equipment, consisting of a large box made from packing cases and lined with tin. Inside, a clay pan of glowing coals kept both plates and food warm until it was needed. The hot case was situated on the butler's verandah at the back of the house, and was necessary because food would otherwise grow cold by the time it was ferried to the table all the way from the cookhouse.

In some rainy parts of India such as Bengal the walkway to the kitchen was covered over, but where it was not, the food was exposed to all weathers, not to mention flocks of crows or kites. There are recorded instances of a kite swooping down on a plate borne aloft by the *khitmutgar* and carrying off a whole roast duck, leaving a bare plate of chips.

Perishables were kept in the pantry, with hooks from the ceiling to hang meat and poultry, wire safes for vegetables and fruits, and wire gauze linings around the windows to keep out flies. Dried and tinned provisions were kept in a separate storeroom, often a separate hut behind the bungalow. A good stock of basic provisions was essential for those who lived out of easy reach of shops and markets, but due to the ravages of insects, careful attention had to be paid to their storage.

To keep the ants out of the sugar, it would be stored on a three-tiered table with legs standing in saucers of water. Some memsahibs even went as far as having a miniature moat of water around the table as a first line of defence, and bricks under the sugar box as a final deterrent. Rice, split peas and grain had to be kept in earthen pots known as *gurras*, which had tightly fitting lids, or in zinc-lined boxes, to keep out the rats and mice. The musk rat was a particularly annoying pest; it would fill a whole room with its scent, and a ham, cheese or whatever it passed over would become impregnated with the smell and taste of musk. 'I had a present of a sack of potatoes,' recalled Mrs Major Clemons, 'a vegetable highly prized at a distance from Nandridrooj, where they grow, but after I had had them for a few days, they were all unfit to eat, a musk rat having run over the outside of the sack.'

It was from this go-down (warehouse) that the daily supplies were weighed out for the cook. Constance E. Gordon gives a suitable list of provisions in her *Anglo-Indian Cuisine and Domestic Economy*:

A little aid to the Bachelors Store List for the month

¼ maund sugar, soft
1 lb tea, makes tea twice a day
1 bottle vinegar
1 bottle salad oil
1 tin cornflour for blancmange etc.
1 bottle Worcester sauce
1 bottle mushroom ketchup
1 tin Bath, or other cheese biscuits
2 pkts lump sugar for use of guests
1 bottle vanilla flavouring
3 tins fish (in case you can't get fresh)
3 jars jam

1 bottle white pepper
1 bottle black pepper for cook
1 bottle salt
1 bottle French prunes for dessert
1 pkt dry ginger
1 bottle anchovies in oil
1 bottle Bovril (to help the soup when you invite an unexpected guest)
2 bars yellow soap for cleaning kitchen
1 pkt matches.

In the eyes of both the Victorian memsahib and her Indian butler, 'Europe articles' held great prestige and the shelves of the storeroom were often lined with rows of bottled sauces, jams and pickles, olives, capers, English biscuits and tinned foods. Such supplies were available at the local 'Europe shop', of which there was one in almost every station. In the cities, there were sufficient shops to ensure healthy competition, but at small up-country towns there was often only one such shopkeeper, who charged exorbitant prices, as Emma Roberts complained:

Establishments at up-country stations, without being nearly half so well supplied, are generally ten times dearer than those of Calcutta. Raspberry jam, the preserve most in request at an Indian table, bears a most preposterous price – a jar which is sold in London for about four shillings will cost from sixteen to twenty-four shillings. The charge at Cawnpore for half a pint of salad oil is six shillings; and in camp, a two pound square jar of pickles, and a pine cheese, have sold for three pounds each – an act of extravagance in the consumer which is without any excuse, the native pickles being infinitely superior to those brought from England, and the Hissar cheeses of far better quality than the importations, which are always either dry or rancid.

One of the best-known up-country provisioners was Havell, who opened what he called a farm at Deegah, on the Ganges near Patna. Bishop Heber, who in 1878 wrote of his travels in *Narrative of a Journey through the Upper Provinces of India*, describes this farm as

a tavern; a large ground-floor house with excellent rooms, very handsomely fitted up, surrounded with some of the most extensive ranges of cow-houses, pig-styes, places for fattening sheep and cattle, dairies, etc., that I have ever saw, all beautifully clean, with a large grass plot full of poultry, and in the middle a very pretty flower garden; to the back is a large kitchen garden, and beyond this, stacks of oats and other grain, not unworthy of an English farmer. The keeper is named Harvell, a very respectable man. He is butcher, corn-dealer, poulterer, wine merchant, confectioner and wax-chandler of all this part of India.

Harvell eventually expanded his business into china, jewellery, millinery, furniture, foreign fruit, jams and preserves, even fishing: his boats would go to the mouth of the Hooghly to catch mango and hilsa fish, which after being cured, were despatched all over India.

In Madras the great Europe store was Whiteley, while in Calcutta, from the late eighteenth century, it was Tulloh and Co.

For many years these regular shopkeepers faced stiff competition from the captains of East Indiamen, who filled the private space allotted them in their ships with goods for resale in Calcutta. As soon as his ship arrived the captain would advertise his wares in the *Calcutta Gazette*, listing such delicacies as tinned lobsters, oysters and reindeer tongues, liqueurs, dried fruits and hams. Some enterprising owners of smaller boats also took these items further up the Ganges from Calcutta, to compete with the Europe shops at riverside stations.

Where there was no Europe shop, the British residents had to rely on Indian hawkers, who carried around a miniature grocery store on their head.

After the introduction of railways, and the consequent speeding up of freight (previously it had taken six months for a bulky commodity ordered from Calcutta to reach an outlying station), most people began to use the mail order service of big Europe shops in the cities. Exorbitant though the packing and freight charges were, the mail order system still proved more economical than patronizing small-town European shop-keepers, who began to pass on to Indians their dusty establishments crammed with strange assortments of stale and sadly tarnished goods.

The Army and Navy Stores, which opened in Bombay in 1891 and in Karachi the following year, and then in Calcutta in 1901, were the most astute of the mail-order suppliers. Their catalogue ran to some 100 pages, and included perishable supplies which were packed on ice and sent by special trains to arrive at the destination on specified dates and times. Their merchandise came from America as well as Britain, and also included frozen meat from Australia, and wines and spirits from France and Spain.

The Army and Navy Store in Calcutta was three storeys high. Directly in from the main entrance there was a Food Hall on one side and a wine and spirits section on the other, with a cold storage unit beyond. In the early years only members of the Army and Navy Stores could shop there, with a ticket which proved membership.

The expense of imported tinned goods no doubt contributed to their snob value, but Colonel Kenney-Herbert, at least, had an enlightened and remarkably modern attitude:

I have long come to the conclusion that the fewer accessories you use in the way of hermetically-sealed provisions in the cooking of a dinner the better . . . Take now for instance a tin of the ordinary preserved mushrooms – those made you know of white leather – what is the use of them, what do they taste of? Yet people giving a dinner party must needs garnish one entrée at least with them, and the Madras butler would be horrified if his mistress were to refuse him that pleasure. The stewed 'black Leicestershire' are the best preserved mushrooms to be had, but even between them and the fresh fungus there is a great gulf fixed.

A few years ago I met an officer of the Artillery, who after having served in various parts of the world had just been appointed to a command in this [Madras] Presidency. Conversation happened to turn upon cookery, and the Colonel soon proved himself to be a man who had for years studied the science con amore. He had had little or no experience of Indian life, and he expressed himself agreeably surprised, rather than otherwise, at the style of living to which he had been introduced. 'But', he said, 'preserve me from your dinners of ceremony.' He had arrived, he told me, quite unexpectedly a few evenings before, and had been at once invited to the mess; the dinner, – the ordinary daily one, – was, he thought, excellent, and so it was on the next day, and the day following, but on the fourth day he was formally invited to dine as a Mess guest, and that was a very different affair. Considerable expense had been gone to, he observed, on this occasion in tinned provisions, but with the worst possible result. There was a dish of preserved salmon hot, and sodden; the entrées were spoilt by the introduction of terrible sausages, and mushrooms; and the tinned vegetables were ruined by being wrongly treated by the cook. 'There are few men', the Colonel went on, 'who have had more to do with preserved provisions than I have, but until I attended this big Indian dinner, I never saw such things actually regarded as delicacies, and put upon the table to the exclusion of the good fresh food procurable at the market.' This is the proper way of looking at this question.

I look upon tinned provisions in the hands of Ramasamy as the cloaks of carelessness, and slovenly cooking; he thinks that the tin will cover a multitude of sins, so takes comparatively little pains with the dish that it accompanies.

One provision to be found in nearly every store cupboard was chilli vinegar, a British Indian invention made by infusing fresh chillies in vinegar (for recipe see page 224). A bottle was commonly seen on the table of every officers' mess, since many officers, accustomed to curries, found soup insipid.

'Amongst sauces', wrote Colonel Kenney-Herbert, 'I consider "Harvey" the best for general use; Sutton's "Empress of India" is a strong sauce with a real flavour of mushrooms; "Reading Sauce" is very trustworthy, and there are others which, no doubt, commend themselves to different palates, but I denounce "Worcester Sauce" and "Tapp's Sauce" as agents far too powerful to be trusted to the hands of the native cook.' Perhaps such advice had something to do with all the chilli and garlic, which abound in the version found in the *Indian Domestic Economy and Receipt Book* of Dr Riddell.

TAPP'S SAUCE

Take of green sliced mangoes, salt, sugar and raisins each eight ounces; red chillies and garlic each four ounces; green ginger six ounces; vinegar three bottles; lime-juice one pint. Pound of several ingredients well; then add the vinegar and lime juice; stop the vessel close, and expose it to the sun a whole month, stirring or shaking it well daily; then strain it through a cloth, bottle and cork it tight.

Obs. – The residue makes an excellent chutney.

Despite its name, Worcester sauce was originally an Indian recipe, brought back to Britain by Lord Marcus Sandys, ex-Governor of Bengal. One day in 1835 he appeared in the prospering chemist's emporium of John Lea and William Perrins in Broad Street, Worcester, and asked them to make up a batch of sauce from his recipe. This was done, but the resulting fiery mixture almost blew the heads off Messrs Lea and Perrins, and a barrel they had made up for themselves was consigned to the cellars. Much later, in the midst of a spring clean, they came across the barrel and decided to taste it again before throwing it out. Wonder of wonders, the mixture had mellowed into a superlative sauce! The recipe was hastily bought from Lord Sandys and in 1838 Britain's most famous commercial sauce was launched.

Within ten years it was being used in the households of many noble families, and exported all over the world. John Lea died a millionaire, and his sauce spawned a host of imitations, many with grand Imperial names such as Nabob's, Mandarin, British Lion and Empress of India. None, however, managed to match the exact flavour of the original. The exact recipe for Worcester sauce remains a secret, but it is based on vinegar, soy and molasses and includes mushroom ketchup, salted anchovies, chilli, ginger, capsicums, shallots, cloves, nutmeg and cardamom.

'The Indian cook cannot live without sauces,' wrote the author of *Things for the Cook*, a 1914 recipe book written in both English and Hindi. 'They are with him, a passion; but his passion must be restrained, or he will use his sauces to drive beneath the surface, the evil flavour of superannuated fish or meat.' The same argument was used with regard to spices, particularly that most celebrated and reviled of all Anglo-Indian concoctions: curry powder.

Nowadays the very mention of the name is calculated to raise the ire of a nationalistic Indian cook, and it is indeed true that curry powder has badly misrepresented Indian cookery to the rest of the world. To a people whose cuisine is centred upon freshly grinding and mixing different spices in varying proportions for each individual dish, the idea that a single ready-made spice mixture can be added to fish, chicken, eggs or whatever to produce real Indian 'curry' is preposterous, to say the least. As Madhur Jaffrey puts it: 'To me the word "curry" is as degrading to India's great cuisine as "chop suey" was to China's.'

However, the mere fact that curry powder has been taken for a purely Indian rather than an Anglo-Indian commodity does not necessarily make it a bad thing in itself. After all, it is not stretching the point to describe curry powder as no more than a version of *garam masala*, the ready-ground spice mixtures which the Indians themselves use every day.

Admittedly these *garam masalas* have fewer ingredients than curry powder and, are not used for the complete spicing of a dish, but merely as a basis. They are also ground at frequent intervals and are never kept on the shelves for years as curry powders often are. Nevertheless, the lists of spices for some of these *masalas* bear strong resemblance to curry powder. A good example is Madras *rasam masala*, which typically contains chillies, coriander, cumin, peppercorns, turmeric, fenugreek, curry leaves and mustard seed. With just a few minor additions, such as small amounts of cloves, cinnamon and nutmeg, this mixture would become what most people would recognize as curry powder.

While the exact origins of curry powder are unknown, it seems most likely it was invented in the seventeenth century as an export commodity for East India Company employees to take or send back to England. The idea of made-up mixtures of powdered spices was by no means new to the English. Recipes for two such compounds were on the rolls of Richard II's master cooks as early as 1390. These medieval mixtures went under several names: 'powder douce', 'powder fort' and 'blanch powder', the last consisting of ground sugar, ginger and cinnamon. In powder fort, hot spices such as ginger and pepper predominated, while milder spices went into powder douce.

In seventeenth-century Britain 'kitchen pepper' came into vogue. One recipe of 1682 called for two ounces of ginger and one ounce each of powdered pepper, cloves, nutmegs and cinnamon, which was then mixed with a further pound of pepper.

Such a strong English tradition of spice mixtures makes it dangerous to assume that an Indian rather than a Englishman made the first curry powder. Whatever the nationality of the inventor, there can be little doubt that he or she was influenced by the spice *masalas* of India. One further thing is certain: curry powder as we know it today could not have come about until the Portuguese introduced the chilli pepper to India in the sixteenth century. As for the name, the consensus seems to be that it is derived from the Tamil *kari*, meaning sauce. 'Curry' is still used in this original sense by Indian cooks when they are speaking, in English, of spiced stew-like dishes with their own sauce. Also possible, but less likely, is that the word was derived from *kahi*, a north Indian yoghurt sauce thickened with chickpea flour, or *kari phulia*, the curry leaf, a common ingredient of Madras curry powder.

The first recipe for chilli-based curry as we know it today was one for *caril* (the Kanarese form of the word) in the seventeenth-century Portuguese cookery book *Arte de Cozinha*.

The British in India certainly used curry powder, but as the recipes in this book will attest, it was not nearly as common as might be thought. Why indeed should they have bothered with bastardized imitations, when an Indian cook was on hand at all times to cook the real thing? Moreover, there was invariably a cook's assistant who could be assigned the laborious task of grinding the spices freshly to order.

To eighteenth-century cooks in England, however, curry powder was no doubt considered a boon, for accustomed though they were to pounding, mashing and sieving, their lightweight mortars and pestles were not up to the task of grinding some of the harder spices such as fenugreek and poppy seed. Even in Indian homes, where they bring into action first a giant stone mortar and an equally outsized pestle held with both hands, and then a stone rolling pin and slab, the grinding of a couple of pounds of spices might occupy the better part of a day.

One of the first British 'currey' recipes appeared in 1747, in Hannah Glasse's *Art of Cookery*. It was essentially a chicken fricassee spiced with turmeric, ginger and pepper 'beat very fine'. In 1772 the author of *The Complete Housekeeper and Professed Cook* also told how make 'curry the Indian way'.

By 1773 curry had become the speciality of at least one London coffee house, and from about 1780 the first commercial curry powders were on sale. In his *Cook's Oracle*, published in 1817, Dr Kitchiner gave a recipe, claiming, in his pompous and self-congratulatory way, that 'the flavour approximates to the Indian powder so exactly, the most profound Palaticians have pronounced it a perfect copy of the original Curry stuff.'

This fashionable revival of piquant food in England (which besides curry powder, manifested itself in bottled sauces, chutneys and relishes) had been brought to England by the returning nabobs and was sustained by their nineteenth-century successors in the civil and military services of India. Queen Victoria herself employed two Indian cooks whose sole duty was to prepare the curry that was served at lunch each day, regardless of whether she or her guests partook of it or not.

During his 1877 Indian tour, Prince Albert was supposed to have been motivated to visit the Madras Club solely by a desire to taste their Madras prawn curry. So impressed was he by the famous curry tiffin they turned out in his honour that 'M. Bonnemain, the chef on board the *Seraphis*, was instructed by native cooks in its mysteries; but the French intelligence, fine and keen as it is, does not penetrate the depths of curry lore, and the dishes, even after a considerable experience in the arts and sciences of several gentlemen of colour engaged expressly to dress curries, never came up to the Indian standard.'

Edward VII, for all his gourmandise, did not inherit this taste, but his son George V showed little interest in anything else. He ate curry almost every day for lunch, having developed a taste for it in India.

By George V's reign however, Victoria's Indian cooks had long gone and the all-purpose sauce his Swiss chef used to smother the royal chicken, pheasant, rabbit or whatever was very typical of the English curry which had evolved by then: curry powder, onions, apples and desiccated coconut cooked with the meat in chicken stock and finished with cream and lemon juice.

In this peculiarly English adaptation, desiccated coconut replaced the fresh, the apple and lemon were perhaps a substitute for tamarind, while the fragrance of other equally unavailable fresh condiments such as ginger root and coriander leaves had been lost completely. Where the idea originated of adding sultanas to the standard English works canteen curry is anybody's guess.

Worst of all was the English tendency to debase the curry to the mean function of using up leftovers. 'You may curry anything,' suggested Mr Arnot of Greenwich, 'old shoes should even be delicious, some old oil cloth or staircarpet not to be found fault with (gloves if much worn are too rich).'

Equally comical because of its factualness is the story in *The Wife's Cookery Book* of 1906. Mrs Franklin writes:

Half the taste and colour of the curry would be destroyed if it were cooked in the very peculiar way that an English woman in England once cooked it.

'This is my rice and curry day,' she explained to an Indian acquaintance who had accompanied her husband's regiment to England. 'Would you like to stay and see me make it? I believe you Indians do not know how to cook.'

Her friend expressed her willingness, and many a time after she told the story with amusement.

The Englishwoman tied a teacupful of rice in a muslin bag, and boiled it in a saucepan of water. She then took a small plateful of cold scraps of meat, one week's savings, and put it in another saucepan with some curry powder, some butter and stock, and proceeded to boil it.

When she thought both rice and curry – save the mark – done, she untied the muslin, served the rice in flat dish, made a hole in the centre of the rice, poured the curry into it and served the unappetising stuff. Yet any native will tell you to avoid twice boiling meat for curry.

Some returned memsahibs such as Henrietta Hervey set themselves the mission of re-educating their English cooks:

The English servant, I find, *is* open to instruction. Ours, a raw country Essex girl, has learnt to boil rice as well as any old 'Thunnikurchi' or Cook-boy out there, and I am hopeful of being able to entrust her with curries &c., at no very distant date. Patience is a virtue and – everything.

Whatever people's usage or abusage of the stuff, there is no denying curry powder's success. Being so easy to use and so readily transportable, it has reached every corner of the earth. Indeed, such far-flung fame must be partly what infuriates the purist Indian critics. In Jamaica curried goat is practically a national dish, as is curried crayfish in New Zealand, and curried chicken in Ghana. In Western Samoa culinary traditions undergo a delightful jumbling with chow mein curry, while in Japan the average family eats curry and rice at least once a week. Even the French, who for all their international acclaim in culinary matters have a minimal understanding of the use of spices, have taken curry aboard, albeit in low forms. Eminçé de volaille au curry or, in more prosaic terms, leftover chicken reheated and disguised by a blanket of curry-flavoured white sauce, emanates from none other than Auguste Escoffier.

In West Africa the local cooks learned and adapted Indian dishes from the cooks who accompanied English expatriates from India. One of the most famous of these is Groundnut Chop, which was served in much the same way as a Sunday curry tiffin in the officers' mess in India, with numerous little side dishes such as grated coconut, roast groundnuts (or peanuts), sultanas, sliced onions and sliced bananas.

GROUNDNUT CHOP *serves* 4

1 lb (500 g) peanuts	1 tsp curry powder
3 tbsp peanut oil	1–2 tsp chilli powder
1 chicken (3 lb, 1.5 kg), cut into pieces	½ tsp allspice, ground
	1 pt (600 ml) chicken stock
1 large onion, finely diced	salt

Roast the peanuts in a hot oven with 1 tbsp of the peanut oil until very lightly browned. Allow to cool, then grind in a food processor. (An equivalent quantity of peanut butter can be substituted, but fresh peanuts taste better.)

Heat the remaining 2 tbsp oil and sauté the chicken pieces and onion until both are lightly browned. Add the curry powder, chilli and allspice and fry for a further 30 seconds, then pour in the stock and add salt to taste. Simmer for 45 minutes. Ten minutes before the end of cooking, add the ground peanuts.

Serve with rice and the accompaniments listed above.

A non-traditional but delicious variation of this recipe is to substitute coconut cream and tamarind water for some of the stock.

While a typical curry powder consists mainly of coriander, turmeric and cumin, with lesser amounts of chillies, black pepper and fenugreek, and smaller amounts still of other spices such as ginger, cardamom, cloves, cinnamon, mustard seed and poppy seed, there is no such thing as a standard recipe. Indeed, the proportions of commercial curry powders can vary wildly. Some Continental brands consist of little more than turmeric (which results in a raw, earthy-tasting curry powder), while others use too much fenugreek, which makes the mixture bitter. Some mean-minded manufacturers also eke out the quantity with ground lentils, or substitute bay leaves for the cardamom, which are far cheaper and yet yield a similarly camphor-like fragrance. Added to this is the fact that many commercial curry powders remain on shop shelves much longer than they should, losing most of their flavour unless the container is kept completely airtight.

All this is a good incentive to grind and mix your own, which in this age of electric coffee mills and blenders is easily done. What follows is just a very few of the many variations included in recipe collections of the era. All make a wonderful change from the average shop-bought powders, but most will need the quantities reducing considerably (Dr Riddell's No. 1 Curry Powder begins with 20 lb (9 kg) of coriander seed!). The spices should be toasted lightly first.

In 1896 the Governor of Bombay gave the following locally produced curry powder his official seal of approval. Henrietta Hervey reproduces it in her *Anglo-Indian Cookery at Home* and it is one of the best for making Anglo-Indian curries.

BOMBAY CURRY POWDER
Take three pounds coriander seed, half pound cummin seed, one and half pound turmeric, four ounces fenugreek, half a pound mustard seed, one pound pepper, one and quarter pound dry chillies. Clean, dry, pound and sift the whole, and keep in well-corked bottles.

For her Bengal Curry Powder Henrietta Hervey included cinnamon and cardamoms, which would increase its cost, but also make a more aromatic mixture.

BENGAL CURRY POWDER
Take three pounds coriander seed, three and a half pounds turmeric, twelve ounces fenugreek, three pounds dry ginger, three pounds black pepper, two pounds dry chillies, one pound cinnamon, one pound cardamom. Clean, dry, pound, and sift the whole, and keep in well-corked bottles.

Madras curry powder, the most famous of curry blends, is given its distinctive flavour by the curry leaves. This version is from *Anglo-Indian Cuisine* by Constance E. Gordon.

MADRAS CURRY POWDER
Clean and roast separately 2 oz fenugreek, 1 oz black pepper, 1½ oz dried chillies, ¼ lb cummin seed, ¾ lb coriander, ¼ oz cloves, 2 oz mustard seed; stir them about on the thoar and roast lightly, then pound very fine and pass through a wire

sieve. Then pound in a mortar, or on a curry stone 1 oz garlic, ¼ lb turmeric, 5 oz salt, less than ¼ oz of dried curry leaf; mix all together, repass the whole mixture through a fine hair sieve again, bottle and cork well, and the curry powder will keep for any length of time.

Harriet Lawrance, in the charmingly named *Cookery for the Million, being 333 practical, economical recipes in Indian cookery* (1908), includes a Madras curry mixture which is preserved in ghee and vinegar, resulting in a paste rather than a powder. (The *venthium* she lists is fenugreek, and – a warning – the inclusion of such a huge amount of saffron as will put it out of the reach of most cooks' budgets!)

MADRAS CURRY PASTE
1 lb coriander seed, ¼ lb saffron, 10 oz dried chillies, 4 oz pepper, 4 oz cleaned mustard, 2 oz dried ginger, 2 oz venthium, 4 oz cleaned garlic, 8 oz salt, 8 oz prepared Bengal gram (cudlay), 4 oz cummin, ½ a pint of English vinegar, ½ a pint of ghee.

Roast all the mussala, this will make it crisp and easily powdered; pound it very fine passing the powder through a muslin, then mix it well up with the ghee and vinegar. Will make 100 dessertspoonfuls.

7

Breakfast and Tiffin

In British India the day often began as early as 5 a.m. with a brisk ride on horseback for an hour or so before the heat of the day set in. A cup of tea and perhaps a little fruit would be taken after such a gallop, and hence the Anglo-Indian institution of *chota hazri* or little breakfast came into being. During the hot weather visitors might be expected during this *chota hazri* hour, but were only ever offered tea, coffee, fruit or biscuits, the *bari hazri*, or main breakfast, being reserved for 9 or 10 o'clock.

Alternatively, the *chota hazri* might act as a wake-up call, a tea tray being taken to the bedroom by a bearer (a custom which still survives in India's 'British clubs', such as the Royal Bombay Yacht Club and the Mahabaleshwar Club).

Returning from his early morning ride, the typical early eighteenth-century Calcutta gentleman, wrote Stoequeler in 1799:

undresses, puts on his loose Turkish trousers, drinks iced soda water, lies down on the couch, novel or newspaper in hand and in all probability, goes to sleep, despite the cawing of crows. Breakfast was at ten and was as lavish then, as now, in Anglo-Indian houses. The said meal consisted in all seasons of rice, fried fish, omelette, preserves, tea, coffee etc, more in the fashion of Scotch than English matutinal recreation. (Quoted in *British Social Life in India* by Dennis Kincaid, 1938.)

Such full-scale feasts were still routine during the next century. A. Fenton, writing his *Memoirs of a Cadet* in the 1830s, describes breakfast at a Calcutta hotel:

Dear reader, picture to yourself a snow-white tablecloth, on which were drawn up, in beautiful array, ham, eggs, a superb kind of fish from salt water lakes, called *bektee* or cock-up, fried, boiled rice, muffins, tea, coffee, & Plantains, radishes, small prints [pats] of butter in a handsome cut-glass vessel of cold water, and a bouquet of beautiful flowers, gave a most cool and refreshing appearance . . . A *khidmutgar*, or native waiter, stood behind each of our chairs, with a *chouree* [fly swat made from a cow's tail] in hand, to keep in awe the flies and a *punkah* waved pleasantly over our heads – and all this lordly service for two cadets!

In the eighteenth and early nineteenth centuries there might be half a dozen servants on duty for breakfast, including one whose sole function was to bring in the tea-kettle from the *ungeeta* (a brazier of hot coals kept out on the verandah) and fill the teapot! During breakfast the *mali*, or gardener, might appear with baskets of fruit and vegetables, and a small bouquet for each lady. His wares, neatly arranged on plantain leaves, would be offered around the table for each person to take something – custard apples, guavas, chillies or cresses.

Later, in Victorian times, there was a reaction against such excessive formality at breakfast, which was, after all, supposed to be an intimate family meal. It was not necessary, wrote Flora Annie Steel, 'to have a tribe of servants dancing around the table ready to snatch away your plate at the least pause.' Rather, the servants should be ordered to remain outside after having handed around the food. Nor should the breakfast table be crowded with formal floral arrangements. Indeed, the redoubtable Mrs Steel had strong views on the subject:

Breakfasts in India are for the most part horrible meals, being hybrids between the English and the French fashions. Then the ordinary Indian cook has not an idea for breakfast beyond chops, steaks, fried fish, and quail; a menu rendered still less inviting by the poor quality of both fish and meat. Tea made and poured out by a *khitmutgar* at a side table, toast and butter coming in when the meal is half finished, and the laying of table for lunch while the breakfast-eaters are still seated, combine to make newcomers open their eyes at Indian barbarities.

When there was a large party for breakfast, wrote Mrs Steel, there should be at least two plates of butter and toast:

In regard to the former, the *khitmutgar* should be generally discouraged from making it the medium for a display of his powers in plastic art; it is doubtless gratifying to observe such yearning for beauty, even in butter, but it is suggestive of too much handling to be pleasant.

Toast was made by holding up a slice of bread against hot embers, and as a result tended to arrive tough and dirty white, streaked with black.

Since the export marmalade industry became established in Britain only in the last years of the nineteenth century, in India they had to make do with 'country marmalade' made from pomelo, the thick-skinned and rather coarse ancestor of the grapefruit. In the hill stations strawberries (both wild and cultivated) and a species of raspberry were so abundant they were used for jam.

During the Edwardian era the so-called Badminton Breakfast at the local club came into vogue, where the wearied players would refresh themselves with barley water and bacon sandwiches and slices of cut cake.

One institution which spanned the entire period of British rule was the public breakfast. This was derived from the common table of the earliest East India Company days and by the mid-eighteenth century had developed into a grand occasion, perhaps in imitation of a new fashion for such public breakfast parties among the aristocracy back in England. In 1775 William Hickey wrote in his diary: 'On the 8th I went to Mr Francis's public breakfast, it being the custom in those days for the Governor-General and members of council to receive visits of compliments or strangers for introduction at breakfast, each having one morning a week for the purpose.'

This was undoubtedly an onerous duty for Francis, who had expressed disgust at the noise of the crowds at such affairs. Obviously they were too popular to be abandoned, although by Edmund Hull's time (1871) they had dwindled to just one or two a year:

These 'governor's breakfasts' are held in some large hall or room in Government House [in Calcutta]: long tables laden with cold viands, being arranged down either side, and a smaller one, on a dais, across the end, for the governor and his more particular friends. At nine or half-past, the hall begins to fill with gentlemen in morning dress, and a few minutes later his excellency enters, followed by his staff, and bowing to the assembled guests. All now take their seats, and in half an hour or so the entertainment is at an end; the company dispersing, every one to his particular business. Gentlemen wishing to have a private interview with the governor must state the wish on their cards (sent in the evening before), and his excellency now remains to grant the desired interviews to each. The object of one is perhaps to ask for a subscription to some charity; another, is in quest of a post for himself; a third, desires advancement for a friend, and so on.

In the 1930s Elizabeth Crawford Wilkin attended, at the unseemly hour of seven in the morning, an almost identical occasion in honour of the Viceroy and Vicereine of India, who were paying a three-hour visit to Krishnabad as part of an official tour of the country in their pristine white private train:

From a culinary point of view the breakfast was not a success – lukewarm coffee and porridge, cold fried eggs and leathery toast – but I doubt its deficiencies were greatly noticed. Their Excellencies were served by their own servants, who had been whisked from the train to Government House, so their meal was perhaps hotter and more delectable than ours.

These Anglo-Indian breakfasts were leisurely affairs, especially in the *mofussil*. There were no trains or school buses to catch, and no early opening of offices, since the Indian clerks had to do their family shopping before they came to work; it was not seemly for an Indian woman to be seen in the bazaar, and due to the heat, perishable foods had to be bought fresh every day.

The startling array of meat consumed at Anglo-Indian breakfasts included crumbed chops, brain cutlets, beef rissoles, devilled kidneys, whole spatchcocks, duck stews, Irish stews, mutton hashes, brawns of sheep's heads and trotters, not to mention an assortment of Indian meat dishes such as *jhal frazie*, prawn *dopiaza*, chicken *malai* and beef *hussainee*. Added to this list were a number of Anglo-Indian concoctions such as kidney toast Madras style (crumbed kidneys on toast spread with curry paste), Madras fritters (ham and chutney sandwiches, battered and deep fried), or leftover meat minced and refried with ginger and chillies.

Such massive consumption of red meat at breakfast was merely an earlier English custom transferred to a tropical climate, regardless of its suitability. The habit of eating fish for breakfast had a more rational basis, since in the hot season, fish caught early in the morning might well have turned bad by the evening. It was in these circumstances that British India's most celebrated breakfast dish, kedgeree, came about.

Kedgeree is a prime example of how one recipe can eventually transmute into another, for, aside from the rice, this delightful Anglo-Indian jumble of smoked fish, rice and chopped egg bears no relation to its parent recipe of the same, or similar name.

Khichri, as it is commonly understood in Indian cookery, means a combination of dal and rice boiled together with spices such as coriander, cardamom, cloves, ginger and chilli (see page 157). There are descriptions of it by travellers to India a thousand years ago, and it probably even predates them, since the name is derived from the Sanskrit *k'ysara*.

When the British arrived in the seventeenth century they adopted *khichri* as a breakfast dish, both in its original form and with flaked fresh fish substituted for the dal. In time they dropped the spices, added hard-boiled egg, anglicized the name, and kedgeree was born.

During the eighteenth century the recipe reached Britain, where its rise to fame happened to coincide with an improvement in communications in Britain, in particular, the stagecoach connection with Findon, just south of Aberdeen. At Findon there was a thriving cottage industry of smoking haddocks, split open and left whole, over fires of seaweed, peat and moss. These haddocks were now able to reach the markets of Edinburgh and eventually as far south as London, and were the ancestors, albeit harder and saltier, of today's Finnan haddock.

These smoked fish were soon associated very closely with kedgeree, which probably explains why kedgeree has so often been mistaken for a Scottish dish. A few nineteenth-century cooks continued to use cold fresh fish, such as salmon or turbot, but most now agreed that smoked fish was central to the character of the dish.

During the Victorian and Edwardian eras kedgeree had a permanent place on the dining room sideboard at the English country house where, in Bertie Wooster's words, 'we really had breakfast . . . fried eggs, scrambled eggs, fishcakes and kedgeree, sometimes mushrooms, some-times kidneys . . .'

Today the prospect of kedgeree may appear more than a little daunting first thing in the morning, but, like all the recipes in this chapter, it serves equally well as a lunch or supper dish.

To define just what constitutes the true kedgeree is a good way to provoke angry letters to *The Times*, but at the risk of doing so, might I suggest its essential ingredients are rice, smoked fish, hard-boiled eggs, onion, butter and chopped parsley:

KEDGEREE *serves 3–4*

12 oz (350 g) smoked fish fillets	2 eggs
oil	1 tbsp butter
1 large onion, chopped	salt and pepper
6 oz (175 g) long-grained rice	2 tbsp chopped parsley

Cover the fish with boiling water and simmer gently over a low heat for 10 minutes. Drain, but reserve the water.

Heat a little oil in the bottom of a heavy saucepan and fry the chopped onion until transparent, then add the rice and stir until it is lightly glazed. Measure a scant ½ pt (250 ml) of the fish water (making up the amount with extra water if necessary), and add it to the rice and onions. Cover the pot tightly and cook for about 14 minutes until all the liquid has been absorbed by the rice.

Meanwhile, hard-boil the eggs (allow 10 minutes) and break up the fish into flakes. Chop or slice the hard-boiled eggs and mix into the hot cooked rice with the fish, butter, salt and pepper to taste. Arrange in a pyramid-shaped pile on a serving dish and sprinkle the parsley over the top. A true daughter of the Empire might also sieve the hard-boiled eggs over the top in the pattern of the cross of St Andrew.

And that, according to the purists, should be all, although of course there are countless variations. You may, for instance, wish to enrich the above mixture with a raw egg and ¼ pt (150 ml) cream. Beat these lightly together and stir into the kedgeree over the heat for a minute at the end of cooking, until the mixture is creamy. If the kedgeree is to be kept on a hot plate, this addition will prevent it drying out.

Curry powder appears in some recipes, and it is especially recommended if you are using fresh or leftover cold fish instead of smoked fish. Allow about a teaspoonful for the above recipe. In her *Book of Household Management* (1861) Mrs Beeton, who suggests fresh fish, recommends adding a teaspoonful of mustard, and other recipes suggest a little cayenne pepper, and enough turmeric or saffron to turn the rice yellow. A pinch of nutmeg can also be added. Some old Anglo-Indian recipes call for anchovy essence (allow about a tablespoonful) and a dash of chilli vinegar (see page 224) to be added at the end. Alternatively, you might use a tablespoonful of tomato sauce, or a good squeeze of lemon juice.

For colour as well as for flavour, try adding any of the following: peas, tinned or fresh sweetcorn, button mushrooms, chopped chives or watercress, green or red capsicums. Almonds and fried onion rings, while not traditional, also add a tasty decoration.

Tinned smoked fish can be used instead, and this may also be supplemented or substituted with tinned salmon, tuna or sardines. You don't even need to be restricted to fish; in his *Tasty Dishes of India* (1980), Colonel Hare recommends minced meat or pieces of cooked chicken.

Kedgeree was not the only fish dish to be served for breakfast. In *The*

Economical Cookery Book (for India) (1926), G. L. Routleff writes that fish moolee is 'a breakfast dish, served with boiled rice or toast handed round, and is much appreciated'.

FISH MOOLEE

One pound of fish cut into squares and fried, a small tea-cup of thick cocoanut milk, the same quantity of stock made from trimmings and bones, two ozs. ghee, two sliced onions, half an inch of turmeric ground, half a dozen very thin slices of ginger, two or three green chillies sliced, half a tea-spoonful of salt, one table-spoonful of vinegar or tamarind juice.

Melt the ghee, fry half the onions in it to a light brown, add the turmeric, ginger and salt, gradually the cocoanut milk; let this cook for a few minutes, then add the green chillies and the remainder of the onions; stir; add your pieces of fish. Keep the pan uncovered and let the whole simmer for a few minutes. Just before serving add the vinegar or tamarind juice.

Because fish did not stay fresh for long in India's climate, cookery and housekeeping books of the Raj all include suggestions for preserving fish and meat. Just how palatable some of these methods were is debatable, and on the whole we can be thankful for fast modern transport and refrigeration! The following both appeared in Harriet Lawrance's *Cookery for the Million.* 'Curry-stuff' would have been a ready-prepared spice mixture like *garam masala*.

PICKLED FISH, A BREAKFAST RELISH

INGREDIENTS:— 2 tablespoonsful of curry-stuff; 12 green chillies; 12 peels of garlic; 6 slices of green ginger; 4 cloves; 1 teaspoonful of whole pepper; ½ teaspoonful of white salt; 1 teaspoonful of common salt; 2 teacupfuls of small fish; about 2 cups of vinegar.

MODE:— Clean the fish and soak it in cold water with the common salt for 1 hour, take it out dry it with a towel, and pack it alternately with the rest of the ingredients in an earthern vessel, mix the currystuff and salt in the vinegar and pour over all, boil til done, cool and bottle. Large fish may be cut up and done similarly.

BALACHONG BREAKFAST RELISH

INGREDIENTS:— 10 oz of minced onions; 2 oz of garlic; 4 oz of green chillies; 4 oz of green ginger; 1 teaspoonful of white salt; ¾ lb tamarind; 1 tablespoonful of ghee; 3 lbs of tomatoes; 1 lb of salt-fish without bones; 1 teaspoonful of ground saffron; vinegar about ½ or ¾ bottle.

MODE:— Soak the saltfish and tomatoes in hot water, remove the skins of the tomatoes and squeeze out the pulp and seeds which throw away, wash the saltfish from all grit and remove the skin, mince all the ingredients, soak the tamarind in the vinegar and remove the fibres, etc.; put the ghee in a vessel and fry the saltfish and saffron till brown; add the rest of the ingredients and boil till quite thick; put up when cold.

Average quantity 5½ lbs.

Then, of course, there were eggs. Always plentiful, eggs in India were very small and somewhat flavourless compared with English ones. 'Singularly adapted to the climate in which we spend our exile, and inexpensive, they are at the same time invested with a certain amount of refinement that to many people is no slight recommendation,' commented Colonel Kenney-Herbert.

Many British kept their own fowls to avoid having to buy eggs of dubious quality from the bazaar. Store-bought eggs had to be subjected to the age-old test of placing them in a basin of cold water: they were stale if one end lifted or the egg began to rise, and downright rotten if they floated.

Scrambled eggs went under the delightful name of 'rumble-tumble', which became 'craggy toast' if tomatoes were included. 'Ox eyes' were eggs baked in rings of fried bread, while 'egg toast' was scrambled egg with chilli on buttered bread.

Omelettes or 'amlates' were (and indeed still are) a very common breakfast dish in India. At the Bengal Club in Calcutta, four cooks were employed to make nothing but omelettes all day long.

'We ought never to be unable to make a good savoury omelette, whether in camp, at a public bungalow, at a picnic, or in the privacy of our back verandah in cantonment,' wrote the Colonel, adding however that

Ramasamy has been led astray altogether with regard to this branch of his art. He sends you up a very nice pudding, symmetrical in design, of a goodly consistency, and of a rich brown colour. You almost require a dessert knife to help it. It is, of course, lighter somewhat than a roly-poly pudding made of paste [pastry], but it greatly resembles that homely composition. It is a first cousin of the pancake, and Ramasamy evidently uses the stuff of which it is made to dip his plantains into when bidden to make fritters. He starts wrongly to commence with, when mixing his omelette: in addition to the eggs he puts in a little flour, some milk or a little water, and, in point of fact, makes a lightish sort of batter. This, I regret to say, he fries in a fair amount of ghee, folding it into shape, and keeping it on the fire till it is nice and firm, and coloured as I before described.

The Colonel tells us he was taught how to make a proper omelette by a civil servant who entertained him in Pennaconda one night when the Colonel was on a march with his regiment from Bangalore to Secunderabad.

Though so far away from any civilised place, the dinner placed before me in the quondam public bungalow in which my host resided might have graced a petit table in the strangers' room of a London Club. His breakfast was an equally artistic meal, and was concluded by an omelette – made on the spot – by my accomplished friend himself.

This was made by mixing, not beating, six yolks and four whites, into which was stirred a teaspoon of shallots, a heaped tablespoon of curly parsley (grown in the friend's garden), and a tablespoon of cream. 'We now left the dining room for the verandah where there was a good charcoal fire in an iron brazier and upon it a pan . . .' in which a pat of butter was heated and the mixture poured, and lifted with a spoon as soon as it set, allowing the uncooked portion to run underneath; the result of course, being a classic French omelette.

The typical Anglo-Indian omelette incorporated minced onion, chillies and fresh mint. It was this mixture which, together with shredded leeks and cloves, went into the King of Oude's omelette immortalized by Eliza Acton in her *Modern Cookery* of 1845. Sometimes, instead of the mint, chopped fresh coriander leaves might be used (an idea borrowed from the Parsis of Bombay).

Eggs also accompanied dal and rice for breakfast, either poached or hard-boiled. Angela C. Spry, in *The Mem Sahibs Book of Cookery* of 1894, added them as a garnish to spiced dal.

DHALL CURRY WITH EGGS
One cupful of parboiled dhall, Two tablespoonfuls Ghee, One teaspoonful salt, Half teaspoonful Cayenne Pepper, Half teaspoonful Garlic, One teaspoonful Coriander-seed, Two sticks Cinnamon, A few Cloves, Three hard-boiled Eggs cut into slices, Six Onions cut into slices and fried brown in butter, One cupful soup or gravy.

Heat the ghee, put in all the condiments and stew brown. Add the dhall, stir all together for five minutes. Pour in the gravy, cover and allow to simmer for 15 minutes until the ghee floats clear on the top. Put out into a vegetable dish, garnish on top with plenty of sliced onions fried brown, and sliced eggs over the onions.

Curried eggs, which have since become so familiar as to be considered an English dish, did equally well for breakfast or lunch. Sometimes they might be simmered with spices in coconut cream (Mrs Bartley suggests hard-boiled eggs as an alternative to fish in her Poorege Fish Curry on page 105), and Angela Spry uses eggs in a curry she describes as molten (even though it is likely to prove somewhat less of a pot of flowing lava than her Dhall Curry with Eggs above).

MOOLTAN CURRY

One teaspoonful Turmeric, Four teaspoonfuls pounded Onion, Half teaspoonful Coriander-seed, Quarter teaspoonful Cayenne Pepper, One tablespoon Ghee, Half cupful Water, Three hard-boiled Eggs.

Heat the ghee; have all the condiments previously prepared. Add them all to the boiling ghee; also add onion. Stir constantly in the sauce-pan and cook until brown. Put in 3 hard-boiled eggs. Pour in half a cupful of water. Simmer until the ghee looks clear like salad oil on the top.

The following, more akin to the traditional English curried eggs, is based on Beatrice A. Vieyra's recipe in *Culinary Art Sparklets*:

EGG CURRY AND RICE *serves 4 as a breakfast or light lunch dish*

1½ oz (45 g) ghee	1 apple, peeled, cored and
1 large onion, sliced	chopped
1 oz (25 g) plain flour	juice of 1 lime
1 heaped tbsp curry powder	4 eggs, hard-boiled
½ pt (300 ml) stock or water	2 tsp tomato chutney
	salt to taste

Melt the ghee in a saucepan and, when hot, fry the onion slices until brown. Stir in the flour and curry powder and mix well. Add the stock or water, apple chunks and lime juice and leave to boil for 10 minutes. Peel and halve the hard-boiled eggs; add to the sauce with the chutney and salt. Stir gently. When the sauce has thickened, remove from the heat and serve on a hot dish with a border of boiled rice.

After such leaden breakfasts, it may be wondered how the British were able to sit down to a midday meal at all, but actually by the early nineteenth century, lunch ('or tiffin as it is called by people who deem Anglo-Indian gibberish better than plain English', fumed Colonel Kenney-Herbert) had become a relatively light meal. The word tiffin itself is thought to be derived from 'tiffing', an eighteenth-century English slang term for sipping.

In 1838 a Mrs Postans was congratulating her contemporaries on their refined tastes in having adopted delicate 'Périgord pies and preserved meats' for lunch in place of the 'hecatombs of slaughtered animals' of former times. In the Victorian era, an economically minded memsahib might now order the previous night's leftovers served up for a family lunch, despite the disdain of the servants who, according to Flora Annie Steel, considered them the sweeper's perk: 'So it is no unusual thing to see puddings served up again as they left the table, and pies with dusty, half-dried smears of gravy clinging to the sides of the pie-dish.'

Many husbands also began to take a packed lunch of sandwiches and a piece of cake to the office in place of the old habit of returning home in the middle of the day.

Sunday lunch, however, remained an occasion for over-indulgence, with mulligatawny soup (always), curry and rice, roast beef and Yorkshire pudding washed down with a bottle of iced beer, and tapioca pudding. This was followed by a long afternoon snooze with the fan swishing gently overhead and split bamboo curtains cutting out the glare of the Indian sun.

Such heavy Sunday tiffins had much to answer for in India, said Flora Annie Steel:

It is a fact scarcely denied, that people at home invariably eat more on Sundays, because they have nothing else to do; so in the hot weather out here people seem to eat simply because it passes the time. It is no unusual thing to see a meal of four or five distinct courses placed on the table, when one light entrée and a dressed vegetable would be ample. Even when guests are invited to tiffin, there is no reason why they should be tempted to over-eat themselves, as they too often are, by the ludicrously heavy style of the ordinary luncheon party in India. If the object of such parties is, as it should be, to have a really pleasant time for sociable conversation between lunch and afternoon tea, stuffing the guests into a semi-torpid state certainly does not conduce to success.

Colonel Kenney-Herbert also advocated lighter menus for these Sunday luncheon parties, despite the fact that dinner was usually delayed until about eight-thirty on a Sunday night to allow the digestion to recover.

An old standing dish to commence a luncheon party used to be a mulligatani. If properly made, this soup is a meal in itself: there are so many condiments, spices, and highly flavoured elements in its composition – not to mention the burning chilli, and the concomitant ladleful of rice which custom decrees, – that he who partakes of it finds the delicate power of his palate vitiated, as far as the application of any dainty plat that may follow is concerned, whilst the edge of his appetite is sorely blunted. So I say, reserve mulligatani for your luncheon at home alone, enjoy it thoroughly, rice and all – and nothing more.

The reason for Sunday being the day for luncheon parties, of course, was that the men had no official duties that day. During the week the wives would have their own tiffin parties at which much lighter fare was served, to the extent that by the 1930s they were holding bridge parties at which there was no formal lunch at all, but merely a side table of finger foods such as sausage rolls and stuffed tomatoes from which the players could help themselves.

Invitations to such lunches nevertheless remained formal, and it was not done to make morning social calls before ten, when the family might be at breakfast, or after two, when they might be having tiffin. Indeed, in the eighteenth and early nineteenth centuries it was considered most improper for the lady of the house to invite any one to join them for tiffin who was not either a relative or an intimate friend of the family.

This made things difficult for the socialite who was not offered refreshments at any of the calls.

At the last house, [one such visitor wrote] we actually listened, with parched throats, to the jingling of glasses and plates, which betokened the preparation of the tiffin table in the adjoining room, without these sounds producing any other effect upon the lady of the house than giving us, by suddenly dropping the conversation, a pretty significant hint to decamp: and accordingly in a state of utter exhaustion we made our parting bows. (Quoted in *Bound to Exile*, by Michael Edwardes.)

8

Soups

—

What varied opinions we constantly hear
  Of our rich Oriental possessions;
What a jumble of notions, distorted and queer,
  Form an Englishman's 'Indian Impressions'.

First a sun, fierce and glaring, that scorches and bakes;
  Palankeens, perspiration, and worry;
Mosquitoes, thugs, cocoanuts, Brahmins, and snakes,
  With elephants, tigers and curry.

Then jungles, fakeers, dancing-girls, prickly heat,
  Shawls, idols, durbars, brandy-pawny;
Rupees, clever jugglers, dust-storms, slipper'd feet,
  Rainy season, and mulligatawny.

(From *Curry and Rice on Forty Plates*,
by George Franklin Atkinson, 1859.)

Before the arrival of the British, the concept of soup as a separate
course was unknown to Indian cookery. Such soups as there were had
been used as thin sauces, poured over plain rice and mixed with dry

curries, but never drunk by themselves, due to the Indian custom of serving all the dishes of a meal at the outset rather than course by course.

The simplest of these 'rice-mixers' consisted merely of spices boiled in water, perhaps with the addition of fried onions. In the north of India the recipe was enriched by yoghurt and known as *shorwa*; in the south, where lentils were often added, the dish was called *saar*. In the Tamil version tamarind was included and the soup called *rasam*. When used metaphorically the *ras* part of *rasam*, like *saar*, means 'essence' – and essences are what they were.

When the British arrived they insisted on a separate soup course, and since *rasam* was the nearest thing to soup their Indian cooks knew, it was anglicized into 'pepper water' and adopted for the sahib's special Sunday curry tiffin. It was a particular favourite of the British at Madras, drunk at the beginning or end of the meal as a digestive.

PEPPER WATER

To one pint and a half of cold water mix in the following ingredients, after being crisply dried in a moderate oven and crushed, so as to draw out the full flavour: one dessert-spoonful of coriander seed, cummin and mustard seed mixed, one tea-spoonful; four or five dried capsicums (or chillies), half a dozen cloves of garlic crushed with the skin on, quarter of a teaspoonful turmeric powder and a piece of tamarind, the size of an egg, broken into the whole, (the garlic and tamarind must not be dried in the oven, but used in their raw state); put all in a saucepan; cover close and boil for half an hour. Allow the pepper water to settle; then strain through a coarse dry towel into a basin; have ready a clean porcelain-lined saucepan, into which put a piece of butter the size of a large walnut, and when it boils, throw in an onion or two finely sliced; fry of a rich brown, then pour in the pepper-water and cover close a few minutes. Serve in a tureen with boiled rice in a separate dish. (From *The Original Madras Cookery Book*, by An Old Lady Resident, 1881.)

Henrietta Hervey, the wife of an Indian Army officer, tells us such plain pepper water 'can be drunk like tea from a cup or eaten like mulligatawny with boiled rice. An excellent remedy for "sick headache".' Her own versions follow:

DHALL, OR RED PULSE PEPPER WATER SOUP I

In two pints of water, boil a large cupful of the grain till sufficiently soft, and strain it. Into the same water put the following, well ground: a small piece of saffron or turmeric, one or two chillies or capsicums, a few cloves of garlic, and a teaspoon each of the following, pepper, mustard, cummin seeds, also a tablespoonful of either tamarind water or vinegar. Boil for twenty minutes. In another pan, fry half an onion in 'ghee' or butter well brown, pour in your pepper water, and give the whole another boil. To be eaten in the same way as plain pepper water.

DHALL, OR RED PULSE PEPPER WATER SOUP II

Preferably in an iron pan, fry an ounce of the pulse and an ounce of black peppercorns with a dessertspoon of 'ghee' or butter; having done which, grind or pound the mixture to a paste. Add two tablespoonsful of tamarind water and two teacups of water, and as it boils add a teaspoon each of cummin, fenugreek and mustard seed, previously fried in 'ghee' or butter. Eat in the same way.

Among the low-caste poor of southern India it was a common practice to add to their pepper water a tiny salt fish known as *karavat*, but naturally it never occurred to the predominately vegetarian Hindus of southern India to beef up the soup with meat stock and add small pieces of meat to the finished product. When the British came along and did just that, mulligatawny soup was born. The name of this most celebrated of Anglo-Indian dishes is a corruption of two Tamil words, *milagu* and *tunni*, meaning simply 'pepper water'.

The dish evolved in the Madras Presidency. Its composition resembles a Madras curry and on some formal menus of British India we find the soup translated into French as potage de Madras. The residents of Madras were even nicknamed 'Mulls' after their famous creation. Mulligatawny became popular with army officers, who carried it in flasks on expeditions in the hills as fortification against the cold.

At its simplest, mulligatawny consists of little more than meat, onions, curry powder and stock or water, as described in E. S. Poynter's curiously titled '*What*' and '*How*' or *What shall we have and How shall we have it?* (1904):

MULLIGATAWNY SOUP

Cut up a chicken or piece of mutton into small pieces and wash well. Fry some onions in 1 oz ghi or drippings, take them out, and fry in the ghi 1 tablespoon curry condiments, sprinkle a little water over them whilst frying, and then add the meat with a teaspoon of salt. When nearly brown, pour in some stock, and the fried onions, close the lid. Simmer over a slow fire until the meat is perfectly tender, about one hour. Serve with rice and lemons cut up.

In the past there has been an unfortunate tendency to relegate mulligatawny to the mean function of using up scraps and leftovers, which has earned the soup a bad press from people such as the novelist Rupert Croft-Cooke:

Mulligatawny is a soup invented by lazy Indian cooks in the days of British rule and given this Tamil name to impress the memsahib with the fact that she was getting something truly of the country. In fact she was getting, as the customers in some Indian restaurants get still, the remains of yesterday's curry and rice stewed and put through a sieve.

The difficulty with mulligatawny is that it has sprouted so many variations that it is impossible to lay down a definitive list of ingredients. There is not even a consensus on the most basic ingredient, the meat. At various times, chicken, mutton and beef have all been used, while old Indian recipes call for venison, rabbit, and even antelope or peacock. Nobody renamed the new versions and the original name persists for some quite different soups. The two recipes below, both from E. A. M. Franklin's *The Wife's Cookery Book*, serve to illustrate just how widely the interpretation of 'pepper water' varied. The first includes okra, or ladies' fingers – 'bendikai' is the Telugu word.

BENDIKAI AND DHALL MULLIGATAWNY

8 bendikai, 4 heaped tablespoonsful of dhall, 12 peppercorns, 3 tablespoonsful of ghee, 2 onions, 2 cupsful of stock, 1 tablespoonful of curry powder, some salt.

Wash the dhall twice in water, place in a chatty with 1 tablespoonful of ghee, the peppercorns and sufficient water; cover the chatty, and when the dhall is three quarters done, put in the bendikai, stock and one onion sliced into thin slices, add the curry powder, and let it simmer till the dhall is as soft as paste, rub through a wire sieve into a bowl.

Place a saucepan on the fire, and slice the remaining onion, put in the ghee, and when slightly brown, pour in the soup, add salt to taste, and serve while warm.

Send to the table with rice.

MUTTON MULLIGATAWNY SOUP

2 onions, half a cocoanut, 1 lb mutton (from the neck or ribs is best), 1 oz ghee, 1 tablespoonful of coriander, 4 dry chillies, $\frac{1}{2}$ tablespoonful of mustard seed, 2 large pinches of cumminseed, 1 clove garlic, 4 peppercorns, 8 curripalli leaves, a small piece ginger, 2 limes, a piece of turmeric about an inch long, salt.

Cut up and wash the mutton, grind the curry stuff (each separately) with a little water to a smooth paste on a curry stone, scrape the half cocoanut and take out the milk, peel the garlic, ginger and onions and mince them.

Take a clean chatty, place the ground curry stuff in it, and put in the second milk of the cocoanut, stirring the ingredients till they are quite mixed, then put in the mutton, ginger, one onion, half the ghee and salt to taste. Cover well and place on the fire for 30 minutes or till the raw smell of the turmeric disappears, then open, stir and pour in the first milk of the cocoanut. Remove from the fire and put in the onion, ghee and the curripalli leaves, allow them to brown slightly, pour in the soup, add the lime juice, and serve at once with rice or bread.

As a variation it is suggested that chicken could be substituted for the mutton. The custom of offering a little rice with mulligatawny is, of course, an echo of its origins as a rice-mixer. Mango chutney might also be handed around separately, or a little mango juice added to the soup itself.

In the early nineteenth century retired East India Company merchants sparked off a fashion for mulligatawny back in England. Inevitably, the soup began to take on the stamp of the English kitchen: apple was substituted for the mango juice of Indian recipes, and the freshly ground spice mixtures replaced by curry powder. Indeed the recipe itself was originally dubbed 'curry soup', as the inimitable Dr Kitchiner indicates in *The Cook's Oracle* in 1817:

Mullaga-tawny signifies Pepper Water. The progress of inexperienced peripatetic Palaticians has lately been arrested by these outlandish words being pasted on the windows of our Coffee-Houses; it has, we believe, answered the 'restaurateur's purpose', and often excited JOHN BULL to walk in and taste: – the more familiar name of Curry Soup – would, perhaps, not have had sufficient of the charms of novelty to seduce him from his much-loved MOCK TURTLE. It is a fashionable soup, and a great favourite with our East Indian friends.

A measure of its popularity was the appearance on the market, about the middle of the century, of tins of 'mulligatawny paste' – condiments to be mixed with meat stock, garlic and onions.

All the great cookery writers of the period gave their own recipes: Eliza Acton, in her *Modern Cookery for Private Families*, included a meatless version with marrow, cucumber and apple, while Mrs Beeton replaced the coconut with ground almonds. Alexis Soyer, the celebrated chef at the Reform Club, concocted a Frenchified version which bore very little relation to the original, incorporating ham, thyme and apple, while Escoffier's was virtually unmanageable. In general, it is the Anglo-Indian variations which remain the most interesting.

There also appeared on menus a clear mulligatawny, also known as consommé mulligatawny or, in the rather contrived French of Victorian menus in India, as consommé à l'Indienne.

CLEAR MULLIGATAWNY *serves 8*

4 tbsp coriander seeds
1 tbsp cumin seeds
1 tbsp fenugreek seeds
½ tsp cardamon seeds
½ in (1 cm) piece cinnamon stick

1 clove garlic, peeled
4 bay leaves
4 pt (2.5 l) good stock
salt, to taste (optional)

Place the spices in a mortar and bruise them, but do not reduce them to a powder. Put them into a piece of muslin along with the garlic and bay leaves, and tie them securely into a bag. Place this into the cold stock, bring slowly to the boil, skim, and simmer for half an hour, by which time the flavour of the spices will have been sufficiently extracted.

Remove the bag, strain the soup through a muslin-lined sieve, add salt if necessary.

'Regarding clear soups,' wrote Colonel Kenney-Herbert,

an idea persists with some people that these require to be assisted with gelatine or isinglass [a gelatine made from fish] to give them a sort of glutinous consistency. Ramasamy has discovered a very pernicious sort of starch which he produces from a raw potato, and by this compound the soup in many houses I know is ruined; the potato imparts a crude, inky flavour to the consommé which is hard to describe on paper, but is fatal in its effects on the palate. Ramasamy should be cautioned on no account to use what he calls 'potato thickening' again, under any circumstances whatever, and, once and for all, let me observe that clear soups require no isinglass.

Such clear soups appeared to be all too popular with Indian cooks. C. C. Kohlhoff, for one, complains in his *Indian Cookery and Domestic Recipes* (1906) of

the eternal clear soups cooks are so fond of serving up. 'Clear' it is indeed of all nutriment or flavour. The Indian cook invariably makes soup of beef bones. It is a mistaken idea to suppose you can get good stock from bones only, for it stands to reason you get no meat juice to form the foundation of stock, that is why a cook's clear soup is little better than hot water with burnt sugar or rung gravy as he calls it for colouring.

Burnt butter was also used to colour soups, but the frugal food manufacturers of India had a better idea. Their tinned soups were made from good fresh meat, but, having boiled every drop of goodness out of it, they proceeded to turn the stringy remains into potted meats! That these were widely acclaimed among the British in India, and even exported, is perhaps a comment on the level of culinary sophistication of the Victorian period.

The great difficulty with making meat stocks in India was that without refrigeration, the heat might ferment them in a matter of hours. Thus, soup had to be made and consumed the same day. If stock was kept for any period, it would have to be decanted and the pot thoroughly scoured and scalded with hot water, and the stock itself thoroughly examined. Only in the hill stations and during the cold weather in northern India could cooks fall back on the never-empty stock pot of English kitchens.

If the making of stocks and soups was a branch of cookery unfamiliar to Indian servants, their employers lost no time in educating them. Colonel Kenney-Herbert, for example, laid down a list of rules, fifteen in all, which he advised the memsahib to have written out in Tamil and hung in the cookroom 'for Ramasamy's edification'.

Another of the Colonel's injunctions concerns the use of herbs:

Country [i.e. Indian] parsley (to my mind) spoils any soup; our natives are very fond of it, I have interdicted its use in my kitchen under pain of a fine. Tarragon is the best flavouring herb you can use in clear soups but we only have the vinegar in India, not the plant itself, and a leaf or two is what we desire in soup. I brought out some dried tarragon leaves from England which I found highly satisfactory, and can safely recommend others to try.

While consommés as prepared in an Indian kitchen might fall short of perfection, they were surely preferable to a heavy potage in the tropical heat? But Colonel Kenney-Herbert assures us otherwise:

I confess that a thick soup is acceptable at times: in cool weather; when you return as hungry as a hunter from some physical enterprise; or when you have a little cosy dinner of only a few items to discuss – a soup, a slice of a joint, a dressed vegetable, and your cheese – but I hesitate to recommend soups of this class for a Madras dinner party – to be placed before men whose labours all day have been sedentary, and ladies who have lunched well, and passed the day in graceful repose.

The English found that *besan*, or dried chickpea flour, could be substituted to make an old favourite:

PEA SOUP
Indian Receipt. Put into a saucepan a broken ham bone and one pound gravy beef, with cold water sufficient to cover; let it boil till the soup has a strong flavour of the ham (any pieces of the meat, if left, may be added to the above); it must be strained into another saucepan and flavoured with sliced onions, mint, parsley and a few celery leaves and set on the fire to boil until the onions are quite cooked; the flavouring may then be removed (but can be left if approved of) and the thickening of peas flour (mixed smoothly with cold water) added; the proportion must depend on the quantity of the soup.

Serve in a tureen with fried bread, lean ham or bacon fried, and green mint fried, all of which must be crisply done and served separately from the soup; a little dried mint rubbed into the soup is an improvement. Pepper and chillie vinegar can be used according to taste. (From *The Original Madras Cookery Book*, by An Old Lady Resident, 1881.)

While her opinion would have fallen largely upon deaf ears, a cookery writer of the period, E. S. Poynter, railed against the excessive consumption of meat-based soups: 'The one idea of the Indian cook is a daily "bone" with which to make the soup for dinner. This is perfectly unnecessary . . . far too little use is made of vegetable purées, or white soups.'

Those Britons who abstained from meat on moral grounds would very likely have belonged to the Theosophical Society, which in 1917 published this recipe in *Vegetarian Menus* by Clara Bemister:

CEYLON SOUP

Put 6 oz of finely sliced onions into a stewpan with 2 oz of butter and fry over a slow fire without colouring it; then stir in (mixed with milk to a paste) a dsp of ground rice, a teaspoonful of curry powder, one of coriander powder, a dessertspoon of cinnamon, with a little salt. Fry this for five minutes, then moisten with a pint of vegetable broth, add 2 tablespoons ground sweet almonds, 2 of grated coconut and one of grated green ginger; bring slowly to the boil, skim, then simmer for 15 minutes, pass all through a hair sieve. Serve very hot with a dice of cucumber in the soup and rice accompanying.

Other vegetarian soups adapted local vegetables to soup recipes from 'home'. This *brinjal* soup is based on a recipe of a doctor working in India, H. Carlton Menkel, who in 1927 wrote *Healthful Diet for India*.

BRINJAL SOUP *serves* 4

2 large *brinjals* (aubergines or eggplants)	1 tbsp butter
	1 tbsp flour
1 onion, chopped	1¼ pt (700 ml) milk
1 tsp fresh sage, chopped	salt

Grill the *brinjals* in their skins until tender. Remove the skins and rub the pulp through a colander, or purée in a food processor or blender. Brown the chopped onion and sage in the butter; add the flour, stir, then add the *brinjal* pulp. Cook for five minutes. Meanwhile, bring the milk to the boil, add to the *brinjal* mixture, cook for five minutes, add salt to taste and serve.

C. C. Kohlhoff describes his recipe for coconut soup as 'a favourite breakfast soup in Ceylon [where] it is called Sorthee'.

COCONUT SOUP

Extract the milk of a large coconut; the first and second draw should fill 2 breakfast cups. Put a very little ghee in a chatty, heat it; and then add a few sliced onions; 2 green chillies, slit lengthways; a bit of maldive fish (well pounded) and the whole of the coconut milk tinged with a little ground saffron.

When well boiled, add some lime juice and salt to taste. As Maldive fish is not to be had in India I use good salt fish (1½ inch square) broken into tiny bits.

ANGLO-INDIAN PUMPKIN SOUP *serves 6*

1 lb (500 g) pumpkin
3 oz (75 g) ghee or butter
2 large onions, chopped
1 tsp turmeric
1 tsp ground cumin
1 tsp chilli powder
2 pt (1.2 l) vegetable stock or water

5 whole cloves
4 cloves garlic, crushed
12 peppercorns
1 tbsp Worcester sauce
½ tbsp vinegar
salt
3 tbsp chopped parsley

Peel the pumpkin, remove the seeds and chop into thin slices. Melt the butter or ghee in a large saucepan, add the onions, turmeric, cumin and chilli powder. Fry gently for 6–8 minutes, stirring regularly. Add the pumpkin and the stock or water, along with the cloves, garlic and peppercorns. Bring to the boil, lower the heat and simmer until the pumpkin is soft. Purée in a food processor or blender, or press through a sieve. Reheat and add the Worcester sauce, the vinegar, and salt to taste. Sprinkle parsley over each bowl before serving.

9

Fish and Seafood

Being expatriates of an island entirely surrounded by fish, the British showed no timidity in experimenting with the profusion of unfamiliar fish they encountered in India. Of India's 2,000-odd varieties, some (such as the shinnara, the pakat and the newta) were tried and soon rejected, but on the whole fish was particularly welcome in a hot, humid climate which was unsuitable for the easy digestion of red meat.

The buyer of fish from the market had to be very careful, however, as the heat of the sun and the lack of refrigeration could cause the catch to go off within hours. Since it was possible in India to be ill one day and dead the next, it is little wonder that Flora Annie Steel considered stale fish 'perhaps the most dangerous of all foods'.

'In purchasing whole fish the only way to tell whether it is fresh is to open the gills and satisfy yourself,' advised G. L. Routleff in *The Economical Cookery Book (for India)*. 'They should be moist and bright red, not dry or muddy brown.' The memsahib was also told to look for bright eyes and firm flesh, all of which is still sound advice for shoppers anywhere.

If fish was not to be eaten immediately, it might still be cooked to extend its shelf life. This left the problem of what to do with the cold fish. Colonel Kenney-Herbert suggested tossing it with hot macaroni and tomato purée, a simple dish which could be put together on a small charcoal fire on the verandah just outside the dining room.

'Cold fish is almost invariably presented to you by Ramasamy in the form of what he is pleased to call "fish pudding",' the Colonel continues. 'This is sometimes nice, and sometimes very nasty. To be nice, a good deal of butter is necessary, Ramasamy at the same time entreated not to make the mould into a pretty pattern with quarters of hard-boiled egg &c., an effect which cannot be achieved without free use of his finger and thumb.'

Another Anglo-Indian cold fish speciality was a variation on the Dutch Sri Lankan fricadellees (see page 138), which involved mashing up the fish and mixing it into balls with nutmeg, Worcester sauce and an egg to bind, and then frying them in oil.

Fresh fish was often salted, pressed with a heavy weight, and then hung up in the sun to dry. Alternatively, it was preserved by smoking over grasses or coir fibre.

At remote inland stations, tinned English salmon, herrings and sardines were often all that was available in the way of fish. These were frequently hazardous as in Victorian days tin poisoning was a very real risk, and the old India hand knew to reject any tinned fish with discoloured labels or the slightest sign of rust.

The most prized of all Indian fish was the seer. It is similar in size to salmon, and although the flesh is white, it also resembles the salmon in flavour. Edmund Hull claimed it 'not unlike the cod in flavour and consistency; and is usually boiled and served up at dinner in the same way as fish at home.'

Plain-boiled, indeed, seems to have been the order of the day, as Colonel Kenney-Herbert tells us:

At the ordinary Madras dinner party, you may rely almost for certain on having boiled seer-fish, with a sauce, and a few slices of cucumber and beetroot at the side of your plate. Or the fish may be pomfret similarly served. 'Tartare', 'hollandaise' and melted butter with essence of anchovy compose apparently the whole repertoire of sauces within reach of the local chef.

Now without wishing for one moment to question the sterling merits of the plain-boiled fish to which I have alluded, I confess that for a dinner party I strongly advocate dishes of a more artistic nature. There are so many easy recipes for cooking fish nicely, that an effort to produce a little novelty in this feature of the menu could scarcely result in failure. In England where you have many varieties of fishes, and some of the best of them only to be seen in the market during their special seasons, a little sameness in the style of cooking may not perhaps strike you. You may boil or fry plainly every day of the week, if each day you are able to present a different fish. Not so with us in Madras. Our supply is good enough, but it lacks diversity.

One way of relieving the monotony was to curry the fish. Mrs J. Bartley's *Indian Cookery 'General'* gives one such simple method. (The *jeera* she lists is cumin, and *kuskus* are poppy seeds.)

MADRAS FISH CURRY

Grind ¼ tsp jeera, ½ tsp kuskus, 4 dry chillies, 6 slices garlic, 1 in turmeric root, ½ tsp mustard seed.

Wash the fish well, place it in a chatty with a sliced onion, tamarind, the ground mussala and sufficient ghee. Place the curry on the fire and cook gently until the ghee appears. Add salt to taste.

N.B. six slices of Seer fish or a large Pomfret will do for this curry.

The following, using the unusual combination of fish and mangoes, is based on a recipe from G. H. Cook's *The English-Indian Cookery Book*. He suggests the dish be served with rice or chapatis.

FISH CURRY WITH DRIED MANGO *serves 6*

2–3 lb (1–1.5 kg) white fish, cleaned and skinned	2 tbsp ghee
	1 tbsp mustard oil
2 onions, roughly chopped	1 pt (600 ml) water
1 tbsp coriander seeds	2 tsp salt
2 tsp turmeric	6 pieces dried mango (known as
1 tbsp cumin	*khatai*)
4 chillies	

Cut up the fish into squares about 1½ in (4 cm) across. Grind the onions, coriander, turmeric, cumin and chillies in an electric coffee mill or blender.

Heat the ghee and mustard oil in a wide pan and add the spice/onion mixture. Fry for a few minutes, stirring all the time; sprinkle a little water on it if necessary, to prevent it from burning. Once the onions have browned, put in the fish, stir gently for a few minutes then add the water, salt and dried mango. Stir, cover and leave to simmer for about 15 minutes. At the end of this time, take off the lid and stir carefully to prevent the fish from breaking up. Take out a piece of fish with a spoon and press between the finger and thumb to see if it is soft; if not, cook for a few minutes longer.

Also highly regarded was a small, sweet-flavoured fish known as the pomfret or pomplet. Writing from western India in 1838, a Mrs Postans enthused:

The delicate highly-flavoured pomplet is unrivalled; this fish, in form, resembles a small turbot, and is justly held at high esteem by all *bon vivants*; it is occasionally caught by the fishermen on the Kattiawar coast, and other places, but inferior in size and quality, Bombay being preeminently distinguished for its pomplets, its shaddock and its mangoes.

Pomfrets were one of the most favoured fish for sousing, and the old Elizabethan recipe was given an Anglo-Indian twist with ginger, garlic and chillies:

SOUSED FISH
Cod's head and shoulders or soles (in India Pomfret) are most suitable for this dish. Wash the fish well, and place in a shallow stewpan; cover with cold water, into which quarter of a pint of vinegar and a tablespoonful of salt should be stirred before pouring over fish; let the whole boil, and when quite cooked, take the fish out and drain it well on a napkin; let it get perfectly cold; then make the souse as follows; to half a pint of vinegar, add a teaspoonful of allspice and a little salt; scald in an enamel-lined saucepan, and having laid on the fish a few slices of green chillies, green ginger and garlic (where the flavour is approved of) pour over the whole of scalding vinegar. The fish will be ready for use in three hours; cayenne pepper can be substituted for the green chillies.

This souse appeared in *The Original Madras Cookery Book* by the pseudonymous 'Old Lady Resident', but C.C. Kohlhoff, in his *Indian Cookery and Domestic Recipes* also recommends pomfret for his 'dhope', in which an egg and vinegar sauce is combined with onions and ginger to make a distant cousin of hollandaise sauce.

DHOPE
This is a tasty way of preparing fish. Select a large pomfret (the black kind is richer) or a bit of seer fish about 6 inches in length. Boil it in water, with a little saffron powder, add a saltspoonful of salt. Make the sauce thus: beat an egg well and then add to it about 3 table spoonfuls of the water in which you boiled the fish, 2 dessert spoonfuls of English vinegar and beat all together. Heat a little ghee, fry a sliced onion, a few slices of ginger, 2 green chillies cut lengthways, 5 garlic sliced very fine and then add the sauce, but take care to stir it all the while till it thickens – now, put in a little salt. Place the boiled fish in a hot plate and pour the sauce over. Serve immediately.

The recipe below is another from Mrs Bartley, in which she uses fruit as a sharp contrast to the fish – bilambees are a type of star fruit.

POOREGE FISH CURRY

Wash and divide a large Pomfret. Prepare the milk of one cocoanut. Grind a salt spoon of raw rice, as much mustard seed, and half an inch turmeric, mix this with the thin milk and strain the latter. Throw in it a sliced onion, 8 pieces garlic, half an inch of fresh ginger sliced, and six green chillies cut half way. Stir the mixture on a moderate fire till it thickens, add the fish, and when cooked pour in the thick milk. Season with salt and acidulate with a green mango sliced, or bilambees or tamarind.

After seer and pomfret, soles came next in order of popularity. Virtually identical to the English species, they were eaten for breakfast.

A great deal of fuss was made in British India over a sun-dried fish known as Bombay duck. Otherwise known as the bombloe (*Harpodon negerus*), it is a small gelatinous fish most common around Bombay but also found to a lesser extent right down the Malabar Coast. They were (and still are) preserved simply by pegging up the fish by their heads to dry, without salting, on huge racks on the beaches of fishing villages near Bombay. The aroma of these villages is as pervasive as a fish glue factory, although much of the overpowering smell of Bombay duck is due to post-mortem treatment with asafoetida.

Exactly how this fish got its name is not known, but it is thought to be derived from the way the fish swims near the surface of the water like a duck. The name is certainly very old, for the seventeenth-century British residents of Bombay were nicknamed 'Ducks'.

It seems strange that a nation of such conservative eaters as the British should have acquired such a taste for this strong, salty titbit, but perhaps smoked kippers set a precedent. In any case, the crispy fried fish crumbled over plates of curry and rice was *de rigueur* as an adjunct to a curry tiffin in the club or officers' mess.

Packets of Bombay duck are available from Indian stores and can be grilled, or fried on each side in hot oil until golden brown, which takes only a minute or two. They should turn crisp when cool. In Navroji Framji's *Indian Cookery 'Local' for Young Housekeepers* (1883) they are called bombloes and form an integral part of some dishes, rather than just an accompaniment:

DRIED FISH STEW

12 dried Bombloes to be cut up into chips and kept aside. Cut in slices four large onions, ⅛ ounce of green ginger, two green chillies, and six slices of garlic. Grind into a paste two or three green chillies, and six slices of garlic, half a tea spoon of jeera and ⅛ ounce of turmeric. Soak two pods of tamarind in half a coffee cup of water, squeeze the pulp and have it ready. Warm a dessert spoon of best sweet oil or ghee, and fry the fish chips crisp, but don't brown them too much or they will

become bitter. Mix the ground mussala and the fried bombloes together, and let them stand until wanted. Place a clean stewpan on the fire, with either a table spoon of ghee or two of best sweet oil, throw in the sliced onions and let them fry till they sink which will be in a few minutes, then add the green chillies &c. then the fish; stir to prevent burning, and when the curry stuff is nicely fried, add the tamarind pulp, and as much water as will be needed for gravy, and salt for seasoning. Simmer the stew for ten minutes longer when it will be ready.

CHILLY-FRY OF DRIED BOMBLOES

A dozen dried Bombloes cut in quarters. ⅛ ounce of turmeric and a bunch of coriander (Kotemer) leaves ground together in a paste. Three pods of tamarind made into pulp with a small teacup of water. Three or four onions, three green chillies, six slices of garlic and ⅛ ounce of green ginger cut in slices, salt to taste and a table spoon of ghee or two of sweet oil.

Brown the onions, then the ground paste, the ginger &c. throw in the bombloes, stir and roast them for two or three minutes, and add the tamarind pulp and as much warm water as will be required for gravy. Stew gently for fifteen minutes.

Around the Bay of Bengal there was such an abundance of fish, both saltwater and fresh, that the British could afford to be choosy. Perhaps the finest and most eagerly sought after was hilsa, which appears only for a short period towards the end of winter, when it begins its migration up the Ganges to spawn. Mrs Beeton (or rather her Edwardian editor, Hermann Senn) claimed the hilsa was 'almost identical with the mackerel', probably because the fish is so rich and oily in texture, but a better likeness is a cross between a salmon and a herring. Its only drawback is that it is full of tiny bones.

The topsee mutchlee or mango fish also appears only briefly in the spring. 'It is as great an object of interest while it lasts, on the banks of the Hoogley, as whitebait is on the Thames,' wrote Sidney Blanchard, claiming that it was the most delicious fish of all. The mango fish, however, is rather small, reaching only 9 in (23 cm) or so in length.

The Calcutta bectie resembles the English cod, both in size and appearance. It is a delicate fish, which I was served in 1985 at the Fairlawn, a delightful Raj-era hotel in Calcutta, by waiters decked out in turbans, white uniforms, brass buttons, cummerbunds and white gloves. Bectie salts well, and provides some of the best 'tamarind fish' – fish preserved in tamarind, vinegar and spices.

Also similar to English cod, only coarser, was gole. It is a large fish, with a particularly firm flesh, often cut into steaks and fried with breadcrumbs. It was not greatly favoured by the British except for the head portion, which was highly prized for its glutinous properties and made excellent curries. This sambal is another of Mrs Bartley's recipes:

SAMBALL OF GOLE FISH
Clean and wash the fish, boil for five minutes in a little water, and salt. Remove the skin and bones, mash the fish well with a spoon, or grind it on a stone. For a tea-cup of mashed fish have ready two thirds of a cup of scraped cocoanut, six green chillies, split lengthways, a garlic sliced, and a dozen curry-pak leaves. Grind for mussala three dry chillies, a level teaspoon jeera, an inch piece of turmeric, and half a garlic. Warm a tablespoon or two of oil, first fry the green chillies, garlic and curry-pak leaves, next the ground mussala, stir in the fish, and fry the whole together. Lastly, put in the cocoanut and simmer the Samball on a slow fire till the cocoanut is well blended.

Of small fish, so-called sardines (they were actually an unrelated species, *Dussumieria acuta*) were popular with Europeans living on the Malabar Coast. Herrings were popular too, featuring as a simple side dish in E. S. Poynter's *'What' and 'How'*:

RED HERRING BURTA
Fry the herring well, clear all the fish from skin and bones, bruise it fine, and mix with very finely minced onions, a chilli and the juice of a lemon. Serve with rice and dal.

Certain genera of tiny fish which only reached a few centimetres in length were indiscriminately termed 'whitebait' by Europeans, particularly a small silvery fish called the chilwa. These were deep-fried on skewers, and often served for breakfast with freshly cut limes.

Of freshwater fish, the greatest prize, for the sportsman at least, was the mahseer, found in the rocky mountain streams of north India. It resembles a salmon, and for anglers took the place of salmon quite nicely, for it grows to a huge size. One type has a bizarre long snout, the other a short, stubby snout. It averages from 3 to 8 lb (1.5–3.5 kg) in weight, although some absolute giants were sometimes caught, as 'Babbott' (Mrs Isobel Abbott) recalled in *Indian Interval*:

When we weighed it, the scales tipped seventy-six pounds, a mighty mahseer. Bashir was delighted. He spent quite some time dividing it up, so much for us, in case we did not catch another, so much for the servants, so much for the horseman, and so much the untouchable of the nearby village who supplied us with eggs and fowls. A diplomat always, Bashir.

Unfortunately mahseer has more bones than most fish and a rather muddy flavour which usually needed disguising with a tasty sauce. Much better eating was the rohu or carp, found in fresh waters from the Sind right across northern India to Burma.

A number of species of *Oreinus* were called trout by the British and cooked as such. These included the Kashmir trout, the Keamon trout and the gourmay. The so-called hill trout (*Discoganthus jamta*) found in mountain rivers was considered good eating, although the flesh putrefied rapidly.

Eels were found in the deltas of large rivers of India, Burma and the Sind, and E. A. M. Franklin described a typical Anglo-Indian way of frying them:

EELS FRIED (INDIAN WAY)

REQUIRED:— 2 eels, 1 inch piece of turmeric, 4 oz of ghee, 1 teacupful of gingelly oil, 2 dry chillies, 1 garlic pod, 16 curripalli leaves and a little salt.
TO MAKE:— Clean and cut up the eels; grind the turmeric, dry chillies, garlic salt and curripalli leaves to a fine paste, which rub on the eel slices. Place a frying pan with the oil on the fire, putting a piece of tamarind and a few curripalli leaves into it. Let the oil boil. When the tamarind is a dark brown colour, take it out together with the curripalli leaves throwing these away. The gingelly oil is now seasoned. Put in the ghee and when the oil has again reached boiling point put in the slices of eel, and fry to a golden brown.

Before the arrival of the British, there was little systematic fishing for crustacea in India. Crab and lobster pots, for instance, were unknown. However, a thriving market quickly grew around Bombay for what were called lobsters, but which strictly speaking were crayfish (being of the genus *Palimonus*). Prawns and shrimps, wrote Edmund Hull in 1871, 'are made by the native cooks into capital curries, seldom appearing on the table in any other form.' Henrietta Hervey gave us this in her *Anglo-Indian Cookery at Home*:

FOOGATH

Shell, head, and tail a dozen prawns. Take a cabbage and steep it in salt water for half an hour, after which, drain and shred it finely; then place it in a saucepan, sprinkle with salt, and steam for a few minutes, or until the cabbage is parboiled. Now drain it. In a frying-pan heat a tablespoonful of 'ghee' or butter; throw in some onion, sliced, two green chillies or capsicums, and four cloves of garlic, chopped fine; also the prawns. Fry the whole together for some minutes, stirring often. Now add your cabbage; mix it well with the other ingredients, pour in the milk of a whole cocoanut; give one boil, and serve with rice.

The prawn curry below is an updated version of a recipe from Beatrice Vieyra's *Culinary Art Sparklets* (1915):

COCONUT PRAWN CURRY *serves 2*

4 oz (125 g) raw prawns, shelled
small ball tamarind (about the
   size of 2 marbles) *or* 1 star
   fruit, sliced
flesh from half a coconut
2 green chillies

6 curry leaves
½ tsp cumin
2 cloves garlic
1 tbsp oil
3 small onions, sliced
salt, to taste

Clean and wash the prawns. Steep the tamarind, if using, in 2 fl oz (50 ml) of boiling water for 5 minutes, then strain.

Grind together in a blender or food processor, the coconut flesh, chillies, 2 curry leaves, cumin and garlic to make a paste. Stir in 16 fl oz (450 ml) water and the strained tamarind flesh (or star fruit).

Heat the oil in a saucepan, then add the sliced onions and remaining curry leaves. Fry until brown, then pour in the spice mixture. Stir, then add the prawns, and salt to taste. Cook over a medium heat, stirring continuously to prevent the oil from separating, until prawns are cooked and the sauce has thickened.

Indian oysters were cheap and much sought after by the British, despite Edmund Hull's opinion that they were 'by no means of superior quality, being exceedingly small, beardy, and protected by great uncouth shells, so that in an uncooked state they are hardly worth attention.' The best-known oyster beds were near Madras, Bombay and Karachi. In the early days the trade was entirely localized, but with the opening up of the railway network in the late Victorian era, oysters began to find their way into the Sind, even as far north as the hill resort of Simla.

Indian cooks put them to good use in pilaus or curries, but their attempts at anglicized dishes were not so fortunate: one shudders to think how many followed the instructions for Mrs Bartley's oyster stew and dutifully cooked them for half an hour!

Following the Victorian vogue for turtles back home, the English ate the green turtle of the Indian seas, as well as their eggs, which were said to taste like marrow. The eating of river turtles was frowned upon, however, because of their reputation as foul feeders.

10

Poultry and Game

Poultry

The 'everlasting murghi' – roasted, grilled, boiled, stewed, hashed, minced, cutleted or curried – appeared on the table week after week with such monotony that for years after leaving India some British retained an aversion to chicken in any form. A standing Anglo-Indian joke told of the Englishman who returned home after a ten-year sojourn in the East, and at every relation he visited was regaled with roast chicken!

At *dak* bungalows, the unvaried menu was chapatis and 'sudden death' – chicken that had been decapitated, plucked, grilled and served up within twenty minutes of being ordered. The bungalow *khansamah* would 'when asked, unblushingly profess to provide every delicacy of the season; but when he appears and uncovers his dishes, there is fowl, and nothing but fowl, of every age, size and degree of toughness,' wrote William Tayler in *Thirty-Eight Years in India* (1881). 'Like the Indian crow he is a character peculiar to the precincts of the *dak* bungalow, and, like "le Roi est mort, vive le Roi", he is always present.'

Capturing the fowl often involved a chase and there were instances of the unfortunate bird taking refuge under the chair of the guest who had ordered it. Tayler tells Philip Robinson's story of the one that got away – almost.

There came up the hill one day some travellers, with whom the cook at the staging house wished to stand well, and when they asked 'What is there to eat?' he replied with suavity, 'Whatever your honours choose to order.' So they ordered beef and then mutton; but there being neither, they desisted from 'ordering', and left it to the cook to arrange the meal; and he gave them soup made of an infant poulet, two side dishes composed of two elder brothers, a fine fowl roasted by way of joint, and the grandmother of the family furnished forth as a curry, and one of the party watched the dinner being caught. With the soup there was little difficulty, for it succumbed to a most obvious fraud. The side dishes fell victims to curiosity, for while they were craning their necks into the cook-room door, a hand came suddenly around the corner and closed upon them. The curry, poor soul, was taken in her afternoon sleep.

But the roast, a fine young cock, showed sport, and well it might. For seven months it had daily evaded death, scorning alike the wiles of the cook and the artifices of his minions. Nothing would tempt it during the day within the enclosure in which so many of his family had lost their lives, and as it roosted high up in the walnut tree behind the bungalow, night surprises were out of the question. Whenever travellers came in sight it would fly on to the roof of the bungalow, and thence survey the preparations for dinner. But its day had come. The travellers had been expected. An hour, therefore, before they came in sight, preparations were made for the great capture; and when, on the appearance of the first horseman, the fowl turned as usual to escape, he found two boys on the roof of the bungalow, six more up the walnut tree, and a cordon of men round the yard. There was nothing to do but trust his wings; so mounting on the wall, he flew for his life. But there was a worse enemy than man on the watch – a hungry eagle grasped him in his yellow talons and winged his burdened way back to the nearest resting place – the roof of the dak bungalow! But his exploit had been watched and hardly had his feet touched the welcome tiles before a shower of sticks and stones rained around him. One pebble struck him, and rising hastily at the affront, his prey escaped his talons, and, rolling over and over down the roof, fell into the arms of the exultant cook.

Added to the monotonous regularity was the scragginess of the fowl itself, which has been described as tasting like one of those indestructible picture books made from cloth. A fully grown roasting fowl was not much bigger than a pigeon and considerably tougher. 'With all the ardour of our being, with all the muscular development of our lower jaw, we strive to masticate the obdurate bird; but no – its flesh is impervious to the sharpest incisor, and spurns the efforts of the most crushing molar, and we rest satisfied with the assurance that we are tackling the identical cock that came out of the Ark,' wrote the satirist G. F. Atkinson.

There was apparently little effort to fatten poultry for the table, although the memsahib was advised to see that the cook left the day's vegetable peelings in a big pan on the warm embers of the stove overnight, to be heated up with grain in the morning and fed to the fowls. 'When they have had this hot chota-hazri' wrote Mrs Temple-Wright in *Baker and Cook*, 'they are less likely to pick up dirty and injurious rubbish and they fatten splendidly.'

Attempts at selective breeding were also limited, although Silver Dorkings were fairly common and were considered India's best all-round breed for both eating and laying. Light Brahmas and Houdans were found at most stations. The latter were good layers but the Brahmas fattened more quickly for eating. Interestingly, India had provided the ancestor of all the domestic cocks and hens of Britain – the red jungle fowl (*Gallus ferrugineus*). Descendants of this bird reached Britain by the middle of the first century BC, having been taken westwards from India and domesticated successively in Persia, Greece, Rome and Gaul.

It was common practice for the Indian cook to kill poultry by cutting the bird's throat and throwing it on the ground to flutter and slowly bleed to death.

Setting aside the cruelty [wrote Colonel Kenney-Herbert], what an idiotic thing it is to waste the very part of the bird from which its gravy and juiciness are derived! White meats are bled in England simply to produce the necessary tint, but they lose much of their nutritious quality in the process. They can afford to do so. Our poorly flavoured birds can ill afford the loss of an atom of the richness they may possess. I maintain therefore that a merciful and instantaneous death, by a heavy blow of a wooden mallet, would be far better for the fowl, and us.

The Colonel was adamant that the cook's habit of plunging the fowl into boiling water to facilitate plucking made the flesh dry and tasteless, and would insist that chickens were brought to him for inspection prior to going into the oven, along with a basket of feathers, so he could see that they were not wet.

Repulsive bread sauces for chicken, made by stirring boiling water into breadcrumbs pepped up with whole peppercorns and cloves, also raised the Colonel's ire (although he was quick to point out that he had tasted 'quite as nasty a composition as Ramasamy's' in England), as did the Indian cook's treatment of stuffing:

If permitted to follow the customs of the cookroom, the uneducated Ramasamy will send up your roast fowl – hardly as large as an English chicken – with its breast strangely puffed out and distorted with a horrible compound called 'stuffing'. This you carefully avoid eating on account of its nastiness, but few, I take it, boldly order their cooks never to perpetrate the atrocity again, being under the impression that stuffing is necessary in roasting poultry. The mixture which tradition has handed down to the Anglo-Indian kitchen for the stuffing of geese and ducks is nearly as disagreeable as that of fowl. Whilst the latter may be described as a consolidated and greasy relation of the 'bread poultice' I denounced when treating of 'bread sauce', the former owes its flavour to violent onion, crude sage, and slices of half-boiled potato, mixed together lumpily and lubricated with some chopped fat. Let me speedily tell you that potato has no place whatever in duck stuffing, and that the crude taste you dislike so much arises from the sage being chopped raw, and the onion being a common one instead of the mild kind called 'Bombay' or 'Bellary'.

The good Colonel has some sound advice for boiling a chicken:

It is a very capital plan to boil a fowl in the soup stock. Herein you have the true essence of economy – no waste. The soup gains all the fowl loses in boiling. I need hardly remind you that in suggesting this to Ramasamy you will meet with opposition. He will tell you, in all probability, that 'mixted the fowl and soup-meat, cannot come the good taste' and when you insist upon a trial, he will go away sorrowful, for the broth produced in boiling a fowl purely and simply, is his perquisite (or rather we do not ask for it) and 'mixted with rice only' makes with a chilli or two – a bowl of 'pish pash' [see page 62]. Nevertheless the fact exists that a fowl is vastly improved by being thus cooked: it remains for you to decide whether, as a matter of policy, it would be wise to vex 'your best friend' by ordering so great an innovation. I confess that a man who, with his eyes open, wars against his chef, is generally the loser before the campaign is ended.

Other cookery writers of the Raj were prepared to give the Indian cook more credit for his abilities with chicken. In her preface to *Camp Recipes for Camp People* (1890), 'Chota Sahib' wrote:

I have given very few recipes for serving the 'Morgee' of commerce, which is the thing perhaps most easily procured in camp, but I would not dare compete with 'Ramaswamy' as the one or two things I have on occasions tried to teach him in this branch, he had always stopped me half way with 'I knowing very well only' and I really think perhaps he does know better how to disguise chicken and more ways of serving it than I could imagine, so I leave it to him.

The Raj's most celebrated chicken dish is undoubtedly country captain, but its origins are not entirely clear. The term 'country' used to refer to anything of Indian, as opposed to British, origin, and hence the country captain after whom this dish is named may have been in charge of sepoys. It seems more likely, however, that he was the captain of a country boat, since the recipe turned up midway through the nineteenth-century at ports as far apart as Liverpool and the American South (where many Americans still mistakenly think the dish originated).

The list of ingredients varies widely, but at its simplest level the dish consists of little more than chicken flavoured with chilli and turmeric:

COUNTRY CAPTAIN

Cut up a chicken as for curry. Melt 2 or 3 oz ghi and fry some onions sliced. Set them aside. Fry ¼ tsp ground turmeric and chillies, then put in the chicken and salt and fry, stirring occasionally, until the chicken is tender. Serve, strewing over the fried onions. (From *'What' and 'How'* by E. S. Poynter.)

Here is a more sophisticated version:

COUNTRY CAPTAIN *serves* 4

l large roasting chicken	¾ tbsp fresh green or red chillies,
4 oz (125 g) ghee or butter	finely chopped
3 large onions	2 cloves, bruised
5 cloves garlic, crushed	up to 6 fl oz (175 ml) chicken
2 tbsp fresh root ginger, grated	stock or water
1 tsp turmeric	juice of ½ lemon
2 tsp ground black pepper	salt, to taste
	red or green chillies, to garnish

Cut the chicken into eight pieces, trim off any fat, and fry in ghee until browned on all sides. Remove and set aside.

To the ghee remaining in the pot or pan, add two of the onions, finely sliced, along with the garlic and ginger and fry until lightly coloured. Add turmeric, pepper, chillies and cloves and cook a few minutes longer, stirring frequently. Add the chicken pieces and some of the stock. Stir, cover the pan, reduce the heat to low, and simmer for about 20 minutes until the meat is tender. If necessary, add more stock or water during cooking to prevent the chicken sticking to the pan. Add lemon juice and salt to taste.

Slice the remaining onion into rings and fry in boiling oil until crisp and brown. Strew these over the top of the dish, along with finely sliced chillies.

When, as was often the case, a chicken curry was served for Sunday lunch, it would be accompanied by a tray of anglicized Indian condiments, such as shredded cooked bacon, shredded coconut, Bombay duck, roast peanuts and chopped hard-boiled eggs.

When interpreted by the British, curried chicken took some rather odd forms. A dish known as Simla Chicken, for example, called for a sauce of whipped cream, to which had been added cayenne, ginger, mustard and Worcester sauce. The next two recipes are more typical. The first is from

Henrietta Hervey's *Anglo-Indian Cookery At Home*, and the second appears in *The Original Madras Cookery Book*.

CHICKEN CURRY

Take a chicken or a young fowl; skin, clean and joint it, dividing the backbone into three. Put a tablespoonful of 'ghee', butter, lard or dripping in a stewpan with one shredded onion, and fry till brown. Now add a few cloves of garlic, and a tablespoonful of curry powder; and fry all together for some minutes, taking care that the mixture does not 'catch' at the bottom of the pan. Throw in your meat and fry for several minutes, stirring briskly. Next pour in a breakfastcup and a half of water with a little salt, give it a thorough stir; cover, and boil gently for fifteen minutes. Now uncover, and as soon as the gravy thickens add a teacupful of cocoanut milk and again boil for five minutes. As soon as the grease rises to the surface, pour in a tablespoonful of tamarind liquid, vinegar, or the juice of half a lemon. Keep on the fire a few minutes longer, then serve.

CEYLON OR COCOANUT CURRY

Ingredients: a tender chicken, one fresh cocoanut, a table-spoonful of coriander seed, a little turmeric powder, four or five green chillies, a piece of green ginger, the peel of half a lemon, four small onions, half a dozen cloves of garlic, a stick of cinnamon, a dozen cardamums in their shells, three blades of mace, eight cloves and salt to taste; cut the chicken into pieces as for other curries; put into a saucepan with a breakfast cupful of thin cocoanut milk, the coriander seeds dried in the oven and then ground to a paste with a little water, the turmeric mixed with a spoonful of cocoanut milk, the whole green chillies, the green ginger peeled and cut into thin slices, the peel of half a lemon, the cloves of garlic peeled whole, the onions cut in slices, the spices tied in a piece of muslin and the salt; stir all together; cover close and simmer for quarter of an hour; the lid must then be removed and a little more than half a teacup of thick cocoanut milk poured in, as well as the juice of a small lemon; the curry must not be boiled after the thick milk is put in, as it will get oily, and when finished, should be of a lemon colour. Rabbit or fish (Soles) can be substituted for the the the chicken.

MRS FRAMJI'S CHICKEN CURRY WITH TOMATOES *serves 4*

1 chicken, cut into 8 pieces
salt
1 tbsp ghee
4 large tomatoes, skinned and
  chopped
1 small onion, diced
6 cloves garlic, crushed
1 in (2–3 cm) ginger root, finely
  chopped

3–4 dried red bird's-eye chillies
  (the hot kind), ground
2 tsp ground coriander seed
1 tsp ground cumin
small bunch coriander leaves,
  chopped
juice of ½ lemon

Lightly sprinkle the chicken with salt and sauté in a little of the ghee for a few minutes. Add the tomatoes, cover the pan and simmer until the chicken is tender. Add water during cooking if necessary.

About 6 minutes before the end of cooking, heat the remaining ghee in a small frying pan and fry the onion for several minutes until lightly browned. Add the garlic, ginger, chillies, coriander and cumin and fry 2–3 minutes longer. Mix in with the chicken and add the coriander leaf and lemon juice just before serving.

KUBAB FOWL *serves 4*

Despite the title this recipe is not for kebabs, but is a whole roast chicken with a yoghurt basting sauce. It is taken from Dr Riddell's *Indian Domestic Cookery and Receipt Book*.

1 chicken	*Basting sauce*:
4 tsp ground coriander	1 medium onion, sliced
1 tsp ground ginger	1 tsp turmeric
seeds of 2 cardamom pods, ground	2 oz (50 g) ghee or butter
	1 tbsp flaked almonds
3 cloves, ground	1 tbsp currants
1 tsp salt	2 tbsp cream
1 tsp ground black pepper	4 fl oz (125 ml) yoghurt

Prick the chicken all over with the point of a knife and rub with a mixture of the coriander, ginger, cardamom, cloves, salt and pepper. Place the chicken in a roasting pan with a small amount of water and place in a moderately hot oven (190°C/375°F/Gas Mark 5) to roast.

Meanwhile, make the basting sauce. Fry the onion and turmeric in butter or ghee until the onion is transparent. Stir in the almonds, currants, cream and yoghurt, warm through gently and remove from heat.

After the chicken has been in the oven 20 minutes, baste with half the sauce. Baste again with the rest of the sauce 10 minutes later and continue to baste the chicken with the sauce from time to time until it is cooked (allow about 1¼ hours). Serve with the sauce from the pan poured over.

Chicken pilau (pullao) would have been in the repertoire of every north Indian Muslim cook in the service of the British. Perhaps better known as pilaf, these spicy rice dishes flavoured with small pieces of meat and vegetables have their origin in the Persian polo, brought to India with the Mogul conquerors. Mrs Bartley's 'pullao' in her *Anglo-Indian Cookery 'General'* is a simple but typical recipe:

PULLAO

INGREDIENTS:— a fine fat fowl, 1 lb table rice, about 2 tablespoons best ghee, a heaped tablespoon plums, 16–18 almonds, blanched and cut into slices, 3–4 onions sliced, 6 cloves, 4 ins cinnamon, 6 cardamoms, 8–10 hard-boiled eggs.

DIRECTIONS:— put the fowl to boil in sufficient water with 3–4 small onions until tender. Fry first the plums in ghee and keep warm, remove the latter and fry the onions. Keep each separately. When the fowl is boiled, brown it also and keep aside. Next fry the rice in ghee, and add it to the broth which must be two and a half fingers above the rice. While the rice is boiling, add a heaped teaspoon of salt and the spice, and stir it occasionally to prevent burning and allow it to simmer until the grains are perfectly cooked. Serve in a flat dish. Place in a layer of rice and then the fowl. Cover with rice. Cut the hard-boiled eggs in halves, and arrange them over the rice, strew over the whole the fried onion, almonds and plums.

A large fowl, if tough, requires 1 or 2 hours to boil and 4 or 5 teacups of water, if tender 3 cups of water and less time. (Pullao is excellent made of a leg of mutton, or with a chuck bone and a pound of nice bones made into broth.) The leg of mutton, after being boiled, must be browned in ghee and served with the Pullao just in the same way as fowl.

While Angela Spry probably had economy in mind in calling for leftover meat for this dish, it is much nicer when begun with boned raw chicken, cut into cubes, threaded on skewers and grilled briefly before being finished off in the spiced stock.

HUSSAINEE CURRY

One and a half chittacks Ghee, Two tablespoonsful ground Onions, Half teaspoonful Garlic, Half teaspoonful Cayenne Pepper, One teaspoonful Coriander-seed, One teaspoonful Ginger, One teaspoonful Poppy-seed, Three blades of lemon grass cut into pieces three inches long, One small teacupful of gravy, Some sliced Ginger, Some sliced Onions, the remains of a Cold Fowl or Mutton cut into rounds.

Prepare the meat, sliced ginger and onions by cutting them all into small rounds about three-quarters of an inch in diameter. Have four silver skewers or thin pieces of bamboo about 4 inches in length. Thread the meat, &c., on this, by putting the skewer through the middle of the round: first meat, then onion, finally ginger, continuing thus until the skewer is filled up. Put the ghee in a saucepan, heat thoroughly, add condiments, pour the teacupful of stock over the whole and allow to simmer slowly for about 10 minutes.

Finally, a classic chicken curry from Mrs Beeton, reminiscent of the famous Parsi dish, dhansak (from *dhan*, meaning 'wealth'), where meat and several varieties of dal are cooked together.

MRS BEETON'S CHICKEN CURRY WITH CHICKPEAS
serves 4

8 oz (250 g) chickpeas, soaked overnight	¼ tsp pepper
1 chicken, cut into 8 pieces	2 in (5 cm) piece root ginger
8 oz (250 g) onions, sliced	¼ tsp ground cinnamon
2 tbsp coriander seeds	¼ tsp ground cloves
salt, to taste	¼ tsp ground cardamom
	2 oz (50 g) ghee or butter

Place the chickpeas in a saucepan with water covering them by a depth of two fingers. Bring to the boil and simmer for half an hour. Add the chicken pieces, sliced onions, coriander seeds, salt and pepper to taste, and cook for another 45 minutes, or until the chickpeas and chicken are tender.

Ten minutes before the end of cooking, strain off most of the cooking liquid. Place in a small pot with the ginger, cinnamon, cloves and cardamom and boil until the liquid has reduced by three-quarters.

Meanwhile, pick out the chicken pieces from the curry and fry them in hot ghee until lightly browned. Place the chicken back in the pot along with the spiced cooking liquid, reheat the curry and serve with plain boiled rice.

Turkeys were introduced into India from America in the eighteenth century, largely to supply a Christmas market. However, they were never very successful – so many died before they reached maturity (particularly in the damp climate of Bengal) that the Indian breeders were obliged to put a very high price on the survivors. Invariably these were overfed and laden with fat, and many people considered them inferior to the peacock which often took their place on the Christmas Day table in the *mofussil*.

Nor were domestic ducks a particularly attractive proposition to householders or farmers, as they consumed a vast amount of feed yet yielded a scrawny carcass. Nevertheless, duck was popular along the Malabar Coast of south-west India. Indeed, this recipe, from E. A. M. Franklin's *The Wife's Cookery Book*, probably had its origins there, among a minority group known as the Syrian Christians. The parent dish, known as duck *mappas*, is still cooked each Christmas day by this

ancient community, descended from some 400 Christians who fled
persecution in Syria in AD 345 and sought refuge in India.

DUCK CURRY

REQUIRED:– 1 fat duck, 3 Bombay onions, 6 dessert-spoonfuls of coriander, 5
dry chillies, ½ teaspoonful of mustard, ½ teaspoonful of cumminseed, 1 inch piece
of green ginger, 1 inch piece of turmeric, 2 tablespoonsful of ghee, 1 wineglassful
of tamarind pulp, 1 garlic, 6 curripalli leaves, 1 cocoanut, ½ teaspoonful of
powdered cinnamon, cloves, and pepper mixed in equal quantities, salt.

TO MAKE:– Cut up, and wash duck thoroughly; grind the curry stuff separately
with a little water on a curry stone; also grind half the cocoanut; scrape the other
half and take out the milk.

Place a vessel on the fire; put in the ghee, sliced onions and curripalli leaves,
and fry to a light brown; put in the turmeric and fry till the raw smell disappears;
now put in the chillies, coriander, mustard and cumminseed, one by one, letting
each fry a little before adding the next ingredient; put in the duck, stir, then allow
it to fry for two minutes. Add the cocoanut milk. Cover and simmer for an hour
on a slow but steady fire.

Now open and add the ground cocoanut, tamarind and salt to taste; allow it to
simmer for a few minutes, then serve in a curry dish.

Potatoes or drumsticks may be added to this curry if desired, but the tamarind
must only be put in when the vegetables are boiled. Lime juice may be substituted
for the tamarind, but must be put in after the curry is cooked.

Beef, mutton and fowl curry may all be made according to the above recipe;
the proportions of ingredients being for one pound of meat.

Buffado (also spelt buffadh or poofadh) was thought to have originated in Pondicherry. 'A dish peculiar to the Eurasians or Indo-Britons,
but one by no means to be despised,' wrote Henrietta Hervey in *Anglo-
Indian Cookery at Home*, no doubt meaning well but speaking volumes
about British attitudes.

BUFFADO *serves 4*

1 small cabbage, cut into four pieces	6 cloves garlic, peeled
1 tsp ground turmeric or saffron	1 in (2–3 cm) fresh root ginger
1 duck	2 tsp ghee or butter
4 onions, peeled	2 tsp salt
4–6 green chillies, slit and the seeds removed	2 tbsp dried tamarind, vinegar or lemon juice

Place the cabbage in the bottom of a large, deep saucepan. Gradually
mix the turmeric into 1 pt (600 ml) water and add to the pan, along

with the duck (left whole) and all remaining ingredients except the tamarind. Cover the pan and steam the duck for an hour, then take off lid and simmer until it is cooked.

Prepare the tamarind (if using) by soaking in boiling water for 5 minutes, then drain and sieve the pulp.

Five minutes before serving add the prepared tamarind or vinegar or lemon juice.

This is the traditional recipe: you may wish to leave the cabbage out until the last 8 or so minutes of cooking, in which case place the duck in a steaming basket to avoid it sticking to the bottom of the pot.

Game

When the British arrived in India they found the countryside literally teeming with game, which in their inimitable fashion they proceeded to annihilate.

Writing in 1878, 'Ex-civilian' recalls four hunters shooting 300 snipe in four hours, and even as late as the 1920s there were reports of over a thousand duck shot in a day by eight hunters, each needing a standby gun as the first became overheated. At big game hunts given for viceroys and Indian princes the bags ran into the hundreds and records were kept to see how one viceroy had compared with another. The result of such excess was that big game such as tigers had been largely shot out of existence by the 1930s. Even some cookery writers, such as G. H. Cook in his *English–Indian Cookery Book* (*c.* 1904), offered advice on hunting:

Some Hints on Large Game Shooting

To begin, don't try to track a wounded tiger unless you know that he is mortally wounded and you have an experienced man with you, as otherwise in perhaps 90 per cent of cases you will be killed, as nothing can stop his charge. He will not move or growl till you are within striking distance say twenty yards then there will be a growl and he will be on you before you can even raise your rifle. An experienced man can tell from the blood marks where the animal is hit, for instance, if hit in the lungs the blood will be dark red and frothy, if in the liver or near the heart it will be dark red, if in the stomach a watery red, and anywhere else it will be a light red colour.

I have often been annoyed at some people chaffing others for not firing at a tiger when turned out in a beat near them. This often happens when a person sees a tiger for the first time in a beat and fails to fire at it even when sitting on a manchan on a tree. This is not due to fright but to a kind of fascination when he sees the animal and is taken up in looking at it until perhaps it crosses him from quite close. Much the same thing happens when birds see a cat or a snake from close. The same person will perhaps easily shoot a tiger when he sees one the next time.

In the early days of British settlement, game was sometimes the only source of meat. John Fryer wrote in 1673 that 'if we expected Flesh, or Fowl, we must take pains for it; no Beef being to be bought here, though up country from the Moors we could; so that our usual Diet was (besides plenty of Fish) Water-Fowl, Peacocks, Green Pigeons, spotted Deer, Sabre, Wild Hogs, and sometimes Wild Cows.'

At the more remote stations, some of which were not served by a butcher at all, game was a welcome change from endless chicken and mutton. Indian hunters, or *shikarrees*, would hawk game from door to door, and sometimes were even retained in European households to provide regular supplies. 'The equipments of these men would astonish the hero of a hundred battus,' wrote Emma Roberts in 1835:

They are armed with an old rusty clumsy matchlock, which they never fire except when certain of their quarry, making up in skill and patience for the inefficiency of their weapons. They go out alone, and never return empty-handed.

Two sauces which go under the name of *shikarree* (hunters') and camp-sauce, are assuredly the most piquant adjuncts to flesh and fowl which the genius of a gastronome has ever compounded.

SHIKARREE SAUCE

8 fl oz (250 ml) claret	juice of 1 lemon
8 fl oz (250 ml) mushroom	1 tsp cayenne pepper
ketchup (see page 224)	1 tbsp sugar

Place all ingredients in a pan and gently heat, stirring to dissolve the sugar. Serve hot with duck and wild fowl.

The sporting year opened with pig hunting which, along with deer and fowl (duck, jungle fowl, quail and peacock), lasted through to March. After a lull during the hot weather, snipe shooting would begin about August and reach its peak in October, when partridge, quail and hare shooting would begin. Christmas time for many meant a shooting holiday in the jungle, spent either in a *dak* bungalow or a tent. This entailed a colossal amount of preparation, to the extent of taking live fowl, gallons of drinking water, and great blocks of ice.

During the Victorian era, the cooking on these expeditions was done on a portable stove such as the American 'kitchener'. This consisted of a benzine-fired stove, a tin pot of about a quart in measure, and a small pan. Both the stove and the pan fitted together into the tin pot, a compact arrangement which was convenient for travelling, but a frustration to the cook, who could not fit a whole chicken or leg of mutton into the pot, or mutton chops into the tiny pan. Invariably the ends of the chops hung over the side, picking up a flavour of benzine.

Colonel Kenney-Herbert had rather more success with his gadget, however:

A friend of mine with whom I used to walk the paddy field, adopted the plan of taking out a digester pot, previously filled with stewed steak and oysters, or some equally toothsome stew, which he trusted to his syce, who lit a fire somewhere or other, in the marvellous way the natives of this country do, and as sure as there are fish in the sea, had the contents of the pot steaming hot, at the proper time, and at the exact spot we required it. He was a bow-legged veteran, this syce, and a most trusty varlet. I almost think, though, that our shooting became a little erratic after our stew, for it was bountiful in quantity, rich in quality, and provocative of beer, whisky and water, or brandy and soda.

The lavishness of shooting expeditions laid on for the British by the Indian aristocracy often bordered on excess, with furnishing firms hired to supply wardrobes, beds, mirrors and dressing tables for the tents, and caterers such as Firpo's, the famous Italian restaurant in Calcutta, brought in to prepare the food.

On a duck-shooting trip in the United Provinces, memsahib Marguerite Bunyard found herself camped next to a rajah, who asked if he might have the honour of entertaining them to dinner. Being a high-caste Hindu, he was not able to eat with them, and only called in for a few minutes beforehand to see that the arrangements were to their satisfaction.

The table was gaily decorated with flowers, and petals and leaves were arranged in intricate patterns on the cloth around the vases and sweet-dishes. The menu ran into twelve courses, and one had, for politeness' sake, to take some of each, so that the whole meal took some time – and effort – to consume.

Hors d'oeuvre of sardines, eggs, and potato slices were followed by soup (probably Heinz). Then came camouflaged tinned salmon with a doubtful flavour, so that one ate warily and hoped for the best, hiding as much as possible under knife and fork. Mutton (or goat) cutlets appeared next, with potatoes and vegetables – beans and eggplant. Next a joint of beef with more vegetables and the same dish of potatoes – slightly cooler and fewer. Minced chicken cutlets, supported by the now fast congealing remnant of the potatoes, were, we fervently hoped, the last of the meat dishes, as a strawberry pudding followed them, but this was rapidly succeeded by snipe, roast with potato chips, most deliciously cooked. Alas! appetites were on the wane by the time these appeared, so that we really could not do them full justice of appreciation. Back we went once more to sweets – an ornate jelly pudding being handed. This was topped with whipped (buffalo) cream and set in a beautiful basket of pulled sugar, of intricate design.

Next, just to give us an appetiser for the dessert and sweets, there came savoury eggs. Dessert consisted of candied fruits, chocolates, home-made coconut ice, roast pistachio nuts, and other confections, and the last lap of hot, strong coffee was more than welcome. (From *The Epicure's Companion*, by Edward and Lorna Bunyard *et al*, 1937.)

The everyday cooking in camp tended to be somewhat dull, however, and Alys Firth, author of *Dainty Cookery for Camp and Other Recipes* (1905), for one, found it greatly lacking in finesse:

How many of us see, year after year, in camp, the haunches of roast venison, the partridge, black or grey, or the rare grouse, also roasted or else made into a sort of apology for a salmi, the poor little quail brought to the table, and presented to you and your guests by your lordly khidmatgar – looking like dried up sparrows on toast.

Game required careful handling as it was liable to go off very quickly in the Indian heat. If a bird was plucked and gutted sooner than necessary it would dry out or become fly-infested, and venison had to be protected with a coating of flour paste before it was hung.

The Indian cook does not in the least understand the treatment of game, (thundered Flora Annie Steel in *The Complete Indian Housekeeper and Cook*). When it goes into the kitchen, it is either left lying in a heap on the ground, or hung up in a bunch, most likely by the legs. At the first moment of leisure the cook-boy is set to work to pluck and disembowel the whole game larder, which is then either put to dry in a strong winter wind, or laid out carefully as a fly trap. When ordered to prepare any for the table, the cook invariably chooses the freshest looking, and thereafter comes to say, with clasped hands and a smirk, 'The rest, by the blessing of God, has gone bad.'

Aside from tigers, British India's most celebrated game animal was the wild pig, which had a huge reputation for aggressiveness.

Our Indian boars have not a curly tail
Like the fat monsters that at home we breed,
That grunt and fatten o'er the swashy pail,
And waddling through our farmyards stoutly feed:
They are quite straight, and cock with wondrous speed,
When their huge bristles elevate with ire,
And turning round – they squat amidst the weed,

And filth and dirt, the brambles and the mire,
With gnashing tusks and eye-balls sparkling full of fire.
.(From *Tom Raw, the Griffin*, by Sir Charles D'Oyly, 1846.)

The two species of wild pig in India were both clean vegetable eaters and their flesh was well-flavoured. The best came from boars which had been feeding in sugar plantations.

Of the many types of Indian deer, the most sought-after by hunters for its venison was the spotted deer (*Axis maculatus*), considered especially good eating during the winter months. Sometimes it was caught young and fed up for slaughter.

The musk deer (*Moschus mochiferus*) was hunted both for its meat and for its musk bag, found at the end of the penis, which was used to treat wounds and venereal disease. Surprisingly, the strong musk odour of the male deer did not seem to taint its flesh.

The hog deer (*Axis porcinus*) found in Sri Lanka was said to have excellent meat, though it may have been all the more appreciated since other red meats were hard to come by in that country. The hog deer found elsewhere in India was somewhat frowned upon for eating since it suffered from internal parasites and its skin was often pierced by the larva of the botfly.

Even less favoured was the coarse venison of the sambar stag, of which the tongue and marrow bone were often all that were saved.

Both of the following recipes are from *Baker and Cook* by Mrs Temple-Wright.

ROAST VENISON

Roast a leg of venison, basting it with fat, only till it is a little more than half done. When cold, cut six or eight good-sized slices from the leg, and let them steep in the following pickle for twenty-four hours: Mix in a bowl a dessert-spoonful of chilli vinegar, a coffeecupful of claret, a pinch of red pepper, and a little salt; lay the pieces of venison in this; then boil six stoned prunes in a little soup; when reduced to a pulp, pass them through a sieve; mince two ounces of the cold venison, pound it to a paste; take the slices of venison out of the marinade, and put them aside; melt two ounces of butter in a pan, add the marinade, prune, pulp, and pounded venison; stir till boiling hot, then put in the sliced venison; let it remain on the fire till quite hot, no longer; then serve *à la Russe* with baked tomatoes or with French beans.

You may treat beef in the same way, but for this purpose the meat should always be a little under-done when roasted.

DEVILLED VENISON

Crush a teaspoonful of roselle or red-currant jelly with a fork; add a small wineglassful of chilli vinegar, a teaspoonful of mango chutney, a mustardspoonful of dry mustard, and mix with a little salt; melt two ounces of butter in a pan, add the mixture, and as soon as it is boiling hot, put in a few slices of rather under-done cold roast venison, and let them heat up thoroughly; place some French toast on a hot dish, put the slices of venison on them, pour the gravy over, and serve.

(Cold beef or mutton may be treated in the same way, and a little soup added to increase the gravy.)

Until the nineteenth century the British practised a particularly bloodthirsty form of hunting they had learned from the Moguls: a captured deer or an antelope would be let loose, and a cheetah set after it, with the 'sportsmen' bringing up the rear on their horses.

Antelope meat was not especially prized as it tended to be dry and lean, needing constant basting with mutton fat during cooking. High up in the Himalayas various species of goat were hunted, but their meat was rarely tasted except by sportsmen and the inhabitants of hill stations. The Himalayan ibex was hunted both by Indians and the British for its quality meat, as was the Nilghiri ibex of the south, whose flesh a certain Rev. Baker considered 'equal to Welsh mutton'.

The same was said of the wild blue sheep (*Ovis nashura*), which probably explains why it was eventually hunted almost to extinction. The female of the thar (*Hemitragus jemlaicus*) was eaten, and although the flesh of the male was considered rather too rank by Europeans, it was favoured by Indians.

The nilgai or blue bull (*Boselaphus tragocamelus*), found throughout India, was hunted and eaten by the British, much to the disgust of the Hindus, who consider it a type of cow, and therefore sacred. It was sometimes stall-fed prior to slaughter in order to overcome the problem of bitter flesh which resulted from its usual diet of *aonla* berries. Emma Roberts considered it rather over-rated 'as the flesh resembles coarse beef, and when made into hams is apt to crumble.'

A variety of bears were hunted in the hills; their flesh apparently had a pleasant if unfamiliar flavour. However, being a muscular beast its flesh was extremely tough and needed to be marinated Russian-style (with vinegar, salt, sugar, bay leaves and peppercorns) for days on end, followed by long slow cooking. Particularly favoured were bear hams cured Russian-style with smoke, then eaten raw. At one time they were sold by Fortnum & Mason in London.

Considering the ethnocentric attitude of the British towards food generally, one can only marvel at the adventurousness the Anglo-Indians displayed. R. F. Burton, author of *Goa and the Blue Mountains* (1851), says of the porcupine:

We advise everyone who has not tasted a *rôti* of these animals to do so *sine mora*, not, however, forgetting to roll up the flesh in a layer of mutton fat, and thus to remedy its only defect – dryness.

Round Trincomalee, the great harbour in Sri Lanka which in the late eighteenth century belonged to Holland, William Hickey hunted the guana lizard: 'They make a rich soup; many people think even superior to turtle. The Dutch eat the flesh too, but that I could never bring myself to do.'

While game birds, hares and other 'small fry' were held rather in contempt by those who were accustomed to stalking a tiger or a bear before breakfast, from the gourmet's point of view such 'cockrobin' shooting often yielded the finest rewards of all. Quail, for instance, was considered better in India than almost anywhere else in the world. At a particular season they were so plump and tender they were likened to 'flying pats of butter' and were sometimes bred for the table in special quaileries. They were usually plain roasted or poached, since their delicate and unique flavour was easily drowned. One Anglo-Indian recipe nevertheless called for a stuffing of green chillies.

BRAISED QUAIL CURRY *serves 6*

6 large quail	2 tsp flour
2–3 tbsp ghee or clarified butter	1 tsp curry powder
1 medium onion, cut into rings	$\frac{1}{4}$ pt (150 ml) stock
2 small carrots, sliced	3 fl oz (75 ml) Madeira
1 stick celery, sliced	

Split the quail down the middle or bone them. Melt the ghee or butter in a frying pan and gently fry the quail until lightly browned. Transfer the quail to a saucepan and add the onions, carrot and celery to the frying pan. Fry until the onions are transparent, then transfer the vegetables to the saucepan holding the quail. Sprinkle the flour and curry powder over and mix well with the quail and vegetables. Pour the stock over. Bring to the boil, stirring, then reduce the heat and simmer lightly for 15 minutes. Add the Madeira and heat before serving on a bed of rice.

Snipe were equally prized, and very abundant. They were best eaten fresh and cooked very briefly, or 'walked through the oven', as the saying went. It was suggested that all the cooking a snipe needed was to be carried twice around the kitchen table!

Snipe were roasted on a piece of toast to catch the entrails, or 'trail', as it came out during cooking. So savoured were these entrails that at the height of the season, when snipe were plentiful, the trail of another snipe might be used for the toast also, the carcass going to make a soup or entrée.

The jungle fowl or mourghi (*Gallus ferrugineus*) was held in far greater esteem in India than its direct descendant, the very much tougher domestic chicken. William Hickey went so far as to claim there was not a more delicious bird in the world. It was not easily found, however, and difficult to shoot, for in spite of its size managed to fly very quickly.

Although some twenty-eight species of wild duck were hunted, only three or four were considered plentiful or good enough to be offered for sale in the towns. The Indian teal was the most common species, but the mallard was regarded as the best eating, followed by the pintail and the gadwall.

WILD DUCK CURRY *serves 4*

1 wild duck	1 tbsp curry paste
2 oz (50 g) ghee or clarified butter	1 tbsp flour
1 medium onion, finely chopped	8 fl oz (250 ml) coconut cream
3 cloves garlic, crushed	juice of 1 lime or ½ lemon
2 green chillies, minced	salt, to taste
2 tbsp tomato paste	

Cut the duck into eight pieces. Melt the ghee or butter in a heavy-bottomed saucepan and briefly sauté the duck pieces until lightly brown, then remove and set aside. Add the onion, garlic, chillies, tomato paste and curry paste, and fry for 2–3 minutes. Sprinkle over the flour and mix in.

Return the duck to the pot and add 8 fl oz (250 ml) of water. Bring to the boil, stirring, then reduce the heat, cover and simmer until the duck is tender (this may take between one and two hours, depending on the age of the duck). Shortly before serving, add the coconut cream and lime or lemon juice, and salt to taste. Serve with rice.

Mrs Temple-Wright offers a fruit sauce to accompany a plain roast duck:

PEAR SAUCE FOR DUCK

Take two or three good-sized country pears, peel and core them, cutting each into quarters, set them to boil till tender in a breakfastcupful of stock, with half a teaspoonful of sugar, and a bit of lemon peel. When the pears are quite soft, put them through a wire sieve. Melt one ounce butter in a pan, and add a teaspoonful of baked flour with a little salt, and a teaspoonful of lemon juice, pour this on the *purée* of pears, heat up well, and serve with roast mutton, duck etc.

Peacocks were to be found in woodland areas all over India, and although they were hunted by the British, they were only occasionally eaten. 'Some Europeans', wrote Emma Roberts, 'have only been reconciled to their admission to the table by an account which has reached them of their appearance at the Lord Mayor's dinners in London: Anglo-Indians, generally, being exceedingly unwilling to judge for themselves where their gastronomic taste can be called in question.

In fact, peacock was also considered very much an oddity in England by this time (1835), having lost favour there in the seventeenth century. Occasionally it might be served at Christmas dinner as a substitute for turkey, which it resembled in flavour. Emma Roberts considered Indian-bred turkeys, which were very fatty, to be inferior to a young peacock, 'which combines the flavour of the pheasant with the juiciness of the turkey'. Other reports, however, indicate that peacock meat was very dry, even if it was an attractive white colour. It was also said to be tasteless and uninviting when not in the proper season. Nor would anybody eat a peacock who was at all sensitive to Hindu religious objections, since the bird was associated with the goddess Saraswati and as such considered sacred.

Despite her high opinion of the peacock as food, Emma Roberts considered it 'must hide its diminished head before the glories of the florikin; the flanderkin of feudal banquets, and the peacock's early rival at baronial feasts of the Montacutes and the Courtenayes.'

The florikin resembles a turkey both in size and plumage, and was found mainly in Bengal and the hills. As a result of clean diet its flesh was well flavoured: the breast and wings were said to taste like wild duck, while the legs were compared to pheasant. The latter was also much sought after by hunters in the Himalayan foothills.

Indian partridge was also considered good eating, even if, as Flora Annie Steel claimed, Indian cooks invariably trussed them wrongly, sticking their legs in unholy positions.

Pigeons were both reared domestically and shot in the wild, a practice which so upset the local Hindus in the days of the early English settlers that they would attempt to bribe the English to spare them.

Other minor game birds included the sand grouse, which had to be hung for a long time to be palatable, and the kulang, a coarse bird considered only good enough for a game soup. Wild geese were never particularly popular either, since their swampy habitat and their diet gave the flesh a rather fishy flavour.

Hares were abundant in some parts, but as a rule were tasteless and dry, and distinctly inferior to the European hare. The one exception was a black-naped variety, described by one writer as 'nearly, if not quite, equal to the English hare in flavour'. Rabbits were found wild but more commonly bred in hutches for the table, where they appeared in place of chicken or mutton in pilaus or in curries:

RABBIT CURRY *serves 2–3*

1 medium rabbit, cut into pieces
seeds of 1 cardamom pod, ground
1 tsp ground coriander seed
2 in (5 cm) piece cinnamon stick
½ tsp turmeric
1 pt (600 ml) yoghurt
salt to taste
1 tbsp dried tamarind pulp

1 large onion, finely chopped
3–4 tbsp ghee or clarified butter
1 green chilli, chopped
4 cloves garlic, crushed
1 in (2–3 cm) fresh ginger root, finely chopped
3 tbsp tomato paste

Soak the rabbit pieces in salt water for 10 minutes. Meanwhile place the cardamom, coriander, cinnamon and turmeric in a heavy frying pan and dry-fry for two minutes over a low to medium heat. Salt the yoghurt to taste and then add the toasted spices. Pat the pieces of rabbit dry and marinate in the spiced yoghurt mixture for at least 30 minutes, but preferably for as long as 24 hours.

Break the tamarind into little pieces and leave for 5 minutes in 2 fl oz (50 ml) boiling water to soften. Press through a sieve to extract the pith and seeds.

Fry the onion in the ghee or butter until lightly browned and then add the chilli, garlic, ginger, tamarind pulp and tomato paste. Add the rabbit and yoghurt mixture and cook until tender (which may take anywhere between 30 minutes and two hours, depending on the age of the rabbit and whether it is domesticated or wild). Pick out and discard the cinnamon stick before serving.

11

Meat

Beef

To this day, many English-speaking people fail to appreciate that the abhorrence they have for the Koreans' custom of eating dogs, or the French horse meat, is identical to the Hindu abhorrence of eating beef.

In India, the cow may be milked and put to hard haulage work, but it is still patted, stroked, washed and fed like any domestic pet. Added to this is the virtual deification of the cow through Krishna, the divine cowherd, and the belief that bad karma befalls anybody who eats its flesh.

The British in India ignored the depth of this feeling to their peril; an immediate cause of the outbreak of the Indian Mutiny in 1857 was a rumour among the sepoy ranks that they would be forced to bite through a new cartridge case coated with either beef or pork fat, an abomination to both Muslims and Hindus.

In practice the British did not eat a lot of beef in India, but this was more for practical reasons than out of respect for Hindus; the brahmin cow was in those days a small animal, and had to subsist on a miserable diet of coarse grasses, particularly during the hot season. Its meat was lean, dark and tough, reared by Indians who had no concept of fattening cattle for the table.

Since the British mostly just drifted into farming after they arrived in

India, there were very few with practical experience of livestock. Even theoretical knowledge was hard to come by in a country where books were both rare and expensive. Furthermore, since most British went into farming for short-term gain only, they paid little attention to the cultivation of grasses or the improvement of pasture. Only in the presidency towns of Bombay, Calcutta and Madras was there sufficient demand for beef to justify full-scale farming around the city fringes. In remote areas of India, beef was a rare luxury indeed, and in the Coorg, in the south-west, the sale of beef was forbidden by law out of respect of Hindu custom.

At smaller towns there had to be sufficient beef-eating Britons to make the slaughter of a cow worthwhile to a butcher. The slaughter of an 'English' stall-fed cow was advertised well in advance in local newspapers, and towards Christmas, the members of the mutton club (see page 144) would arrange buyers, in advance, for every joint and cut of the beast to be slaughtered. This was particularly necessary in view of the short shelf life of meat in the tropics in the days before refrigeration.

The Amateur Butcher

'Sir, to-day is Saturday.'
  'Yes.'
  'They have killed an ox.'
  'Where?'
  'Outside the office.'
  'What a pity. You shall keep the flies out of the office yourself. Well?'
  'The master would like some meat?'
  'Yes, please, some meat.'

  'Cook.'
  'Yes, sir.'
  'Has the meat come?'
  'Yes, sir.'
  'Cook, I have eaten 12, 39, or 364 chickens since we last had meat.'
  'Yes, sir.'
  'I do not wish this meat to be finished or go bad in one day or two, for I have no wish to eat another chicken until I must.'
  'Yes, sir.'
  'I will eat the liver for lunch.
  'I will eat the brains for dinner followed by the grilled fillet or tournedos.
  'I will have kidneys and bacon for breakfast.
  'I will have steak and kidney pudding or pie for lunch tomorrow, and roast meat (sirloin or fillet) for dinner tomorrow which I will eat cold the next day.

'In the meantime you will be preparing the oxtail and the tongue and this piece of silverside or brisket we will put into salt and I shall eat them next week. Tomorrow we must roast a bit of the meat which is not cooked, or it will go bad. Out of it we will make a casserole, mince, curry, and Headless Sparrows. These bones are for soup. By Friday I shall be able to face tinned fish again, but not before.'

'Yes, sir.'

'In fact I shall even be glad to see a chicken on Saturday next.'

'No, sir.'

'Perhaps you are right.'

(From *A Household Book for Tropical Colonies*, by E. G. Bradley, 1948.)

In the absence of refrigeration, salting was a necessary way of preserving any surplus beef. A favoured method, known as hunter's beef, was to rub it with salt and place it between two boards with heavy weights over. Dried beef, picturesquely known as Ding Ding (see page 228 for recipe), was also common, especially in households on the move, since the meat, once dried, was easily portable. The pickling of beef in spices and vinegar was very popular since it served the dual purpose of tenderization and preservation. Even the hump of a brahmin cow was pickled or corned.

A popular Anglo-Indian story told of an Englishman in Agra who, visiting his cookroom one day, found the cook sitting in an apparently uncomfortable position. As he would not budge from his 'seat', the sahib demanded an explanation. It appeared that a round of beef, originally symmetrical, had, in the hot weather, become flattened and misshapen. The cook, with a professional eye, had noticed this and come up with a novel solution: he had bandaged the beef very tightly with cotton, and was using his backside as a press at the time of the interruption!

Pineapple Beef is said to have been invented by the French Count Benoît La Borgne, better known as the military adventurer General de Boigne. The marinade would, if necessary, have helped disguise any hint that the meat was past its best.

PINEAPPLE BEEF *serves 3*

1 lb (500 g) beef sirloin, cut into rounds the size of a pineapple ring
4 cloves garlic, crushed
salt
½ tsp chilli powder

2 tbsp Worcester or soy sauce
1 tbsp oil
1 small pineapple, peeled and cut into rounds
2 oz (50 g) butter

Rub the beef with garlic, then place in a bowl and sprinkle with the salt, chilli powder, Worcester sauce and oil. Leave to marinate for four hours.

Fry the pineapple slices in the butter while you grill the steaks, then serve the beef steaks topped with the fried pineapple slices.

For reasons of nostalgia, if not the weather, roast beef had to be accompanied by Yorkshire pudding, cooked in ghee if the beef had yielded insufficient fat.

'Horseradish sauce', wrote Colonel Kenney-Herbert, 'is a good standard adjunct to our national food, "the roast beef of old England", and beef in India cries out for help far more piteously than its rich relation far away. Horseradish grows well at Ootacamund, and I grew some with success at Bangalore, but the scraped root of the moringa, or "drumstick tree" provides so good a substitute that we may rest contented with a sauce thus composed.'

That stolidly British dish, beef olives, underwent indianization with the addition of fresh ginger, mint and cinnamon to the traditional bread-crumb and bacon stuffing. With *jahl frazie*, the process was reversed, the Mogul dish becoming a way of using up a Sunday roast:

JAHL FRY *serves 4*

1 lb (500 g) leftover roast beef or lamb	2 fresh chillies, deseeded and sliced
1 heaped tbsp dried tamarind	1 tsp ground cumin
2 oz (50 g) ghee or clarified butter	1 tsp ground turmeric
3 large onions, sliced	1 tsp salt
	3 cloves garlic, crushed

Trim the meat of fat and cut into slices. Put the tamarind into 2 fl oz (50 ml) of boiling water and leave to soak for 5 minutes, then squeeze and strain out the pips and pith.

Meanwhile heat the ghee or butter and fry the onions, chillies, cumin and turmeric for several minutes until the onions are lightly browned. Add the salt, garlic and tamarind liquid, and then the meat. Cook, uncovered, until the meat has heated through.

SANDHURST CURRY *serves 4*

Served in the officers' mess, typically for Sunday lunch, this would be accompanied by side dishes such as sliced apples, bananas, shredded coconut, and more chilli powder for those who wished to make a show of their bravery.

2 lb (1 kg) beef	¾ pt (450 ml) beef stock
2 small onions	½ tsp salt
2 tbsp oil	¼ pt (150 ml) coconut cream
2 tbsp Bombay curry powder	½ tsp sugar

Cut the beef into 1 in (2–3 cm) cubes and dice the onions finely.

Heat the oil in a pot and fry the onions until transparent but not browned, then add the beef and brown on all sides. Add the curry powder and stir fry for a further minute. Pour in the stock and add the salt, and simmer slowly for an hour or more, until the beef is tender.

Before serving, stir in the coconut cream and the sugar.

It is interesting to compare Sandhurst Curry, with its sugar, beef stock and ready-mixed curry powder, with a similar recipe adapted from Navroji Framji's *Indian Cooking 'Local' for Young Housekeepers* which lists individual spices for roasting and grinding.

NAVROJI FRAMJI'S MAHRATHA-MODE MEAT CURRY
serves 2–3

1 tsp caraway seeds	1 large onion, chopped
1 tsp anise seeds	1½ tsp ground turmeric
6 peppercorns	small bunch coriander leaves
2 in (5 cm) piece cinnamon stick, broken up	1 in (2–3 cm) fresh ginger root
	2 green chillies, finely chopped
seeds of 2 cardamoms	1 clove garlic
2–3 cloves	1 lb (500 g) mutton or beef, cubed
1 tbsp coriander seeds	
4 tsp ghee or butter	salt, to taste
flesh from ½ coconut, cut into pieces	4 fl oz (125 ml) coconut cream (optional)

Place caraway seeds, anise seeds, peppercorns, cinnamon, cardamoms, cloves and coriander seeds in a frying pan and toast over a medium heat for several minutes, shaking the pan from time to time. Grind the spices in a blender/coffee grinder, or with a mortar and pestle.

Heat 1 tsp of the ghee in the frying pan and fry the coconut pieces and onion until lightly browned. Add, together with turmeric, coriander leaves, ginger, chillies and garlic, to a food processor or blender and grind; or chop finely by hand.

Heat the rest of the ghee in a pan, brown the cubes of meat and then add all the ground ingredients, along with 8 fl oz (250 ml) water. Cover and simmer until the meat is tender. Just before serving add salt to taste, and, if liked, the coconut cream.

From the same source comes the following, in which the dal would have soaked up the fat from the meat and formed a thick sauce.

DHALL AND MEAT CURRY

Put ¾ tea cup of dhall in 3 tea cups of boiling water and boil till the grains are soft. Strain the pulp through a coarse towel or bit of curtain net, saving the gravy. The mussala to be ground – 1 dessertspoon of coriander roasted and husked, ½ tea spoon jeera, ½ tea spoon pepper, 4 red chillies, 6 or 8 cloves garlic, ¼ oz fresh ginger, 1½ inches turmeric. Warm a tablespoon ghee, and brown a sliced onion, then the mussala and a 1 lb of fat mutton or beef cut in inch pieces, when both are nicely browned, add the dhall pulp with salt to taste; have a very slow fire and let the meat &c. cook gently for 10 minutes, then pour in the dhall gravy and the mussala water and as much warm water as is needed to cook the meat and form a sauce.

Hyderabad curry was another British Indian recipe, in which peas were added but the only spice used was chilli. Beatrice Vieyra gave a more elaborate version in *Culinary Art Sparklets*.

BEEF CURRY

REQUIRED:– 1 lb good beef, 8 dried chillies, 1 tablespoonful of coriander, 2 pinches cumminseed, 4 cloves of garlic, 1 small bit of saffron, 4 cloves, 1 small bit of cinnamon, 3 tablespoonsful well heaped of grated cocoanut, 4 onions, 1 tablespoonful of ghee, 2 tablespoonsful of vinegar, a few curry leaves, salt.
METHOD:– Broil the cocoanut, a few curry leaves and curry stuff, but not the spices and saffron, to a brown colour, then grind to a fine paste while warm; while grinding add the spices and saffron and grind these also.

Peel and slice the onions thinly. Place a chatty on the fire, put the ghee into it and when well heated, thrown into it the onions and a few curry leaves; when the onions are brown, add the curry stuff and the meat washed and cut into small pieces. Pour in the vinegar, and water to cover the meat, and let the curry simmer covered.

When the gravy gets thick and the oil clears on top of the curry, take it off the fire. Add salt to taste, and serve hot.

If preferred, tamarind could be used instead of vinegar, and oil instead of ghee for seasoning.

MUSSALA BEEF, OR MUTTON STEAK

1 lb meat. Rub it over with the following powder: 1 dessertspoonful coriander seed, mustard, spoonful cummin seed, 3 red chillies, roasted in a pan and ground. Rub into the raw meat. Melt 1 oz of butter in a pan, and put in the meat until half done, covering it with the butter from time to time. Then sprinkle some salt over. Take a dessertspoon tamarind pulp, mix it with half wineglass water, pour it over the beef. Let it cook in this sauce a few minutes longer. Then take it out of the pan, cut the meat into neat fillets, put them in a dish, pour the tamarind sauce over them and serve as a breakfast dish. (From 'What' and 'How' by E. S. Poynter.)

Mrs Poynter also gives instructions for bobotie. This is generally thought to have been taken to South Africa by Malay immigrants, although the presence of curry powder in many recipes tends to suggest an Anglo-Indian influence.

BOBOTIE

One onion, 1 oz butter, one cupful milk, 1 slice bread, 6 sweet almonds, 2 eggs, ½ lb minced meat cold or uncooked, 1 Tb curry powder. Slice an onion and fry it, soak in milk a small slice of bread and grate 6–8 sweet almonds. Beat 2 eggs in ½ cup milk, and mix all well together with the minced meat, a small lump of butter and the curry powder. Rub a pie dish with butter and piece of lemon, and bake the curry in an oven not too hot. Serve with boiled rice in a separate dish.

Vinthaleaux, or vindaloo, originating from Portuguese Goa, would traditionally have used lamb or mutton, and would have been extremely hot from the amount of chillies used. Milder anglicized versions using beef or even pork were soon popular.

BEEF VINTHALEAUX *serves 4–6*

2 lb (1 kg) cheap cut of beef (shin or braising steak)	pinch of cardamom
	1 stick cinnamon
2 tsp ground chillies	2 tbsp crushed garlic
1 tsp ground coriander	4 tsp chopped root ginger
½ tsp ground cumin	½ tsp salt
2 cloves	2½ fl oz (70 ml) vinegar
3–4 whole peppercorns	4–5 tbsp ghee or clarified butter

Cut the meat into large squares. In a frying pan, assemble the spices and dry fry them for a minute to allow the flavours to mellow. Grind in a coffee grinder or with a mortar and pestle and add the remaining ingredients except the ghee. Mix well with the meat and allow to marinate for 24 hours. Stir occasionally.

Heat the ghee or butter in a heavy-bottomed casserole and add the meat mixture. Cover and simmer over a very low heat for two hours, stirring occasionally, until the meat is tender.

Spicy meatballs in a curry sauce were a favourite with British communities all over India, but were most closely associated with the Punjab and the Deccan plateau. A direct descendent of the *kofta kari*, the Anglo-Indian version differs from the original in that coconut cream rather than tomatoes were used for the sauce. The use of egg to bind the meatballs was also a British innovation.

This recipe, based on an entry in E. A. M. Franklin's *The Wife's Cookery Book*, is one of the best; others called for leftover meat or sausage meat eked out with mashed potato and breadcrumbs. Also popular with British Indians in the south were a variation on the Italian *polpetti* – meatballs mixed with grated cheese and lime juice.

BALL CURRY *serves 3–4*

1 lb (500 g) beef or mutton, minced	½ tsp ground cinnamon
	½ tsp ground turmeric
1 large onion, finely chopped	½ tsp chilli powder
3 green chillies, finely minced	1 egg
¼ tsp ground black pepper	oil for deep frying

Mix all the ingredients and shape into small balls about the size of a walnut. Deep fry them in hot oil and drain on absorbent paper.

SAUCE:

1–2 tbsp ghee or clarified butter	½ tsp mustard seeds
3 large onions, sliced	½ tsp ground cumin
8 curry leaves	8 fl oz (250 ml) coconut cream
2 tsp ground turmeric	salt, to taste
½–1 tsp chilli powder, according to taste	1 clove garlic, crushed
	juice of 2 limes or 1 lemon
2 tbsp ground coriander	

Melt the ghee or butter and gently fry the onions. Throw in the curry leaves and the turmeric and fry until the raw smell disappears; then put in the chilli, coriander, mustard seeds and cumin one by one, letting each fry a little before adding the next. Stir in the coconut cream and add salt to taste. Now add the garlic and the fried meatballs.

Cover the pot and allow to cook for about 10 minutes. Remove from the heat, mix in lime juice and serve with plain boiled rice.

As a variation the coconut cream in the sauce could be replaced by 3–4 large tomatoes, peeled and chopped, 2 tsp of grated fresh ginger and 1½ tbsp of fresh mint or coriander leaves.

Until they emigrated *en masse* in the 1970s, the so-called burghers, or descendants of the Dutch who settled in Sri Lanka in the sixteenth century, had a significant influence on the social life of that country, especially as they were seen as neutral in the conflict between the Tamils and the Sinhalese. Here is one of their meatball recipes, based on the Dutch dish known as *frikkadels*.

FRICADELLEE *serves 3–4*

1 egg	2 tsp *garam masala*
1 lb (500 g) minced beef	1¼ tsp ground fennel seeds
1 small onion, finely chopped	¼ tsp ground nutmeg
2 cloves garlic, crushed	1 tsp salt
1 in (2–3 cm) piece green ginger, finely chopped	rind and juice of ½ lemon

Beat the egg in a bowl, add the remaining ingredients and mix together thoroughly. Roll into balls about 1 in (2–3 cm) in diameter.
Assemble the following ingredients:
flour
1 beaten egg
dry breadcrumbs
oil for deep frying
Roll the balls in flour, then dip in the beaten egg and roll in the breadcrumbs. Heat the oil and deep fry the balls 6 to 8 at time, allowing 4–5 minutes for each batch to cook. Drain on absorbent paper before serving.

Navroji Framji's minced meat curry can also, she says, be formed into meatballs. (*Kotemer* is coriander leaf.)

MINCE MEAT CURRY WITH GREEN MUSSALA
INGREDIENTS: 1 lb of mutton or tender beef minced, an onion minced. Grind up one bunch of kotemer, two or three green chillies, six cloves of garlic, ¼ teaspoon of jeera, and turmeric and fresh ginger of each one inch piece.

DIRECTIONS: Mix the curry paste and the minced meat together, with a little salt, warm a dessertspoon ghee, brown the onion first, then stir in the mince and fry it nicely, then add a small tea cup of water, and let the curry simmer gently with a slow fire below and a coal or two and hot ashes on the cover. Renew this last as the heat dies. There must be very little gravy. This mince curry is very nice put into paste and fried as patties.

As E. G. Bradley's 'amateur butcher' makes plain at the beginning of this chapter, no part of a precious cow would be wasted once it had been slaughtered. The rather alarming amount of chilli in Harriet Lawrance's recipe from *Cookery for the Million* might be safely reduced by two thirds.

TONGUE CURRY

INGREDIENTS:— 1 bull or cow tongue; 1 tablespoonful of curry-stuff; 12 green chillies; 8 peels of garlic; 12 slices of green ginger; 6 cloves; 1 piece of cinnamon; 8 leaves of currypillay; 2 tablespoonsful of sliced onions; 1 tablespoonful of ghee; tamarind and salt to taste.

MODE:— Boil the tongue with enough water to cover it and a little salt, till tender enough to be pierced easily with a broomstick, add more boiling water if necessary, cut off the root, which will do for your dog's dinner, peel the skin of the tongue off (if properly boiled the skin should peel off quite easily), cut up in 12 inch squares, put in a clean vessel on the fire with the ghee and the onions in it with the green chillies slit, ginger, garlic cleaned, currypillay and spice, when brown add the curry-stuff, add the tongue and 1 teacup of the broth left from the boiling of the tongue; the rest will make a very good pepperwater or stock for any other dish; add salt to taste in the curry and simmer till the gravy is thick enough to serve, add tamarind juice to taste, boil up once or twice, and serve. Sufficient for 4 persons.

In many areas of India the British residents were loath to trust the local meat at all, and fell back on that staple of the army, tinned corned beef. This typically Anglo-Indian concoction was served cold as an adjunct to dal and rice, or with mashed potato flavoured with fresh mint and marjoram.

CORNED BEEF BHURTA

1 medium-sized tin corned beef
1 large onion, finely chopped
3 green chillies, finely minced

rind of 1 lemon, grated
juice of 2 lemons

Mash the corned beef with a fork and work in the remaining ingredients. This can also be made with tongue and other cold meats.

Pork

Since pork was considered unclean by both Muslims and Hindus, the British had to make their own arrangements for pig farming right from the earliest days in India. In the seventeenth and eighteenth centuries, every well-appointed British household had its own piggery, where pigs were fattened for the master's table. By the nineteenth century, however, an emerging class of European provisioners was setting up piggeries in the cooler climate of the hills to avoid the problems of keeping pigs in a tropical climate, and curing the resulting bacon and ham. The fame of one such establishment, Harvell's Deegah Farm near Patna, spread to the Viceroy himself, as Edmund Hull recounts:

Mr Harvell's pigs had the honour to detain the most distinguished personage in India from the expectant garrison of Dinapore, drawn out to receive him. After waiting for several hours in the sun, the sepoys, who do not comprehend the distinction between pigs of quality and those of plebeian origin, were not a little amazed and scandalized when they saw the great man ride up in his deshabille, and understood that he had been solacing himself in the pig-sties of Deegah, instead of appearing, at the appointed time, in full costume before the troops anxiously desirous to catch a glimpse of the Burra Sahib.

At remote stations on the plains, the curing of bacon could only take place in the cold weather. Both this and the job of rearing the pigs would typically be entrusted to a retired butler from the local officers' mess or club. English hams, packed in canvas and sent overland before the days of the Suez Canal, were extremely expensive – to the extent that retailers in India were often accused of reaping excessive profits, even allowing for a large proportion of the hams turning bad *en route*.

While the wild boars of the jungle were considered fine eating, there was a great deal of prejudice against the long-legged, bristly-maned domestic breed. This was not without foundation, for the keepers of these animals – the low castes and the Christians of Goa – fed them a foul diet consisting largely of human excrement, a custom which survives to this day in Goa.

Since the majority of the cooks employed by the British were Muslim, this created difficulties when pig-meat of any kind was to be cooked. Lady Mary Hay remembers that her Muslim cook did not mind handling English bacon as it was 'Blighty bacon', but not all were so accommodating. A tactful memsahib would know not to bring home bacon from the club and hand it to her Muslim cook. Instead, she would leave it on the table for one of the low-caste Hindu servants, such as the sweeper, to cook.

Naturally, the British were careful not to include pig-meat on the menu when entertaining Muslim dignitaries, but inevitably the *faux pas* occurred, as Isobel Abbott recalled in *Indian Interval*:

At dinner I found I was seated next to the big landowner, a quiet, thin, good-looking Muslim in his late fifties. His short, well-trimmed beard was almost white, and his heavy-lidded eyes gave him a most distinguished appearance. He knew very little English and spoke in a confused, halting way, but he seemed to understand better than he could speak and nodded and smiled when I made idle conversation. But it was heavy going, from soup to fish, entrée to roast, and when finally an iced pudding was put before us, I was utterly exhausted. I made one last effort.

'Oh, isn't this charming? Our puddings are all like little animals, all different. Look, mine looks just like a little rabbit. See his long ears and bunny nose?'

'Yes, yes, I can see you are right.' He sounded quite delighted and excited. 'I can see the resemblance. What do you think mine looks like?'

'Oh, yours is easy, it's perfect – a little pig.'

I didn't notice the silence. I was only aware he pushed the pudding plate on one side, untouched, and as soon as possible hurriedly left the room . . .

Not all Muslims were so sensitive however, and some were even known to partake of ham in the company of Europeans, particularly if the Muslim's servants were not present or if his social standing was sufficiently high as to place him beyond reproach of the Muslim clergy:

> And I have known Nabobs their bellies cram
> With many of the saints' forbidden dishes
> Waillaitee mutton, styling – Yorkshire ham;
> And freely eating – what his soul must damn,
> If he the true faith owns. But if he rich is,
> His deviation from it is a flam;
> 'Tis the poor wretch without a rag of britches,
> And starving, who of conscience only feels the twitches.
> (From *Tom Raw, the Griffin*, by Sir Charles D'Oyly, 1846.)

Another Muslim euphemism for ham was 'Belatty herron' – English venison.

The best pork dishes of British India came from Goa, where local spices had been incorporated into the culinary repertoire of eighteenth-century Portuguese colonizers.

Chourisam, a famous offspring of this marriage, was a sharp, gingery version of Portuguese *chouriço*, a garlic pork sausage. Similarly, the pickled pork and liver curry known as sorpotel had its roots in the Portuguese tradition of marinating pork in wine and vinegar.

Accompanied by fluffy white rice bread leavened with toddy (the fermented sap of the palm tree) sorpotel was an essential part of any Goan Christian feast. It was also served from time to time by the British, who greatly favoured Goan cooks because their religion placed no ban on the handling of beef or pork.

SORPOTEL *serves 10–12*

4 lb (2 kg) boneless pork from loin, leg or shoulder, with all fat left on
2 lb (1 kg) pig's or calf's liver
1 lb (500 g) pig's heart
1 tbsp salt
1½ tsp ground turmeric
2 tbsp dried tamarind pulp
4 tbsp oil
2 medium onions, finely chopped
8–10 cloves garlic, pulverized
2 in (5 cm) piece fresh ginger, pulverized

1½ tbsp ground coriander seeds
1½ tbsp ground cumin
2 tsp ground cinnamon
2 tsp ground black pepper
1 tsp ground cloves
¼ tsp ground cardamom
2–4 fresh or dried red chillies, pulverized
1 pt (600 ml) coconut vinegar or malt vinegar
1 tsp sugar

Put the pork, liver, heart, salt and turmeric into a large pot with enough water to cover completely. Bring to the boil, then reduce the heat, partly cover, and simmer for an hour.

Remove all the meats and set the cooking liquid aside. Trim all the fat off the pork, but do not discard. Cut all the meat into ½ in (1 cm) cubes. Transfer to a large bowl and cover with the cooking liquid. Cut the pork fat into ½ in (1 cm cubes), too.

Break the tamarind pulp into small pieces, cover with a cupful of boiling water, and leave for five minutes. Squeeze the pulp to remove the stones and pith, strain off the thick brown liquid, and set aside.

Wash and dry the cooking pot, then return to the stove with the oil, onions and cubes of pork fat. Over a medium heat, stir-fry the onions until transparent but not browned. Add the garlic, ginger, coriander, cumin, cinnamon, black pepper, cloves, cardamom and chillies, along with most of the vinegar, retaining 4 fl oz (125 ml). Turn up the heat to high, and continue to stir for 10 minutes, until most of the liquid has evaporated and the mixture has thickened. Add the meats and the cooking liquid. Bring to the boil, then reduce the heat, cover tightly, and simmer for 30 minutes. Five minutes before the end of the cooking time, add the remaining vinegar, the tamarind water and the sugar.

Once cooled, store the sorpotel, well covered, in the refrigerator. It may be eaten after two days, but reaches its best after two weeks, and will keep up to six weeks under refrigeration.

Heat thoroughly before serving.

Mutton and Goat

So ingrained was the English taste for great joints of roast beef and mutton that it followed them even to the tropical heat of India. To their disappointment, however, they found the Indian sheep small and lean, yielding small, tough joints only about half the size of those in England. The only way to improve matters was to take up stock breeding themselves:

We have a farmyard, as a matter of course; and our every need is supplied from within the mud-walled boundaries of our grand estate. Herds and flocks, and much cattle, do we possess. We have our shepherd (that sable fellow there, carrying almost his entire wardrobe on his head, in the form of a long cloth in many folds), who tends our flock, taking them out to graze by day, and protecting them in their mud-walled fold by night. And high-caste sheep are ours, albeit they are black, and albeit they are diminutive; but, encouraged by grain, their little plump carcasses yield us delicious mutton, that a Leicester would be proud to have afforded, and a South Down get emaciated on beholding.

George Franklin Atkinson, of course.

Another Victorian writer claimed that the mutton of the Patna breed from the north-west was 'as good as any that Wales ever produced'. The green pastures of the Deccan also yielded sweet-flavoured mutton, but even more celebrated was the gram-fed mutton of Bengal. The cheapness of gram in Bengal meant that sometimes whole flocks of sheep were fed on it, although the high quality was probably due equally to the shepherds turning the young males into wethers, then a rare practice in India but essential to producing good lamb and mutton.

Coming from better-fed sheep, the joints of Bengal mutton were much larger than those found elsewhere in India, but were also more expensive. In the nineteenth century a leg of mutton in Calcutta might cost up to six times as much as the same joint in Madras. There was a great scarcity of quality meat in Madras, a state of affairs for which, in the opinion of Colonel Kenney-Herbert, the English of Madras had only themselves to blame:

If the butchers were certain of sales at remunerative prices they would produce a far better article than they do, but when people grumble at an extra anna charged on a seer of well-fed meat, you can scarcely expect much improvement.

Indeed, the expense involved in providing top-quality feed meant the best Indian mutton ended up costing very nearly what it would in England, as the statistics of the old up-country mutton clubs show.

The mutton club was a co-operative of English residents who kept their own flock of sheep, a necessary feature of every regiment and smaller up-country station in India, since goat meat was usually all that was on sale locally. By the 1890s, however, the mutton clubs had almost died out, as good gram-fed mutton became available from village bazaars.

The club was managed by an honorary secretary, who supervised the accounts, the shepherds, feed, and delivery of the meat. When a sheep was killed each week, it would be butchered into five parts – necessitating that the number of mutton club members be five, or multiples of five – and each member would take, by turns, one of the two forequarters, the legs or the saddle. This arrangement had the effect of controlling the station dinner parties. A dinner at the Judge's or the Collector's could be foretold as accurately as the appearance of the full moon, by calculating the date on which the succulent saddle was due to them, for it must be remembered that in India before the days of refrigeration an animal had to be eaten within twenty-four hours of its being killed.

Since the mutton could not be hung it was almost invariably tough, and a number of tenderizing techniques were used. Of these, the most scientifically sound was to wrap the meat in papaya leaves, which contain a tenderizing enzyme, papain. Some Indian cooks added a pinch of quick-lime to a tough curry or a mulligatawny soup, while others were adamant that putting a bit of broken china in with the meat rendered it tender. The truth is that the china absorbed the heat that too fierce a fire produced, and thus did what the Indian cook claimed for it, but a slow fire would have had the same effect.

Marinating the meat had the double benefit of tenderizing it and preserving it for the next day, while meat could be kept for up to four days even in the hot weather, by placing it in a box with smouldering charcoal and sulphur. In *Indian Cookery and Domestic Recipes* C. C. Kohlhoff provides instructions for pickling meat to avoid the excess being wasted.

PICKLED MEAT

Take 3 lb of fresh mutton or pork without a bit of bone, cut it into pieces of about 3 or 4 inches square and 1 inch thick; rub well into it ¼ lb of salt (white), and allow it to remain in the brine 48 hours. In the meantime, prepare the following ingredients, each separately cleaned and ground with vinegar to a fine pulp, viz; ¼ oz dry chillies, and the same of saffron, garlic, cummin, mustard and coriander seed and green ginger.

Drain the meat from the brine and put it into a small, clean, dry jar. Mix a pint of good vinegar with the ground massala, and pour it over the meat. Shake the whole well up for five minutes. Close the mouth of the jar and keep it in a dry place. It will be fit for use in a couple of days.

Up until the early nineteenth century the English insisted upon their roast mutton being done the traditional way, on a spit, despite the complete unsuitability of the lean, scraggy Indian joints for this method of cooking. Towards the end of the century, however, the penny finally dropped, and pot roasting became the norm. Some ghee or dripping would be put in a heavy pot, and the meat would be turned from time to time until it was browned all over. Hot embers placed on the cover of the pot ensured more even cooking. A joint might also be braised in broth and then fried briefly in ghee to give it a roasted appearance. The memsahib had to guard against the old cook's trick of roasting the joint long before it was needed and keeping it warm until it was required, resulting in dried-up meat.

Another common way with meat, well out of fashion today, was politely termed *rechauffé*: in other words, the remains of yesterday's roast heated up in some hefty disguise such as a sauce or a curry. Nobody pretended, however, that this was any substitute for a good fresh meat curry: 'The Quoorma', wrote Colonel Kenney-Herbert in his *Culinary Jottings for Madras*, 'if well made, is undoubtedly an excellent curry. It used, I believe, to be one of the best at the Madras Club, in days when curries commanded closer attention than they do now.'

QUOORMA CURRY

Cut up about a pound of very tender mutton without any bone, and stir the pieces about with a dessertspoonful of pounded green ginger, and a sprinkling of salt. Melt a quarter of a pound of butter in a stew-pan, and throw into it a couple of white onions cut into rings, and a couple of cloves of garlic finely minced. Fry for about five minutes, and then add a teaspoonful of pounded coriander seed, one of pounded black pepper, half one of pounded cardamoms, and half one of pounded cloves. Cook this for five minutes, then put in the meat, and stir over a moderate fire until the pieces seem tender and have browned nicely. Now, take the pan from the fire, and work into it a strong infusion obtained from four ounces of well-pounded almonds, and a breakfast cupful of cream. Mix thoroughly, adding a dessert-spoonful of turmeric powder, and a tea-spoonful of sugar. Put the pan over a very low fire, and let the curry simmer as gently as possible for a quarter of an hour, finishing off with the juice of a couple of limes. This, it will be perceived, is another curry of rich yet mild description. The total absence of chilli, indeed, constitutes, in the opinion of many, its chief attraction.

Writing at the beginning of the twentieth century, Harriet Lawrance and C. C. Kohlhoff both assumed reasonably tender meat would be available.

A MADRAS CURRY

INGREDIENTS:— ½ a cocoanut; 4 pods garlic; ½ teaspoonful mixed cummin and mustard; ¾ of a teacup of coriander seed; 2 dried chillies; ¾ teaspoonful ground saffron; 1 tablespoonful minced onions; 1 tablespoonful ghee; meat ½ lb; the juice of half a lime.

MODE:— First prepare the ingredients. Broil well the coriander seeds, rub between the hands and sift well, then grind with the two chillies. Grate the cocoanut, set aside about 1 tablespoonful of it. Pour on the rest ½ a big teacupful of hot water and extract the first milk. Then pour on the cocoanut 2 big cups hot water and extract the second milk. Take the cocoanut that is set apart and grind together with the garlic. Take the ghee and put in a saucepan and place on the fire. When all the ghee has melted, put in the onions and fry till they are a pale yellow, then put in the saffron and fry a few minutes, then put in the coriander and chillies and fry a few minutes, lastly the meat which has been cut up into dice, fry until all the raw smell has departed from the curry-stuff. Then put in the second milk, now boil till the meat is cooked and then simmer till all the liquid disappears. Then put in salt to taste, the first cocoanut milk and the lime juice. Cook for a few minutes and serve. (*Cookery for the Million*)

MUTTON CURRY

One lb of mutton cut up into small pieces, 1 tea cup of coriander leaves ground, 1 dozen green chillies ground, a handful of sliced onions, 8 cloves of garlic ground, 1 cocoanut half-ground and the thick milk of the other half, extracted; a dozen cloves and an inch of cinnamon ground, a small piece of green ginger ground, a teaspoon of ground saffron, 2 teaspoons of ground coriander, ¾ tea cup of curds or tyre, a little salt, and, if needed, the juice of half a lime, 2 tablespoons of ghee.

Fry the onions in the ghee. Mix with the meat, in a separate dish, a little salt and all the ground ingredients, throw it into the ghee and mix thoroughly. After a minute or two, cover the chatty and let it boil for about 10 minutes. Take off the cover, and fry the meat until only some thick gravy is left, when add the tyre, and continue frying till only ¼ the gravy is left. Now, add the thick cocoanut milk, and let it simmer on a slow fire until the gravy is of the consistency required. Lime-juice may, or may not, be added. (*Indian Cookery and Domestic Recipes*)

Yet Mrs Bartley, in her *Indian Cookery 'General'*, recognized both the need for long slow cooking to tenderize stringy meat, and the value of cooking meat to keep it for a day or two. Her recipe for Jewish Curry probably originated in the famous community of Jewish spice merchants in Cochin.

JEWISH CURRY

Grind one coffee-cup coriander seed, four inches turmeric, one tablespoon of black pepper (level) three ounces of garlic, and four dry chillies. Boil two tablespoonfuls of ghee or four tablespoonfuls of salad oil. Fry a sliced onion, then brown in the mussala, pour in a wine glass of vinegar, then two pounds of meat cut in pieces and washed, cover the chatty and cook the curry on a slow fire till the meat gets tender. This curry will keep two days.

A popular way of dealing with tough meat of all types was to mince it thoroughly (some cooks even went to the extent of pounding it and then passing it through a sieve) to make the ever-popular cutlets. This is one of Henrietta Hervey's versions:

ANGLO-INDIAN MUTTON CUTLETS

Most old Indians, will, I think, admit that the cutlets out yonder are far superior to the home production; so I give the following recipe, which I always find successful, not only with mutton, but with beef and chicken. In a machine, mince a pound of lean meat; mix with a finely chopped onion, a tablespoonful of chopped sweet herbs, and a little pepper and salt. Then mix in the yolks of two eggs; shape into flat discs, about three-quarters of an inch thick; dip each first into egg, then into bread crumbs (on one side only) and fry till brown, turning occasionally.

Goat meat was even tougher than mutton, but considerably cheaper. This is what the average Indian tended to eat, and since the Anglo-Indian term *muttongosht* (i.e. 'mutton flesh') referred to the meat of both sheep and goats, there was often considerable confusion among the servants. Memsahib Mary Fitzgibbon noted in her diary: 'At Bangalore at dinner in seeing the curry I asked "What curry is this?" He said "mutton". I replied, "but I told the cook to kill the kid for curry." He said, "Yes too kid mistress." '

Goat meat never gained complete social acceptability among the English, although at dinners given by the Mogul nobility, they would politely pick at whole carcasses covered in gold leaf. The finest goat meat, much prized around Bombay, came from the kid of a round, short-legged breed from Surat. A later edition of *Mrs Beeton's Household Management* noted acidly that while goat meat was sometimes cooked in India, 'it is anything but pleasant to English tastes'.

In view of the price difference, it is not surprising that certain unscrupulous butchers and *khansamahs* tried to palm off goat as mutton. There was no difficulty in distinguishing goat from mutton after it had been cooked, as goat was considerably tougher and more highly flavoured, but there was little difference in the appearance of the two meats when raw. Some memsahibs insisted on being shown the meat with the hoof on, but even with this precaution they were advised to examine it very carefully, as a sheep's hoof had been known to have been sewn on to a goat's leg!

C. C. Kohlhoff provides an interesting recipe for curried goat in *Indian Cookery and Domestic Recipes*, in which eggs are added to the gravy.

KID CURRY

Wash and cut into pieces 1 lb of kid. Now, rub the meat well with a little salt, the juice of 6 onions, 1 garlic, and a bit of ginger. Heat a tablespoonful of ghee and fry in it 6 sliced onions and the meat with the juice. Add a little water and boil till the meat absorbs the gravy. Now, add 2 more tablespoonsful of ghee and, when three-fourths fried, add a little pounded spice, and fry well; break 3 eggs in a bowl with a little water and warm them on the fire, stirring all the while with a spoon till done. Add this to the meat, together with a little water and 2 tablespoons of thick tamarind pulp and let it simmer for quarter of an hour.

For historians of Mogul cookery, Dr R. Riddell's *Indian Domestic Economy and Receipt Book* of 1849 must rank as a key text, for among a wad of pedestrian advice on plain English cooking, there is a treasury of 'Persian receipts' set down with military exactitude in Bombay bazaar weights, possibly for the first time ever. Little is known about Dr Riddell, except that he was also the author of the *Manual of Gardening for Western India*. However, from a note on what is meant by a measure of water, it is obvious that he had not recorded these recipes first hand. Many are extremely long and complicated, but the following should be within the bounds of the modern cook. A note on seers, tolahs and other weights and measures can be found on page xi, although it may be wise to moderate the amounts of ghee and salt the recipe calls for. ('Tyre' is curds or yoghurt; 'chenna dhall' are chickpeas, and to 'give a bughar' is to fry rapidly, shaking the covered pan over the heat.)

KULLEAH BUNGOODAY

kid's meat	1 Seer	Cream	⅛ Seer
Ghee	⅓ Seer	Chennah dhall	2 Tolahs
Coarse tyre	¼ Seer	Turmeric	1 Tolahs
Onions	¼ Seer	Garlic	2 Tolahs
Green ginger	2 Tolahs	Cardamoms	2 Mashas
Salt	2 Tolahs	Cinnamon	2 Mashas
Blanched almonds	⅛ Seer	Cloves	2 Mashas

Cut in thin slices some onions, garlic and green ginger; put in a frying pan with a little ghee, and fry till brown; keep it on one side; then strain the ghee and put it in another saucepan and keep it hot; cut the meat in small slices and season it with a part of the curry-stuff, onions, green ginger, and garlic; mix these together with a little tyre, and rub over the meat and give it a bughar in ghee; then put in the chennah dhall and boil it with the rest of the tyre, until it is dried up; fry it well; add a little water and simmer it until the meat in tender; grind the almonds with rice water and mix it with the cream, and, stirring it together pour over the meat; then put the onions fried with the rest of the curry-stuff to it, adding a little ground saffron, and squeeze over it the juice of a lime and boil for a short time.

12

Dal, Roti and Rice

———

This is a handful of cardamom,
This is a lump of ghee
This is millet and chillies and rice,
And Supper for thee and me.
(From *Kim*, by Rudyard Kipling, 1901.)

The humble lentil stew known as dal and its accompaniment of rice or unleavened flat bread (roti or chapati) has always been daily fare for hundreds of millions of India's poor, and is central to the diet of the vegetarian south.

In Britain, dried pulses beefed up the everyday pottage of the medieval peasantry and the monasteries, and were considered excellent horse and cattle fodder, but were hardly a delicacy befitting the table of a household with genteel aspirations. Hence, in British India pulses might be mixed with rice and fed to children or animals, served for a homely lunch, or even dinner at the spartan table of a missionary family, but to have served dal roti at a grand station dinner would have raised eyebrows and provided gossip about the host's eccentricity for months afterwards.

Of the many dals eaten in India, the most familiar to the English was a small salmon-coloured variety known as masoor or mussoor dal. This is almost identical to the common red lentil, and has the advantage of not needing prior soaking, and being exceptionally quick to cook. This 'dholl' recipe, typical of many, is from C. C. Kohlhoff's *Indian Cookery and Domestic Recipes*:

DHOLL CURRY

Pick, clean and wash a teacupful of red or any other dholl, boil it till quite tender in 3 tea cups of water, drain and set aside. Heat a table spoon of ghee and fry in it 1 sliced onion, a tea spoon each of ground ginger, garlic and saffron, add a little salt and then boiled dholl; stir it well with a pestle, adding about 3 green chillies, well chopped. Let it simmer for five minutes. Before taking it off the fire, put in a tablespoonful of very thick cocoanut milk.

In *Indian Cookery 'General'*, Mrs Bartley includes a spicy variation which she desribes as 'Mahratta mode'. The fierce Hindu warrior caste known as the Mahrattas were well respected by the British military. From tiny hilltop forts in the Western Ghats near Bombay, their leader Shivaji had inspired fierce though ultimately unsuccessful resistance in the seventeenth century. As cooks, they had a reputation for bagging any game or vegetable that came their way – and cooking it up with plenty of chilli to match their fiery temperament.

MUSSOOR DHALL CURRY (MAHRATTA MODE)

INGREDIENTS:— a tea cup of dhall to be put to boil in six tea cups of boiling water. It will be soft in an hour or less. The curry stuff as follows: ½ a tsp of 'shajeera', ½ tsp of kuskus, ½ tsp jeera, 2 red chillies, 3 cloves, a stick of cinnamon, 2 ins long, one cardamom seed, an inch of turmeric, a tsp aniseed, a dsp coriander, ¼ of a cocoanut, 1 onion, and 2 peppercorns.

First fry all the curry stuff in ghee on a thoa and grind it all together, stir in the curry stuff in the boiled dhall, cover the chatty, warm a dsp of ghee, brown well some slices of garlic, covering chatty while doing so, then add curry which must only boil up once.

Curries made of curds thickened with ground dal were a speciality of the Parsi sect of Bombay. Followers of the ancient prophet Zarathustra, the Parsis fled from Iran to India in about the eighth century AD to escape persecution from the invading Arab Muslims. Although originally rural artisans and labourers, the Parsis were greatly favoured by the British and quickly became Westernized in outward ways. During the Raj, they moved in large numbers to Calcutta and Bombay, where they went into the professions, established India's first cotton mills and, in the twentieth century, founded the huge Tata conglomerate of chemical and heavy vehicle manufacturers.

Mrs Bartley again:

BUTTER MILK CURRY

Grind one third of a small cocoanut, one teaspoon jeera, one onion, one red chilli, half a garlic, two or three pepper-corns, a bit of turmeric, and a small bunch of kotemer leaf. Warm three tea cups of buttermilk, mix in the mussala, with salt taste, stirring all the time till it boils, when remove from the fire, and let the curry cool. In another chatty warm a heaped teaspoon of ghee, fry half a garlic sliced, and pour in the curry. Stir and simmer a few minutes longer.

CURRY OF CURDS

A tea cup of curds, four tablespoons of gram flour, a dessert spoon of ghee. Grind a small green bunch of green kotemer leaves, an inch piece of turmeric, two red chillies, a quarter teaspoon jeera, and six slices of garlic.

DIRECTIONS:– Mix the curds, gram flour, and mussala together. Warm the ghee and fry half a garlic sliced. Add the curds and let the curry boil with enough salt.

The 'khurhi' in G. H. Cook's *The English-Indian Cookery Book* is flavoured mostly with garlic or *maithi* (fenugreek), but could be further spiced with grated ginger, turmeric and cumin.

KHURHI OR GRAM FLOUR CURRY

INGREDIENTS:– 6 oz gram flour, 1 teaspoon salt, 1 teaspoon ground chillies, 2 teaspoons ghee or butter, 2 lbs butter milk, or curds (dahi), four or five pieces garlic, or maithi seeds.

Place all the ingredients excepting the ghee and garlic into a deckchi with the buttermilk and boil for about 15 minutes until it gets like a thick gruel.

Put ghee and garlic into another deckchi and fry for a few minutes until brown. Then put into the deckchi containing the gruel and cover up quickly not to allow the aroma or scent to escape. Stir well before serving. This is eaten with rice, chapatties or poories.

In 1925 an Englishman, V. H. Mottram, published a book entitled *Food and the Family*, in which he attempted to give a physiological explanation of why the traditional English cooked breakfast should be part of the natural order of things for the whole of humanity.

After twelve hours' fasting, he insisted, the body needs the immediate energy provided by easily digested carbohydrates like porridge, which pass through the pylorus into the small intestines, leaving behind in the stomach the eggs and bacon to be duly digested as to 'provide the sense of satisfaction, which no breakfast, except the British and the American, can provide.'

No doubt a memsahib somewhere in southern India read these lines with a grunt of satisfaction, thinking disapprovingly of the everyday breakfast eaten by her servants and the local populace generally – a hot spicy, protein-rich family of dishes based on a batter of ground lentils and rice: masala dosa, idlies and a fried savoury doughnut known as the vada.

It may not have occurred to her, or to the good Mr Mottram, that Indians happened to find these assaults of protein and carbohydrate every bit as satisfying as porridge, eggs and bacon.

While the vada was not often seen on British breakfast tables in India, it did make an occasional appearance as a snack for tiffin, which is how it is recommended by Beatrice Vieyra in *Culinary Arts Sparklets*.

DHAL VADA

REQUIRED:— 8 ozs of dhal, 3 dried chillies, a very small bit of saffron, 12 green chillies, 10 small onions, a tablespoon of picked curry leaves, 3 tablespoons of rice-flour, ¼ bottle cocoanut oil, and salt.

METHOD:— Clean and wash the dhal well and boil it in enough water. When quite soft drain well from the water, and grind coarsely, next grind to a paste the dried chillies and saffron and mix up well with the ground dhal.

Chop up the green chillies and onions and add these to the dhal, also the curry leaves whole; mix up thoroughly, add the flour, and salt to taste, then form into biscuits making a hole in the middle, and fry brown on both sides.

Serve warm. The remaining oil might be used for seasoning curries.

A little fenugreek may be used with the dhal, if preferred.

These currystuff cakes and their variation, pagodas, are heavily spiced cousins of the vada.

CURRYSTUFF CAKES

Soak and grind 2 large tea cups of Bengal gram; chop very fine 4 bundles onion stalk, 2 handfuls of onions, 3 bundles coriander leaves, 1 piece of green ginger, a dozen green chillies; grind a coffee cup of prawns, and add a little salt according to taste.

Heat a sufficient quantity of ghee; mix all the above ingredients together; form into small patties on a wet cloth and fry, a few at a time, in the heated ghee.

If you wish to make pagodas, the same mixture, with the addition of a few more chillies, will answer; only you must put in about a teaspoonful each pagoda, without forming them into cakes. (From *Indian Cookery and Domestic Recipes*, by C. C. Kohlhoff.)

Good, yeast-risen bread was more hankered after than actually eaten in most of British India. While Bombay, Madras and Calcutta all had clean, European-managed bakeries in the central business districts, in remote up-country stations there was no such convenience.

In 1893, after years of impatience with makeshift baking arrangements out in the *mofussil*, Mrs R. Temple-Wright, wrote *Baker and Cook: A Domestic Manual for India*. Its unassuming cloth and cardboard cover emblazoned with willow-pattern crockery motifs, the little book was an instant success, and over the next two decades ran to three revised editions.

In exhorting her readers not to eat bazaar bread, Mrs Temple-Wright doubtless fed popular prejudice with her account of a leper waylaying a baker's carrier on his way from the bazaar to the station, and fingering every loaf in the basket. She also claimed to have seen a leper employed as a baker in a bazaar shop, and 'the family blanket pulled off the bed of sickness and death, and used in the bazaar bakehouse to keep warm the dough which would presently appear in the form of bread for European consumption!'

Mrs Temple-Wright suggested her country readers form bread clubs along the same lines as the popular mutton clubs, with a co-operatively owned mill, bakehouse, and oven, and a trained *roti-wallah* with wages paid from members' subscriptions.

There is little evidence of this having happened, however. Few memsahibs went to the effort and expense of training a *roti-wallah* from the bazaar, for not only would he have to be taught how to bake the bread, but to make the yeast as well. The so-called German yeast used by bakers in Britain could not be bought in India, so yeasts had to be home-made, often with great difficulty. Soda bread was common after baking powders became widely available in the 1860s, but the sandy, tasteless results wrapped in waxed paper (still seen in India today) appealed only to those who wished to maintain British decorum at the breakfast table at all costs.

Chapatis were thus commonly eaten by the British out in the *mofussil*, albeit mostly under sufferance. Even Reginald Heber, the poetry-writing Bishop of Calcutta whose palate was generally receptive to 'Hindoo messes', had to confess in his journal during a journey through Rajasthan in 1825, that a delivery of fresh yeast-risen bread 'came at a very good time, as we were just commencing on a course of Hindoostanee chapatees, which are not a very good substitute.'

Over time, however, many British developed a taste for all the famous flat unleavened breads – phulka (a thinner, more refined chapati), the puffy nan cooked in a Punjabi tandoor, and the fried, flaky paratha. They were after all, the breads the *bawarchi* knew how to cook best of all. George Franklin Atkinson's *Curry and Rice on Forty Plates* carries a description of one such cook at work:

Look at that individual seated in front of the kitchen door. He is cooking unfermented bread. See there, again, the simplicity of an Oriental's wants; for there before him is his kitchen range, – there is the stove, the grate, his fire – his every need. Three small heaps of clay has he rudely knocked up, and the surface has he smoothed with diluted mud; he has gathered a few sticks; he has a thin globular sort of saucepan; and with these alone is he prepared to make your bread, which, with some water and flour, that he has kneaded into dough, he flattens into circular cakes with his hand, and bakes them on the bottom of his pot. There in a few minutes will he bake you unfermented cakes; and if you have good butter to spread on them, and eat them when hot, you will have no reason to complain.

This is the breakfast, the dinner, the tea, the staple food, the aliment, the nutrition, the staff of life, of millions of the indigenous, who live upon these 'chupatties', which the poor eat plain, the wealthy with oil and butter, and other supplementary condiments. This is the food of the native soldiery – of high and low, or rich and poor.

Chapatis, or hand cakes, 'are made with wheat flour (don't attempt to make with maida or finely ground flour as they are not tasty),' warns *The English-Indian Cookery Book*. 'They are made easily. The majority of English cooks cannot make them, as they have no experience in rolling or cooking them. The cook's wife will make them better than him.'

CHAPATTIES

Take say a pound of flour and knead it with water until it can be rolled. Then take a pat of flour and roll it in the hand until it gets round and the cracks are closed. Sprinkle a little dry flour on the board and roll it into the shape and size of a quarter plate frequently turning it over until it is about an eighth of an inch thick, then place on an iron plate known as a tava which is previously placed to warm on a choola fired with wood. Let it harden for about half a minute then turn it over until the other side hardens and then place it on side standing inside the choola until it swells up, then turn it over on the other side and allow it to cool. These taste better than toasted bread when eaten hot with butter and salt. The secret in making them tasty lies in not cooking them entirely on the tava as this prevents them from swelling and getting light.

C. C. Kohlhoff provides an attractive variation on the standard chapati recipe by adding mashed sweet potatoes – rather in the tradition of Irish potato cakes:

SWEET POTATO CHUPATTIES

Boil two lbs of sweet potatoes, skin and mash them smooth; before they are cold add flour gradually to the potatoes, make the mass into a dough, no stiffer than can be rolled out without breaking. If too stiff add a little milk, form into cakes, and bake one at a time on a 'Thoa' over a coal fire. While baking move the cake about with your hand, wrapped in a napkin, turn the cake every two or three minutes, till you find them baked sufficiently.

Pooree, or puri, is a famous Indian bread made simply with flour and water and perhaps a little ghee, rolled out and deep fried until puffy. On special occasions, however, the puri came with a stuffing of dal:

DAL POOREE

Five units of dal washed. Boil till tender. Add 1 unit ground onions, ¼ of ground chillies, ¼ of ginger and turmeric mixed, a clove of garlic, and ¼ unit salt. Brown 6 onions in 2 units butter and stir to the dal. Make a flour-and-water paste as for water biscuits. Take a piece of this the size of a walnut and hollow into a saucer, put into this sufficient quantity of the prepared dal. Lay on another similar saucer, flute the edges, and roll out as thin as possible. When the size of a dinner plate fry in boiling ghee. (From *The Complete Indian Housekeeper and Cook*, by Flora Annie Steel and G. Gardiner.)

Unlike their cousins back in England who considered rice just another form of starch (and inferior to potatoes at that), old India hands appreciated the huge variation in quality among the estimated 10,000 types of rice grown in British India; in particular, they came to relish what their servants referred to as 'table rice'. This was the famous hard, long-grained, pearly Patna rice grown in the north. It was eaten by the wealthier Indians and by the Anglo-Indian community as well. Even more prized was (and still is) basmati rice, whose distinctive, faintly nutty scent and flavour improves with keeping (usually about six months, although there are stories of basmati having been aged for fifteen years!) and whose extraordinarily long grains swell twice their length when cooked. The process baffles scientists to this day. Much is grown in Pakistan and Bihar State in north India ('patna basmati'), but the aristocrat of basmatis is from Dehra Dun in the northern state of Uttar Pradesh.

Due to the laborious hand harvesting, husking and winnowing of the grains, many foreign bodies such as dust and bits of gravel found their way into the rice, and a lowly servant, usually a woman, would be given the daily task of sitting and sorting through the rice grains, picking out the unwanted matter, along with any broken grains. The latter were often doled out by the handful to passing beggars, the rest being meticulously washed in specially designed wooden bowls prior to cooking.

The rice of Bengal tended to be a very much smaller grain, while the staple grain of the rice-eating south was of a much coarser texture, though richer in flavour.

The servants would have to be satisfied with these lesser varieties, though generally it was at least polished, or white rice; *ukad*, the rough, unhusked village rice, coloured a shade of red by the wrapping of bran around the kernel, was left to the Ryot caste, and much, much later, to the hippies.

For the rice puddings demanded by homesick English exiles, the cook would, of course, have chosen a short grain variety, and this was also the type of rice which went into Indian sweets, cooked for the household staff at festival time. For pilaus and the chota-sahib's kedgerees, however, only the best would do.

The original version of kedgeree, and according to Yule and Burnell's *Hobson-Jobson* (1903) the only correct one, was based on rice and lentils, not fish. We read in the Rev. F. Ovington's *A Voyage to Suratt in the Year 1689*:

Of this [kedgeree] the European Sailors feed in these parts once or twice a Week, and are forc'd at those times to a Pagan Abstinence from Flesh, which creates in them a perfect Dislike and utter Detestation to those Bannian Days, as they commonly call them.

Along with fried fish and green chutney (see page 225), the following was, says Lady Mary Hay, a favourite Bombay breakfast dish. (For more on kedgerees, see pages 83–5.)

KEDGEREE *serves 3–4*

1 lb (500 g) long-grain Patna rice	2 sticks cinnamon, each 2 in
4 oz (125 g) lentils	(5 cm) long
4 oz (125 g) butter	½ tsp allspice
2 tbsp chopped onions	6 thin slices green ginger
1 clove garlic, chopped	½ tsp ground turmeric
	salt

Wash the rice and lentils thoroughly and leave to soak in cold water for an hour or so.

Use a large saucepan with a close-fitting lid. Put in the butter, onions, garlic, cinnamon, allspice and ginger. Cook until the onions are soft but not brown. Drain the rice and lentils and add to the pan. Add the turmeric and salt. Toss together and cook for four to five minutes. Add boiling water to cover the mixture by about 1½ in (4 cm). Cover the pan and cook very slowly until the rice is cooked and all the water absorbed – about half an hour.

Serve sprinkled with raisins and sliced hard-boiled egg. The raisins are best 'plumped' in butter for a few minutes.

'ENGLISH' PULLOW:
'This is the recipe for the dish as generally seen on Anglo-Indian tables,' writes Henrietta Hervey. 'The same process is observed, with but little variation, throughout the empire.'

Wash and soak in cold water for twenty minutes a pound of Patna or other fine rice. In a large stewpan bring to boil half a pound of 'ghee'or butter, in which fry a finely shredded onion to a crisp brown. Remove the onion, but not the butter, and into which last put a small handful of allspice, frying briskly for a minute; then add the rice, keeping it stirred till the grain turns colour. Now pour in some previously prepared stock, sufficient to more than immerse the rice; stir in a little salt, cover, and boil gently. As the liquid evaporates, uncover and stir constantly till the rice is cooked. Now let it steam by the fireside for ten minutes, stirring frequently, till the grain separates, when serve; garnishing with hard boiled egg, your crisped onions, and some lightly fried raisins and sliced almonds.

A fascinating source of pilau recipes is the *Indian Domestic Economy and Receipt Book*, in which Dr Riddell recorded his unique collection of Mogul 'pullows'. His measures are precise (see page xi for an explanation of bazaar terms), but include alarming amounts of ghee, salt and butter, which can safely be reduced to suit modern palates and health-consciousness.

MOORGHABEE OR FOWL PULLOW

Mutton	1 pound	Mace	4 Blades
Fowl	1	Cloves	10 or 12
Rice	8 ounces	Cardamoms	10 or 12
Onions	5 or 6	Green Ginger	1 Tolah
Eggs	3 or 4	Salt	1 Dessertspoonful
Butter	½ pound	Currypak leaves	2 or 3
Black pepper	10 or 12 Corns		

Put the mutton cut in slices, with four onions whole, into water six quarts; boil all this together until reduced to one third; take it off the fire; mash the meat into the liquor and strain through a towel and set it aside. Take eight ounces of rice; wash it well and dry by squeezing it firmly in a towel; put half a pound of butter into a saucepan, and melt it; fry in it a handful of onions sliced lengthways; when they have become a brown colour, then take them out and lay aside; in the butter that remains, fry slightly a fowl that had been previously boiled; then take out the fowl, and in the same butter add the dry rice and fry it a little; as the butter evaporates, add the above broth to it, and boil the rice in it; then put in the cloves, cardamoms, pepper corns and mace (be cautious not to put too much of the latter); then add the currypak leaves and salt, with the green ginger cut into thin slices; when the rice is sufficiently boiled, remove all but a little fire from underneath, and place some [çoals] on the pan cover; if the rice be at all hard, add a little water to it and put into it the fowl to imbibe a flavour; then cover it over with the rice, and serve up, garnished with hard boiled eggs cut either in halves or quarters.

SHERAZEE PULLOW

Meat	1 Seer	Raisins	2 Tolah
Eggs	No. 5	Cinnamon	2 Mashas
Ghee	⅓ Seer	Cloves	1 Masha
Onions	¼ Seer	Cardamons	1 Masha
Green ginger	1 Tolah	Black pepper	1 Masha
Apricots, dried	2 Tolah	Cummin Seeds	1 Masha
Pistachio	2 Tolah	Rice	1 Seer
Almonds	2 Tolah		

Take three-fourth seer of the meat and cut into large slices; put it into a saucepan with a proper quantity of water with the onions and the ginger sliced, also some salt and coriander seeds, ground in a little ghee; boil till the meat is tender; then strain off the gravy into another saucepan, and give a bughar to the meat with the cloves in ghee; pound the cumin seeds and a part of the spices and put it in with the meat into another saucepan; parboil the rice in plain water; remove it and put it with the gravy, and boil till the rice is done; then place it over the meat with some ghee; cover the saucepan close and let it simmer gently for an hour; mince the remainder of the meat and give a bughar to it in ghee; add some pounded salt and coriander seeds with a little water and boil it gently; when done and the ghee and gravy well mixed, put in the raisins, pistachio, apricot, blanched almonds, and spices, with the white of the eggs beaten up, and let it stand on the side of the fire till cooked; then fry the yolks of the eggs in a little ghee and all is ready. When you serve the pullow, spread the minced meat, &c. over it, and fried eggs on top of that.

13
Vegetables

___

While the British may have had only a minimal influence on Indian cookery directly, the impact of the vegetables they introduced to India has been enormous. Nowadays, potatoes, cabbages, tomatoes, lettuces, runner beans, avocados and corn are well integrated into the Indian diet and countless 'traditional' recipes exist for them, yet the cultivation of them all dates only from the arrival of the British and the Portuguese.

Understandably, the Europeans in India wished to eat vegetables which were familiar to them, and where these were not available, sought to introduce and grow them. The *Madras Dialogues* in 1750 listed the following vegetables as grown in Madras: 'Cucumbers, Country Beans, Peas, Colewort, Cabbage, Corriander, Lettice, Mint, Radish, Garlick, Melon, Leeks and Chitterlings.' Sixty years later, Williamson's *East India Vade Mecum* mentioned 'Cabbages, Cauliflowers, Lettices, Celery, Carrots, Turnips, Pees, Cucumber, French Beans, Radishes and Potatoes' as being acclimatized, and stated that 'Love Apples, Egg Plants, Gourds, Calavans, Yams and Sweet Potatoes' were also grown.

The difficulty with English vegetables was that many could not be grown on the plains during the hot weather, although in the hills and in relatively cool places such as Poona they were available during the monsoon. Especially in the north, the seeds of European vegetables were sown after the rainy season, and matured during the cold weather: green peas, cauliflowers and cos lettuces appeared at Christmas, surviving frosts which would kill them in their native climates. Either the cultivation of these relatively delicate vegetables was better understood, or the soil was more suited to them, for they succeeded better than hardier plants such as celery, beetroots and carrots, which never grew to their full size, and were frequently lacking in flavour.

Since produce bought from up-country markets was often inferior and not fresh, many British maintained their own vegetable gardens. (Of peas, Colonel Kenney-Herbert commented: 'You never get a dish of peas equal to those gathered in your own garden: those bought in Indian markets are, as a rule, far too old, having been allowed to attain the largest size possible.')

The English were little influenced in gardening technique by the Moguls, whose gardens they generally did not see until they were in a state of decline, but in eighteenth-century Madras they borrowed ideas and bought many seeds from the nearby Dutch settlements. The gardeners they employed were generally Hindus, whose skill in irrigation was considerable. The beds were enclosed by raised walks, so that they could be flooded at various times with water, which was soon absorbed into the sun-baked soil. The flow was controlled by tiny sluice-gates made of clay, from a reservoir fed laboriously by buffaloes carrying leather bags of water. Generally, however, the Indians' knowledge of horticulture was limited, and from the eighteenth century onwards, the most esteemed vegetable gardeners in British India were the Chinese, who filled the gaps in the local knowledge.

By Victorian times large-scale market gardens on the fringes of the big towns were providing steady supplies of European vegetable varieties, and the hill stations were also well served in this respect.

The shortage of water up in the hills meant the buyer had to be very careful, however, as the vegetables might well have been washed in infected water. Once home, the conscientious memsahib would supervise the scrubbing of the vegetables in bowls of water mixed with potassium permanganate.

In the absence of refrigeration great attention also had to be paid to storage. Generally fresh vegetables were laid out on a stone floor in a cool and airy place. Vegetables such as potatoes, onions and pumpkins, which could be kept for longer, were hung up in baskets, out of reach of rats.

As for the cooking of vegetables in India, we must turn once again to Colonel Kenny-Herbert: 'Critics on English cookery seem to agree in saying that, wanting as we are, as a rule, in our general knowledge of kitchen work, our ignorance of the treatment of vegetables is greater than in every other branch of the art.' An illustration of this is to be found in *Indian Cookery for Young Housekeepers*, where the instructions for boiling cabbage blithely inform us: 'it will take about an hour'. Flora Annie Steel, for her part, blamed the Indian cooks:

Indian vegetables are often called insipid, but the fault lies chiefly in the disgraceful way in which they are cooked. It is no uncommon thing to find them all boiling in one saucepan, or even in the soup, the result being one confused in flavour. The habit should be sternly reproved, and the cook taught that it is better to have one vegetable decently cooked than half a dozen which are not worth eating.

Another common habit was to boil green vegetables long before dinner time, soak them in cold water, then warm them up before they were to be served. The cooks claimed this preserved the colour.

Thankfully, however, there were reformists at work: 'Boil all vegetables quickly,' urged E. S. Poynter in her little recipe book published in 1904, adding that a little vinegar in the water would remove insects. Writing in 1878, Colonel Kenney-Herbert thought he had detected an improved attitude towards vegetable cooking brought about by more English people travelling abroad.

A fillip has, in this way, been given to vegetable cookery in England, and people with any claims to refined taste have at last come to perceive the absolute barbarism of heaping up two or three sorts of vegetable on the same plate with roast meat and gravy. From time immemorial tinned asparagus has occupied a prominent place in the menu of a dinner in India: I have often wondered how this spark of civilisation became kindled, and why the example thus was never more generally followed with regard to other vegetables.

It will be, I think admitted nem con that we live in a climate out here especially demanding vegetable diet. With the thermometer indicating 90 or thereabouts, plain animal food is not only distasteful to many, but absolutely unwholesome. We cannot therefore, devote too much attention to the cookery of vegetables.

A small minority of Britons in India were indeed devoting much attention to vegetables. In March 1887 the inaugural meeting of the Calcutta Vegetarian Society was held, at which one Leopold Salzer delivered a lecture on 'The Psychic Aspect of Vegetarianism'. The Theosophical Society published books such as *Vegetarian Menus*, and other titles such as *Healthful Diet for India* gave sensible recipes for Simla Nut Loaf, a relative of the much-satirized nut cutlet.

This desire for dishes to have the appearance, if not the substance, of a flesh-based meal led to a number of 'mock' meat or fish recipes, such as this one from Navroji Framji, in which aubergine stands in for fish.

BRENJALL OR MOCK FISH CURRY

Cut in slices a large Brenjall, and prepare it for frying as directed in the batter recipe below; fry it in the batter and let it stand till wanted. Add ½ a tea cup vinegar to the scraping of one or half a cocoanut, and keep the pressed liquid. Again press the milk with ½ a tea cup of warm water, pour this into a separate bowl, repeat the process till you have as much liquid as you need for the curry gravy. Colour the latter with ground turmeric, throw into it one or 2 sliced onions, 5 or 6 green and red fresh chillies cut down ½ way; ½ a garlic, and one square inch fresh ginger sliced. Stir the mixture on a moderate fire till it begins to thicken, then put in carefully the fried brenjalls; shake the handee, but don't use a spoon or the slices will break. Add the thick milk mixed with vinegar 10 minutes or less before the curry is served. Serve with rice and tamarind fish, or salt fish fried.

Batter for Benjalls: Brenjall for the above curry is to be dipped in batter made thus, break an egg in a chatty, beat it for 4 or 5 minutes, mix it with ¼ lb flour and 1 coffee cup of water. Dip the slices of brenjalls in the batter, and fry in plenty of ghee.

Country Captain was well known as a chicken dish (see page 114), but it too evolved a vegetarian variation.

COUNTRY CAPTAIN OF VEGETABLES   *serves 3–4*

2 tbsp dried tamarind	8 oz (250 g) cooked peas
6 spring onions, sliced	8 oz (250 g) cooked beans
4 cloves garlic, crushed	2 tsp curry powder
2 tbsp ghee	salt to taste
8 oz (250 g) cooked potatoes	2 oz (50 g) freshly grated or
8 oz (250 g) cooked carrots	desiccated coconut

Break the tamarind into small pieces and place in a cup. Half fill with boiling water, leave to soak five minutes, then press through a sieve to remove pips and pith.

Sauté the spring onions and garlic in the ghee and add the vegetables, tamarind water and curry powder. Heat the vegetables through, add salt to taste, then serve with coconut sprinkled over.

The cabbage was introduced to India by Europeans at a very early date, and by the nineteenth century was being widely cultivated, both in the plains during the cold weather, and in the hills during spring and summer. It was largely grown near towns and cantonments, and was as much eaten by Indians as Europeans. Drumhead, a large, coarse Savoy-type variety, was extensively planted by Indians and by the late nineteenth century had become perfectly acclimatized, the early cabbages on the market being the young heads of this plant.

'I ought to call attention to a bad habit that the native cook indulges in,' wrote Colonel Kenney-Herbert. 'I mean that of chopping up a plain boiled cabbage before serving it: setting aside the ugly appearance that the dish presents when thus maltreated, it is a wasteful practice. The chopped cabbage dries quickly, and will not be found worth dressing up a second time; whereas if served whole, the portion that may be left after dinner, will remain nice and juicy, and form a rechauffé.' (The cook was perhaps blamed too often for such mishandling of vegetables, if Isobel Abbott's experience with her father-in-law's cabbage – see page 53 – was typical.)

Peculiar to British India was 'cabbage loaf' – a whole cabbage with minced meat or prawns stuffed down between its leaves, which was then cooked in coconut cream. Another popular Anglo-Indian way with cabbage was as a foogath, a dish which uses precooked vegetables fried with onions and coconut. This is from Navroji Framji's *Indian Cookery 'Local'*:

CABBAGE FOOGATH
Brown slightly 2 minced onions, 3 green chillies, 10 cloves garlic and ⅛ ounce of green ginger sliced fine; cut in pieces the heart of a cabbage half boiled, put this in the chatty with some salt, and when nearly fried, mix with the scraped flakes of a half a cocoanut. The latter must not be browned. Stir and fry and cook it gently.

Another way:
Boil, shell and clean 2 tablespoons of small prawns and put it with the cabbage, just before the cocoanut scrapings are added, and proceed to make the foogath in the same way.

In her *What's What in Cookery* (2nd edition 1910), Maud Wells suggests another brassica which can successfully be curried:

DRY CAULIFLOWER CURRY
Parboil a cauliflower and cut it up small, melt a dessertspoonful of ghee in a saucepan, add one onion cut in slices, fry it a light-brown, then add a saltspoonful of powdered turmeric, two or three green chillies cut in slices, the cauliflower and a little salt, fry for five minutes, then add half a grated cocoanut, stir it over the fire till it gets quite dry; before serving add a dessertspoonful of vinegar. Cabbage and French beans made in the same way are very nice.

Celery, a native of England and other parts of Europe, was cultivated in different parts of India during the cold weather, mainly as a garden crop in the vicinity of towns, for the British. It was also grown in the Punjab for its root and in Bengal for its seed, which was eaten by Indians.

While several wild species of asparagus were eaten by the hill-peoples of eastern India, the cultivated forms did not do well, and most asparagus seen at Anglo-Indian dinner tables was imported in tins from Europe.

'There is a custom,' wrote Colonel Kenney-Herbert, 'followed by ignorant English as well as native cooks, of placing a slice of toasted bread in the dish destined to receive a bundle of asparagus, &c., over which a plentiful bath of white tasteless flour and water is finally poured.'

The broad bean, a native of the Mediterranean, was introduced to China, then to Japan, and much later to India. It was commonly grown in Kashmir and at high altitudes, and in the nineteenth century reached the plains. It was only grown to any extent in the North West Provinces, in British gardens for British consumption. Colonel Kenny-Herbert described French beans as being well worthy of attention 'for we can get them when other vegetables are out of season'.

BEAN FOOGATH
REQUIRED:— 1 lb of French beans, 1 large cocoanut, 8 peels of garlic, 5 green chillies, 8 Bombay onions, 1 inch piece of green ginger, 2 tablespoonsful of ghee, salt.
TO MAKE:— Clean the beans, slit them, and mince very fine; wash and place in a sauce-pan on the fire with a small coffee cupful of water, a little salt, two minced onions and the garlic peels; boil till the beans are cooked, then allow the water to evaporate and remove from the fire.

Scrape the cocoanut and mince the onion and chillies.

Place a saucepan with the ghee on the fire, put in the onions and chillies, and fry a light brown; throw in the beans, and stir the foogath for a few minutes, remove from the fire; then add cocoanut, more salt if required, stir and serve.

(Snakecoy, drumstick leaves, four-o'clock leaves, greens, parvakai and spinach may all be made into foogath, the above recipe being intended for all foogaths.

Cabbage may be made into foogath, but pepper must be used, not green chillies.)

(Interestingly, in this recipe, Mrs Franklin advises against the use of green chillies in a cabbage foogath, whereas Navroji Framji's cabbage foogath used them liberally.)

Several varieties of American bean were introduced by Europeans to India, the most popular being the runner bean and the sword bean (*Canavalia gladiate*). The young tender half-grown pods of the sword bean usually constituted the so-called French beans at the tables of Europeans.

The Americas were a source of several new foods: corn and maize came to India from America and, like chillies, guavas and pineapples, were probably introduced by the Portuguese. At the beginning of the nineteenth century maize was still hardly known but it spread rapidly and by the century's end had become almost as important a crop in India as wheat.

The tomato, introduced from South America, grew most luxuriantly in the hills, but was cultivated all over India. Colonel Kenney-Herbert reported that they were easily grown in the Madras Presidency and were often available during the hot weather when the stock of garden stuff had sunk to its lowest state. 'Natives are beginning to appreciate the fruit,' wrote George Watt in *A Dictionary of the Economic Products of India* (1889), 'but the plant is still chiefly cultivated for the European population. Bengalis and Burmans use it in their sour curries.'

In *Indian Cookery and Domestic Recipes*, C. C. Kohlhoff provides a very concentrated form of spiced tomato to accompany rice and fish.

TOMATO CURRY

Take about three dozen large, fresh tomatoes; put them into boiling water for a few minutes and then skin them. Remove the seeds, and secure the juice and pulp separately. Express the milk of a large cocoanut with the aid of the juice. Strain and add 2 tablespoons of curry stuff. Chop very fine about 1½ inch of green ginger, 8 onions, 8 cloves of garlic and half a tea cup of green coriander leaves. Now, put in the pulp and cocoanut milk, together with 3 or 4 tablespoons of ghee. If you like, add a few prawns, or some saltfish. Mix in salt to taste, and boil until the curry attains the proper consistency. Guard against burning the curry. This curry can be kept for a week, as no water is used in its preparation.

A sambal is a side-dish of either meat or vegetable made fiery hot with chillies and, although of Malay-Javan origin, many varieties were enjoyed by the British in India. This is from *The Original Madras Cookery Book*:

TOMATO SAMBAL

Three good sized tomatoes, four green chillies, four onions (or spring onions when in season) salt to taste and a small lemon; scald the tomatoes in a basin, pouring boiling water over them and covering close for a few minutes; drain well from the water; remove the stalk and peel off the skin; then mash the fruit in a soup plate with a little salt; slice the chillies (after having removed the seed); add the tomato; shred and wash the onions; mix together with the other ingredients; squeeze in the lemon juice and serve in a glass dish.

The capsicum or bell pepper was presumably introduced to India at about the same time as its close relative, the chilli (see page 6). It was mainly grown for Europeans. C. C. Kohlhoff gives a recipe for stuffed peppers:

CAPSICUM CURRY

Remove the seeds and fibres of a dozen or more large capsicums by slitting them neatly on one side. Fill either with mince mutton or prawn curry, the latter is better, and sew up the opening. Fry in ghee till the skins of the capsicums shrink. Heat a table spoon of ghee in another chatty; fry in it a table spoon of curry stuff, add a small cup of thick cocoanut milk, throw in the capsicums; stir and then serve. A little lime juice may be added.

Another South American introduction, the avocado, is today very popular on the Malabar Coast, but British India was rather indifferent towards it. 'The praise bestowed on it is absurd,' sniffed the authors of *Hobson-Jobson*, the celebrated glossary of Anglo-Indian words and phrases: 'With liberal pepper and salt there may be a remote suggestion of marrow: but that is all . . . Its introduction into the Eastern world is comparatively recent; not older than the middle of the 18th century. Had it been worth eating it would have come long before.' One well-documented early importation of the plant was in 1819, to the Botanical Gardens in Bangalore.

Of root vegetables, the most important to the British was the potato. While there is no doubt that the potato is of South American origin, the date of its introduction to India is unknown, and few facts can be gathered to give even an approximate date. It must, at any rate, have been widely cultivated in India before the beginning of the eighteenth century, since Roxburgh, who wrote his classic *Flora Indica* at the end of that period, says that in his time it was grown largely in the cold weather and produced abundant tubers, and that this cultivation had been going on for some considerable time. The potato was most probably introduced to India from Spain, whether directly or indirectly, some time between the end of the sixteenth century and the beginning of the eighteenth.

The best potatoes were grown in the hills, and those of Nundigrog, about 200 miles (320 km) from Madras, were sent all over India. Potato salads, such as this from G. H. Cook's *The English-Indian Cookery Book*, were not so very different from Western equivalents.

ALOO OR POTATO SALAD

INGREDIENTS:— Two pounds potatoes, Two onions peeled and sliced fine, 1 teaspoon ground pepper, 2 teaspoons salt, 1 teaspoon mustard oil, 3 tablespoons lime juice, 1 cup curds (Dahai), 4 teaspoons ground sugar.

Boil and peel the potatoes and cut them up into pieces about half an inch in size. Put the pepper, salt, lime juice, sugar and curds into a small bowl and mix up thoroughly with a spoon. Put the potatoes into a large bowl and pour the mixture over it and mix, taking care that the potatoes are not broken up.

The Jerusalem artichoke, which is native to north-east America, was grown in India mainly for the British, although by the end of the nineteenth century it was slowly making its way among Indians also. In Kathiawar, says George Watt, 'it is boiled in milk and is considered, by the Natives, a strengthening vegetable.' The plant was brought to

Europe, and was probably introduced to India from there. Colonel Kenney-Herbert commented that it was 'a vegetable which, as a rule, people either dislike exceedingly, or are very fond of. I place it amongst the best we have.'

The beetroot was probably another European introduction, since it has no Sanskrit name and various early Indian botanical works describe it only as a cultivated plant.

Although a hardy type of greenish-white carrot is thought to be indigenous to India, it had little of the flavour of the European carrot. For this reason English varieties were introduced, but they failed completely in the plains until they had first been successfully grown in Darjeeling and acclimatized seeds produced.

During the hot weather, many types of cucumbers, marrows, aubergines and other tropical vegetables came into their own, and as they were virtually all that was available, the British were forced to be adventurous in trying them. Often these 'country' vegetables were sent to the table in the form of curries. The aubergine was the clear favourite of the British. The Anglo-Indian name 'brinjal' was derived from the Portuguese *brinjella*. Its alternative name of eggplant derives from a white variety, now less often seen, which in size and shape resembles an egg.

BRINJAL CURRY

REQUIRED:— 2 round brinjals, 1 heaped tablespoonful coriander, 3 cloves of garlic, 2 pinches cummin, 4 dried chillies, ¼ of a large cocoanut, 6 green chillies, 8 slices ginger, 2 tablespoonsful vinegar, 1 tablespoonful oil, 10 small onions, saffron, salt and curry leaves.

METHOD:— Grind a small bit of saffron and a little salt to a fine paste, slice the brinjals round, about ⅛ of an inch in thickness, rub the slices well with the ground saffron and salt and keep aside.

Next grind to a paste the coriander, garlic, cummin, dried chillies, and a small bit of saffron. Extract the milk from the cocoanut properly. Keep by the first thick milk.

Place the oil in a chatty on the fire and when heated throw in about 4 small onions sliced and a few curry leaves; when the onions are brown, add the ground curry stuff and fry for a time, then pour in the 2nd and 3rd milk extracted from the cocoanut, mix well, add a little water if necessary to boil the curry stuff; and then put in the green chillies sliced or cut lengthwise, slices of ginger, and the remaining 6 onions sliced, together with the vinegar. Keep stirring to prevent the curry from curdling when the vinegar is poured in; after one boil add the first thick cocoanut milk. When the gravy is thick, and the oil has cleared on top of the curry, take it off the fire.

Put the saffron-smeared slices of brinjal fried quite brown, into the gravy while warm. Add salt to taste, and serve.

Serve carefully, so as not to mash up the fried slices of brinjal. (From *Culinary Art Sparklets*, by Beatrice Vieyra.)

'If you have cooked eggplants for some other purpose,' writes Harriet Lawrance, 'it is a good idea to reserve a little to make this sambal as a side-dish.'

BRINJAL SAMBAL
INGREDIENTS:— 1 dessertspoonful each of minced onions, thick tamarind juice, and tomatoes with the skins and seeds removed, and mashed; 2 dessertspoonfuls of brinjals, roasted and mashed; 3 green chillies minced; ¼ teaspoonful of white salt; ¼ teaspoonful of ghee.
MODE:— Roast the brinjals in the fire, remove the burnt skin, and mash them with all the other ingredients, except the ghee in which fry the sambal till all the ghee is absorbed in it, serve hot or cold.

Sufficient for 2 persons.

Mrs Bartley uses aubergine skins to encase a curried stuffing:

BRINJALS WITH FRIED MUSSALA
INGREDIENTS:— two brinjals, salt, ghee, grind one table-spoon of roasted coriander, an inch of turmeric, ten corns of pepper, a salt spoon of jeera, two or three red chillies, four or five slices of garlic and half an inch of ginger with a teaspoon of salt.
DIRECTIONS:— Cut the brinjals in halves, scoop out some of the pulp, mince it fine, mix it together with the ground curry stuff, place the mince in the brinjal skins, rub over with beaten egg, sprinkle thickly with breadcrumbs and fry a nice brown.

COLONEL HARE'S BRINJAL BHURTA

2 medium-sized aubergines
1 tbsp butter
3 small onions, sliced
1 tsp ground cumin
seeds of 3 cardamom pods, ground

¼ tsp ground cloves
1–2 green chillies, minced
15 fl oz (450 ml) yoghurt
1 oz (25 g) fresh mint, chopped
salt to taste
juice of 2–3 lemons

Make a slit down the side of each aubergine and place under the grill, turning until the skin is blackened on all sides and the flesh is soft. Scrape out and mash, or purée in a food processor/blender.

Melt the butter in a large pan and fry the onions until golden. Add the ground cumin, cardamom, cloves and chillies and fry a minute or two longer. Pour in the yoghurt and mix well, then add the mint. Add the aubergine purée and simmer until the mixture has evaporated slightly, then add salt to taste and mix in the lemon juice.

Serve, like a fresh relish, to accompany meat and rice.

Moringas, or drumsticks as they were dubbed by the British, were also greatly eaten during the hot weather when European vegetables refused to grow. These hard fibrous beans, long and green with ridges, have an asparagus-like flavour when young and tender. The flowers went into sambals, the leaves into foogaths, while homesick British found the roots an acceptable substitute for horseradish. (Drumsticks are available from Indian stores in Britain.) Beatrice Vieyra cooks them with cashew nuts and coconut:

DRUMSTICK GRAVY CURRY

REQUIRED:— 6 fresh and tender drumsticks, 30 green tender cashew nuts, 1 heaped tablespoonful of coriander, 3 large dried chillies, 1 pinch cummin, 1 bit saffron, $\frac{1}{2}$ of a well-seasoned cocoanut, 1 tablespoonful vinegar, 8 green chillies, 10 small onions, 4 cloves of garlic, 1 tablespoonful oil, few curry leaves, and salt.
METHOD:— Scrape off the outer top green skin from the drumsticks, wash and cut each into 6 pieces. Slit the cashew-nuts and take out the kernels, throw them into boiling water and then wash in cold water and peel them.

Put the drumstick pieces and cashew nuts into a chatty with a little water, cover up and allow them to simmer.

Take a tablespoonful of the grated cocoanut and grind to a paste, and grind also the coriander, dried chillies, cummin, and saffron to a paste.

Take out the milk from the cocoanut, but reserve of the first milk $\frac{1}{2}$ a teacup. Slit the green chillies lengthways, slice the cloves of garlic and 6 of the small onions.

Place the oil on the fire and when heated, throw in the 4 small onions sliced and curry leaves, and when they are brown, add the ground cocoanut and curry stuff and fry for a time in the oil then pour in the cocoanut milk, a little water if necessary, and the vinegar, cover up and allow to boil once, then add the first milk and put in the boiled vegetables and the sliced ingredients; simmer till the gravy turns thick and the oil clears on top of the curry. Add salt to taste, and serve.

Given sufficient water, pumpkins and other gourds grew well all over India and, as William Tayler indicates in *Thirty-eight Years in India*, their use was not simply culinary:

No unimportant plant is this pumpkin (kudoo); not only does the fruit, or rather vegetable, afford excellent and nutritious food for native stomachs, but a material by no means to be despised for the English cuisine, where it is concocted into sham carrots, soup-fritters, fictitious apple-sauce, and sundry other delicate and ingenious purposes. Its utility, however, does not stop here; dried pumpkins, with their interiors scooped out, are used all over India as water-bottles, and seem to have suggested the idea of the favourite serai, which we have also adopted and placed of late years in crystal glass on our dessert-table as a decanter. Nor does the pumpkin minister only to the refreshment of men's bodies or satisfaction of the appetites, but travels to the intellectual, and appears in many a melodious instrument. The sitar – Anglice, a guitar – the classical cithara, with others, all are split pumpkins. Nature's ready-made sounding boards.

RED PUMPKIN FOOGATH

Remove the skins and seeds, and mince small a slice of red pumpkin, two inches thick, slightly brown a minced onion in a dessert spoon of ghee, two green chillies, and half an inch of fresh ginger minced. Add the pumpkin, and fry for five minutes. Put in gradually a little water with salt to taste; boil till the vegetable gets soft. (From *Indian Cookery 'General'*, by Mrs J. Bartley.)

The karela or bitter gourd, which has been known in Britain since the sixteenth century, was frequently seen on Anglo-Indian dinner tables during the hot weather, although it was never a favourite. As to why, we are given a clue by Rudyard Kipling's *Second Jungle Book*, in 'Mowgli's Song Against People':

> I will let loose against you the fleet-footed vines –
> I will call in the jungle to stamp out your lines!
> The roofs shall fade before it,
> The house-beams shall fall;
> And the karela, the bitter karela,
> Shall cover it all!

Indeed, so bitter was the karela that it needed special treatment to make it acceptable at all to the British palate. Navroji Framji gives instructions:

KURILLA FOOGATH

Cut the vegetable [karela or bitter gourd] in slices, sprinkle well with salt, and leave it for one or two hours. Mash it well and wash it in cold water. Repeat this operation 3 times to extract the bitterness. Roast and grind the same mussala put in meat curry, with a slice of roasted cocoanut. Place the mashed Kurilla in a bowl of cold water. Mince the same amount of onions as there is Kurilla, and brown them either in ghee or oil, add the ground mussala, when the latter is nicely browned, fry some minced meat. The latter can be ½ the amount of the Kurilla. Drain well the vegetable and fry it with the rest, add the mussalla water and as much was as will be needed to cook the vegetables. When they become soft the foogath is made. Prawns can be put in place of the minced meat.

(Karelas are available from Indian shops in Britain, as is another hot-weather vegetable of the Raj, the snake gourd.)

The aptly named Mr Cook describes a way of drying and preserving pumpkin for the store cupboard.

BARIES OR DRIED PUMPKIN (INDIAN DISH)

1 lge white pumpkin, known as bartha kamrah, 4 lb Uorda dal, 2 oz dried chillies, ground, 2 oz green ginger, 2 oz Dhania coriander seeds, 1 oz Jeera [sic] caraway seeds

Grind the white dal on a grindstone. Peel the pumpkin and mince in a machine. Grind all the masalas and mix with the dal and the pumpkin. Spread on a clean sheet on a bed in the sun and with the hand drop small pats of it on the sheet til all is finished. Then dry for 2 or 3 days in the sun and store in airtight tins or bottles. These are cooked the same way as potato or vegetable curries.

Mushrooms were abundant in fields of some parts of India, especially the Punjab, and were described as excellent and equal to the English mushrooms by those nineteenth-century Europeans who tried them. However, most mushrooms eaten by the British in India were tinned imports.

What was called a truffle was eaten in Kashmir by Europeans, who said it resembled the Piedmontese truffle. Actually this so-called Indian truffle was later identified as of the genus *Melanogaster* rather than the true truffle genus, *Tuber*.

Other 'country' vegetables included wall-paper beans, mochekoy, goonsalle, and a number of spinach-like greens.

Spinach itself was at one time mainly cultivated in the gardens of Europeans in India, but by the late nineteenth century it had been generally adopted by Indians as part of their diet. From the British point of view its great advantage was that it was one of the few European vegetables available during the hot weather. The following recipe for *sag* or spinach comes from Alys Firth's *Dainty Cookery for Camp*.

KULLEAH CHOWLAHEE

Take a seer of fresh chowlahee sag, pick it well and wash till the leaves are quite clean. Cut up into small pieces and put into a pan with some water, and boil. Drain off the water, throw it away and lay aside the pan of greens. Brown some onions in ghee and put it over the green with some salt and pepper, pounded fine. Fry some sliced garlic in ghee till it becomes brown, then put in the greens and give them a baghar. Grind a little dhunia leaves and add to the sag when cooked; add the masalas and shake the pan at intervals. Boil 5 eggs hard, cut them in halves and place them over the greens and let the whole simmer till cooked. Serve with poories or chappaties.

Other leaves also found their way into Anglo-Indian cuisine. 'Sorrel,' wrote Colonel Kenny-Herbert, 'is not half enough used:'

Your cook will know it if you order 'sorley' (Ramasamy's pronounciation of the double 'r' being peculiar) – and nothing is nicer than a mutton (neck) cutlet with a sorrel purée, for the pungent taste of the vegetable suggests a novelty to your palate. My readers who are now enjoying themselves in the Neilgherries [a range of hills in Southern India] ought to try a dish of pork cutlets with a purée of sorrel, for such a rich white meat, sorrel is especially agreeable.

Navroji Framji suggests coriander (*kotemer*) or fenugreek (*methi*) leaves for flavouring small fritters.

BUGEAS

Grind a bunch of green kotemer, $1\frac{1}{2}$ inches turmeric, $\frac{1}{2}$ tea spoon jeera, 2 inches fresh ginger, a garlic and 8 or 9 green chillies. Dry chillies will answer when green cannot be had. Mix the mussala and its water with a lb of gram flour, salt to taste, and 3 large onions minced very small. Fry the bugeas in ghee or oil just like fritters. An egg may be mixed with the flour &c., if liked.

Bugeas (Another way): Mix the flour, mussala &c., together with a table spoon of small prawns shelled and washed, and a table spoon of young methe bajee cut in bits, washed and drained.

Thought to be of African origin, bhindi, or ladies' fingers (okra), were a favourite both with the British and the Indians. In making soups for the British, cooks would use its mucilaginous property as a thickening agent, and Mrs Bartley's *Indian Cookery 'General'* has an okra foogath.

BENDA FOOGATH

Fry a sliced onion in ghee or oil, put in a dozen Bendas washed and sliced. After three of four minutes add a tablespoonful of scraped cocoanut, two green chillies, a bit of fresh ginger, and six inches garlic all minced; add salt to taste and cook gently till the vegetables are done.

During the hot weather, nobody needed to be urged to eat salads. They did, however, need to be careful about the preparation of raw vegetables, to the extent of washing lettuce in water in which boracic powder had been dissolved.

Lettuce appears to have been used from very remote times. Herodotus informs us that it was served at the tables of Persian kings as early as 400 BC. It is thus surprising that all knowledge of its cultivation for food appears to have died out in India until comparatively recently, when it was reintroduced by Europeans. In the late nineteenth century it was grown all over the country as a cold season crop for the British, but was rarely if ever eaten by Indians. The *qui hais* would enliven it with all manner of mayonnaise substitutes.

QUI HAI SALAD DRESSING

2 tbsp oil

2 tbsp vinegar

2 tbsp anchovy essence

3 tbsp mushroom ketchup (see
  page 224)

1 tbsp cream

3 hard-boiled egg yolks, mashed

1 large cooked potato, mashed

Mix together all ingredients and serve over lettuce.

Cucumber, on the other hand, is native to northern India. The rainy season varieties were most common, and were eaten by both the British and Indians of all castes, in curries and in salads – even if Mrs Bartley's recipe does bring to mind Dr Johnson's stern advice that the cucumber (after careful preparation) should be 'thrown out, as good for nothing'!

CUCUMBER SALAD

INGREDIENTS:— one cucumber, one onion, quarter inch of green ginger, a green chilli, a salt-spoon of pounded pepper, vinegar.

DIRECTIONS:— Peel the cucumber and cut it into thin slices, sprinkle with salt and let it stand for some minutes, pour away all the water that it gives out, pressing it gently with the back of a small plate to get as much more as you can. Cut the onions in round rings, and mince the chilli and ginger, mix the cucumber with the last two articles, sprinkle pepper over, garnish with onions, and add sufficient vinegar to flavour and moisten the whole.

Not all dishes labelled 'salad' might be recognized as such:

BRINJAL SALAD

REQUIRED:— 8 small brinjals, 3 Bombay onions, 2 tablespoonfuls of ghee, 2 hard-boiled eggs, 3 green chillies, $\frac{1}{2}$ oz of salt fish, 1 wineglassful of cocoanut milk, 2 tablespoonsful of vinegar, salt to taste.

TO MAKE:— Cut the brinjals, each in half and each half in fours. Wash and place in a vessel; mince two of the onions and add with the cocoanut milk; boil until the vegetables are quite soft, then remove from the fire.

Place another vessel with half the ghee on the fire, and fry the salt fish a light brown, which take out and set aside. Slice in the remaining onion and two green chillies; put in the remaining ghee; fry the onions a light brown; pour in the cocoanut milk in which the vegetables were boiled, and allow it to come to the boil; add the vegetables and salt fish, having first shred the fish with two forks, and remove all the bones.

Allow the salad to boil for five minutes, then remove from the fire and add the vinegar. Serve warm.

(This is an Indian dish, and if properly seasoned, the salad should retain the

smell of the fried onions when done.) (From *The Wife's Cookery Book*, by
E. A. M. Franklin.)

To broaden the repertoire of salad ingredients, Beatrice Vieyra turns to
that favourite fruit, the mango.

MANGO SALAD
REQUIRED:– 4 large well seasoned mangoes, 6 green chillies, 10 small onions,
½ cocoanut, and salt to taste.
METHOD:– Skin and chop the mangoes finely and throw away the nut. Pour over
the chopped mango a few tablespoonsful of salt water, mix thoroughly, and keep
by for a few minutes, then drain it well; this process removes a great deal of the
acidity. Grate the cocoanut finely and take as much thick cocoanut milk as
possible. Pour this on the mango, add green chillies and onion chopped; mix well
and place in a salad bowl. Add salt to taste.

When green and unripe mangoes and papayas were treated like
vegetables. For her mango cucumber (a fresh relish made daily), Mrs
Bartley instructs: 'Pare and mince a green mango, mince also one onion,
two green chillies, and half an inch of fresh ginger, mix the whole
together with salt to taste, and lastly stir two table spoons thick cocoanut
milk.' She also gives a recipe for curried mango.

MANGO CURRY
Roast on a thoa a dozen dried chillies and half a teaspoon methe seed, and two
inches turmeric. Grind these with half a teaspoon jeera, a piece of ginger and half
a garlic. Boil half a small tea cup of fresh oil, throw in half a teaspoon mustard
seed, next add and brown the mussala. Stir carefully in the fried mussala, for
three minutes, [add] six green mangoes halved and a garlic sliced. Add one or
three table spoons water, and simmer the curry till the mangoes are soft. Season
with salt.

Beatrice Vieyra treats papaya similarly:

PAPAIYA CURRY
REQUIRED:– 1½ cupsful of papaiya cut into small bits, saffron, 5 green chillies, a
pinch of cumminseed, 4 small onions, 1 tablespoonful oil, few curry leaves, and
salt.
METHOD:– Wash the papaiya bits, put them into a chatty, add a little water, a
few curry leaves and salt; cover up and boil. As soon as the bits are half boiled,
add the curry stuff ground to a paste and cocoanut ground coarsely, cover up the
vessel and allow contents to simmer; when the water is well dried, take off the
fire and season the curry in another vessel with the oil, onions, and curry leaves,
add salt to taste, and serve.

14

Desserts

———

Rich as it may be in confectionery, Indian cuisine has never been noted for its desserts, and an everyday meal is more likely to be rounded off quite simply with fresh fruit. The British, however, maintained a strong sentimental attachment to their puddings, however unsuitable they may have been for the sweltering climate, and set about teaching their Indian cooks how to make them.

They met with only limited success, as Colonel Kenney-Herbert notes: 'Many of my readers have experienced the pleasure, no doubt, of the pudding being served in a crumbled state, and Ramasamy's admission:– "Din't stand uff praperly the pudding" is, of course, well known.' The near-impossibility of maintaining even temperatures in primitive wood-fired ovens did not help matters, yielding puddings with burnt surfaces or underdone interiors.

Some Indian cooks never graduated much beyond caramel custard, which was easy to make and convenient because there were always plenty of eggs and milk. However, it became so overworked it was nicknamed '365' – served every day of the year! Lady Hay recalls that they refused to have caramel custard at home, since it was served in *dak* bungalows and railway stations *ad nauseam*.

The Indian cook's custard, claimed Colonel Kenney-Herbert, 'is a floury composition, its colour is not prepossessing, and its flavour is generally derived from nutmeg or some spice or other.' He advised the memsahib to supervise the weighing out of the ingredients exactly to the recipe, as the only means of avoiding over-sweetened puddings:

The native cook oversweetens everything unless carefully watched, besides taking 'small sugar balance only for own-self coffee'. I once knew of an establishment in which these 'small sugar balances' proved so outrageous that a Chubb's lock was purchased as an antidote, and a system of supervision inaugurated. The consequence was that the monthly expenditure of sugar was absolutely reduced by nearly two-thirds.

The Colonel approves of the Madras Club's pudding recipe he gives in his *Sweet Dishes*, which relies mostly on dried fruit rather than sugar for its sweetness.

MADRAS CLUB PUDDING

The Madras Club Pudding (called 'St George' after the club crest) is a good one: Eight ounces of sponge cake; two ounces of pounded ratafias; two ounces of breadcrumbs; eight eggs; four ounces of finely chopped suet; four ounces of preserved apples; four ounces of currants; two ounces of raisins; four ounces of mixed dried fruits; five ounces of sugar, one ounce of candied orange peel, one ounce of preserved ginger, the juice of a lime, a few drops of almond essence, half a wine glass of brandy and a liqueur glass of curaçao. Stone the raisins, wash, pick and dry the currants, chop the suet as small as possible, and mix them with the sponge cake (crushed to crumbs), the pounded ratafias, and the breadcrumbs; add the candied peel shredded, the apples cut into dice, the dried fruits and ginger minced, the five ounces of sugar, the almond essence, and a saltspoon of salt with a pinch of nutmeg. When all ingredients are well blended, stir the mixture together with the well-beaten eggs, the brandy and curaçao, and half a pint of milk. Butter a pudding mould, fill it with the mixture, cover the bottom of the pudding with a sheet of buttered white foolscap, tie it up in a cloth, and boil for four hours. Turn it out, and serve with Sauce Royale as follows:

Beat eight ounces of butter to a cream, sweeten it with two ounces finely powdered sugar, add half a liqueur glass of brandy and the same of Madeira. Keep it quite cold, and serve it in a boat!

Refined white cane sugar was regarded as a luxury. More common were the lumpy brown products known as *gur*, made from date palm sap, or jaggery, which was unrefined cane sugar. Often these needed to be refined further at home by boiling and skimming off impurities.

Given the abundance of local ingredients such as fresh ginger, limes, ground rice and fresh coconut, it is hardly surprising that traditional English puddings began to take on the stamp of the Indian kitchen. Some of these Anglo-Indian variations were remarkably successful:

GINGER PUDDING

½ lb flour, ¼ lb suet, ¼ lb sugar, 2 Tbs grated ginger. Shred suet very fine and mix with flour, sugar and ginger: put mixture dry into a buttered basin, tie cloth over and boil three hours. (From *Every-day Menus for Indian Housekeepers*, by W. S. Burke, 1909.)

And from Mrs Bartley's *Indian Cookery 'General'*:

PUMPKIN PIE

Cut two lbs of ripe red pumpkin in bits, and boil it in very little water, with quarter a teaspoon salt. When cool, mix in the boiled fruit, the thick milk of one cocoanut, four eggs well beaten, two teaspoons of aniseed pounded, sugar to taste, and as much rice flour as will form the mixture into a thick batter. Line an earthenware chatty with buttered plantain leaves, pour in the batter, cover and bake the cake till firm.

COCONUT PUDDING

Australians and New Zealanders will recognize this as an interesting variation on pavlova.

4 egg whites	8 oz (250 g) freshly grated
pinch salt	coconut
8 oz (250 g) sugar	1 tbsp brandy
2 tsp cornflour	1 tsp rosewater or orange flower water

Beat the egg whites with a pinch of salt until stiff, then gradually add the sugar, beating after each addition to dissolve it. Fold in the remaining ingredients.

Pile the mixture into a round buttered pie dish. Place in an oven, preheated to 180°C/350°F/Gas Mark 4. Immediately reduce the heat to low, and bake for 1½ hours.

'Hurry-scurry' was an Anglo-Indian variation on French toast, presumably so-named because it could be made at short notice. It consisted of bread slices cut into fingers, dunked in egg and milk, then fried in ghee, and spread with jam. 'Pomfrete' was French toast spiced with nutmeg and served in a stack with sugar between the layers. Henrietta Hervey, in *Anglo-Indian Cookery at Home*, calls her version Bombay Pudding. Two other puddings shared this name during the British Raj, which may explain her difficulty in finding a cook to produce what she wanted. One was a sort of summer pudding, the other a halva-like mixture of semolina simmered with milk, thickened with eggs, and then cut into diamond shapes, fried, and served with a sugar syrup.

BOMBAY PUDDING

This is a misnomer; for strangely enough, during our stay in the Bombay Presidency, we never had a cook who understood the making of this dish. Make a good sweet milk and egg custard, and in it soak some moderately thick slices of stale bread, and fry in ghee or butter to a light brown. Make a syrup of lemon juice and sugar; serve with the 'fry', grating a little nutmeg and sifting a little white sugar over the whole.

Gulabies (or the many variations in spelling) were a favourite Indian sweet, made from rings or circles of batter deep fried and then immersed in syrup to make a light but sticky treat. Margaret Denning, in *Dainty Cookery for the Home* (1911) uses cottage cheese to make her batter:

BENGALI GULABIES

2 cups of fresh cottage cheese, 1 cup of rice flour, clarified butter, 1 cup of granulated sugar
Work the cheese and flour smoothly together, adding a little cream if too dry. Form into little round cakes and drop into the boiling butter. When done a nice brown drop into the thick syrup, which should be hot. Let them cool in this and stir slowly and carefully until well coated with the sugar.

Rice flour, which Mrs Denning advises for her gulabies, was much used as a substitute for ordinary wheat flour. Until quality kiln-dried flour became available from the newly opened mills at the end of the nineteenth century, the only alternative source was American imported flour, which was expensive and not always available. Colonel Kenney-Herbert uses rice flour successfully to make pancakes in this recipe from his *Sweet Dishes*:

GROUND RICE PANCAKES

Put half a pint of new milk upon the fire in a very clean saucepan; when it all but boils, stir in a good table-spoonful of ground rice, previously mixed smooth in a little extra cold milk. Keep the saucepan on the fire until its contents thicken, but do not let the mixture boil; next, pour it into a basin to cool, stirring into it two ounces of butter: when cold sweeten it with sugar and give it any flavour you like with essence or spice; add two eggs well beaten (whole) and a pinchlet of salt. When thoroughly incorporated proceed to fry pancakes in ghee or butter; sift powdered sugar over the cakes, and serve hot as you can.

Hesitation while making a pancake is fatal. The moment the morsel is ready, it should be served.

To enjoy pancakes properly, indeed, they should be cooked in the verandah hard by the dining room door, and sent in 'hot and hot' as the saying is. Lime juice and powdered sugar is the correct dressing for them.

Rice flour would also be used to produce Anglo-Indian equivalents of the milky semolina or sago puddings remembered with affection from nursery days.

RICE MOULD

Combining elements of both British and Indian cuisine, this dessert clearly reflects its origins in the Anglo-Indian (mixed ancestry) community. It can also be made with semolina and is much improved when served with a coconut sauce.

4 oz (125 g) rice flour   almond essence or orange flower
1¾ pt (1 l) milk   water
sugar, to taste

Mix a little of the milk into the rice flour to form a paste, then stir in the rest of the milk and bring the mixture to the boil. Add sugar to taste and boil for about 20 minutes, until the mixture has thickened considerably. Add a few drops of almond essence or orange flower water to taste, then turn out and serve with a coconut sauce, made by blending some tinned or instant coconut cream into an egg custard.

BEVECA

This is an Anglo-Indian classic.

6 oz (175 g) sugar   14 fl oz (400 ml) tinned or instant
6 oz (175 g) rice flour   coconut cream
     few drops rose essence

Boil the sugar with a little water to make a syrup. Slowly work this into the ground rice and then stir in the coconut cream. Replace the mixture in the pot and bring to the boil, stirring continuously, until the mixture thickens. Add a few drops of rose essence to taste. Transfer to a buttered dish and bake to a light brown.

Beveca goes well with a fruit salad. Sliced almonds are added in the Portuguese Goan version, which also includes eggs. Caraway seeds can also be added, and Colonel Kenney-Herbert recommends a tablespoon of any liqueur or brandy. This mixture was also put into a special iron mould used to cook a Portuguese-Goan speciality called Rosa Cruickeese, a waffle shaped like a rose with five petals.

In the heat of the plains, pastry-making was not to be contemplated lightly and only in the cool of the hill stations could good results be expected. Ingredients, too, worked against the Indian cook: before decent flour became available, the coarse semolina-like *suji* was not conducive to good pastry, and nor was the butter produced in India very suitable, as it contained too much water. Even clarified beef suet was not always available. South Indian 'cream' was also very poor, according to Colonel Kenney-Herbert, who fumed: 'The stuff that is sold as cream in Madras is scarcely better than rich milk, and sometimes not as good . . . The Madras milk-man should be suppressed by Act of Parliament.'

While Indians had been turning out a superb form of condensed milk ice cream (*kulfi*) for centuries, the British ignored this in favour of Western-style ice cream, made possible with the importation of American and British ice cream churns in the mid-nineteenth century. The local club might have one of these machines, which could be borrowed by members for use in their homes. The results were often erratic, however: one day the mixture might be a mass of lumps and liquid, the next a block of frozen snow.

Sorbet-style ices were hawked by street-sellers, who found ready customers in the 'griffs', freshly arrived in India and blithely unaware of the hazards of the local water. In *Eastwards, or the Realities of Indian Life* (1874), C. P. A. Oman describes the docking of a steamer at Madras:

Had it not been for the heat, the constant rolling motion and the glare, the different groups on board the steamer at this time would have been highly amusing. Here are half-a-dozen men with enormous turbans, balancing, carefully, high-heaped glasses of suspicious looking ices. The look of melancholy on the poor fellows' faces, as they see the coloured delicacy fading gently away, while your lordship will not look around and buy, is highly ludicrous. Have they any consciences, these ice-men? If they have, would they allow the thirsty griffs on board to eat half a dozen of their concentrated essences of cramp?

Of the many new fruits the British encountered in India, it was the mango which most caught their fancy. Dr John Fryer, who went out to Persia and India with the East India Company in the 1670s and later wrote of his experiences (*A New Account of East India and Persia, 1698*), claimed the apples of the Hesperides were nothing but fables to a ripe mango – 'for Taste, the Nectarine, Peach and Apricot fall short'.

A sign of this esteem was the proliferation of recipes in England in the eighteenth and nineteenth centuries which sought to imitate the flavour of the fruit. Predictably, there were dissenters: 'As for the far-famed mangoes,' sniffed Fanny Parkes in *Wanderings of a Pilgrim in Search of the Picturesque* (1832), 'I was disgusted with them, all those to be had at that time being stringy, with a strong taste of turpentine.' Even she changed her mind, however, after tasting a ripe specimen.

The English name comes from *manga*, a corruption by the Portuguese in Goa of the original Tamil *mankay*.

Such a juicy fruit as the mango was impossible to eat tidily, leading the British to jest that it was best eaten in the bath. They would have been advised to adopt the Indian method, which is to knead the unpeeled fruit to a pulp, then cut the top off the narrow end and suck the pulp out. There was, however, a more refined means of preparation:

COLONEL KENNEY-HERBERT'S BRANDIED MANGOES

No one will regret trying a liqueur glass of brandy with a ripe mango, as follows:

Having before you an iced mango of a really good variety, and in perfect condition, slice off the upper piece as you would decapitate an egg, with this difference, that the mango must be sliced as it rests naturally on its side, lengthwise, and not be set up on end as an egg. Well, having sliced off this piece, put it on one side of your plate, and proceed to scoop out the stone with your silver spoon, detaching in that operation as little of the flesh of the fruit as you can. Having extracted the stone, scrape the pulp out of the slice you first cut off, and empty it into the cavity left by the stone; now detach the rest of the pulp round it, and mix the whole well together, adding a liqueur glass of liqueur brandy, and a dessert spoonful of powdered loaf sugar. If the mango be really well iced and a good one, the result will be found very pleasing.

Inasmuch as at a dinner party the eating of a mango may be considered out of the question, slices of the fruit, dressed as I have just described, iced, and served as a salad, form a very nice dessert dish. (From *Sweet Dishes*.)

The pulpy flesh of the mango was eminently suited to making into fool, an English dish of sweetened puréed fruit mixed with cream, which dated back to Tudor times.

Pineapples were equally sought after wherever they could be grown. They were good in Bengal, and even better in Burma. At Calcutta markets at the end of the nineteenth century a pineapple could be bought for a pice (less than a halfpenny).

John Huyghm van Linchoten, who arrived in India in 1576, tells us the pineapple was 'first brought by the Portuguese out of Brasille'. It seems to have reached parts of India by 1548 and was introduced into Bengal by the Portuguese in 1594.

Pineapple balls were an original, if somewhat heavy, Anglo-Indian invention, consisting of chopped pineapple mixed with a stiff batter, formed into balls and deep fried.

The papaya, the guava and the custard apple are also believed to have been brought from Latin America by the Portuguese. The non-Asiatic origin of the papaya is now conclusively proved, since it was not known before the discovery of America. It has no Sanskrit name and its modern Indian name is evidently derived from the American word 'papaya', itself a corruption of the Carib *ababai*. Its Burmese name, *thimbawthi*, means 'fruit brought by ocean-going vessels'. In 1626 seeds were sent from India to Naples, so the tree must have been introduced to India shortly after the discovery of America. Some say the papaya came to India via Malacca.

The guava in India is first mentioned by the early seventeenth-century traveller W. Bruton. While the Indians savoured its strong aromatic flavour, the British preferred to tone it down by stewing it, or making it into fruit cheese.

While there is no doubt that the custard apple is native to America, some dispute the assumption that it was introduced to India by the Portuguese, claiming it was possible that plants were taken across the Pacific hundreds of years before Columbus. During the Raj, the fruit was often made into iced puddings.

Both the shaddock or pomelo and the durian found their way to India from the Malay archipelago.

The shaddock was introduced to India by the master of an East Indiaman, a Captain Shaddock. He also took it to the West Indies, where it became the forerunner of the modern grapefruit.

The durian is a spiky fruit, looking like a large hard grenade. Its strong odour, which resembles that of putrid flesh and rotten onions, was considered highly offensive by the British but once the prejudice to its smell was overcome, the fruit found some converts among the Europeans. A Colonel Biggs claimed it was the finest fruit in the world and said the odour only develops when the fruit is not fresh.

The melon, which grew well in northern India, was much eaten by the British, as was the lychee, following its introduction into Bengal from China at the end of the eighteenth century. They also enjoyed the acid, primrose-scented mangosteen, introduced from the East Indies and cultivated in Burma and around Madras from the 1880s, but it was never a common fruit.

The pomegranate was eaten by some, despite Emma Roberts' opinion that it was 'crude and bitter', but the British seem to have largely shunned the fresh figs imported from Afghanistan. The cape gooseberry, the carambola (star fruit) and the carissa (a yellowish green fruit sometimes called the Natal plum) went mainly into jams and pickles, while the wild Himalayan cherry made an acceptable cherry brandy.

Despite such abundance of exotic fruit, it is understandable that after lengthy spells in the tropics, the English began to yearn for their familiar apples, pears and peaches. These could be grown at Bangalore in the south, because of its relatively high altitude, but not with great success. Florence Marryat wrote in *Sketches of Anglo-Indian Life and Character* (1868):

Some English fruits and vegetables certainly do grow there, but they grow like English children, stunted and sickly. I had a few little green sour apples presented to me once; but they looked too much like an embodiment of cholera morbus to tempt me to do more than taste them; and although peach-tart is a common dish at the dinner-table, it always reminded me of those we use to have at home in the early spring, when the gardener thinned his wall-fruit, which does not say much for the size attained by Bangalore peaches.

In the Nilghiri hills west of Bangalore, however, peaches grew very well, and those of Bengal also had a good flavour, ripening to a 'soft pinkish pulp'. Wild peaches grew in the north-west Himalayas, although they were never eaten as their fruits were small and green, the rains apparently preventing their ripening. But in the neighbourhood of British hill stations, these wild peaches were cared for and the fruits brought to market to sell to Europeans.

Indeed, all Western fruits could be persuaded to grow well in the hills. Lady Mary Hay recalls of Parachinar on the frontier in the Kurram Valley: 'It is about 7000 feet up with a perfect climate and in our garden grew apples, pears, plums, peaches and apricots, while at the lower end of the valley – about eighty miles away – oranges, lemons and limes flourished.' Excellent apricots were to be had in Kashmir, while inferior apricots were also grown in the Punjab and along the Western Himalayan chain.

While apples grow wild in the Himalayas it is thought they must have been introduced at some early stage; certainly the introduction of finer British strains into the Kulu Valley about 1870 improved the quality, and Kulu apples were soon considered to be almost equal to the best grown in Europe. Throughout most of the nineteenth century American ice ships brought in large supplies of apples, but they were good only when first taken out of the ice and soon turned mealy. They were, however, always good for a fruit cheese. This recipe is from Mrs Bartley's *Indian Cookery 'General'*:

APPLE CHEESE
Pare, core and cut in pieces 1 lb apples; add ½ teacup water, boil till soft, mash until smooth, put in ¾ lb sugar to mashed apples with water they were boiled in. Boil slowly till cheese formed.

While Mrs Bartley makes no mention of stirring the cheese during cooking, this is essential. Frequent stirring will prevent the mixture from catching on the bottom of the pot and burning. The cheese is ready when a spoon drawn across the pan will leave a neat trough or trench. Apple cheese makes an excellent spread for scones, muffins or bread, and can also be used as a filling for cakes.

In many areas apples were not available at all, forcing the homesick Englishwoman to seek substitutes in green mangoes or to make mock-apple preserves and sauces from papayas, dillpussums (a variety of small marrow) and pumpkins. The flavour of these preserves was heavily disguised with spices, wine, citrus juice and sugar.

The fruit of the wild pear trees found in Kashmir were generally hard and flavourless, and though eaten by Kashmiris were rarely used by the British except in cooking. The following recipe, from Mrs Temple-Wright's *Baker and Cook*, is suitable for any inferior or unripe pear.

GINGER PEARS
The hard, tasteless Indian pear is very nice treated in this way. Peel, core and cut into slices as much as will weigh half a pound, boil two ounces of crushed green ginger in a large breakfast cup of water, till the flavour is fully imparted to the water, strain the juice and put it on the fire; when boiling slip in the slices of pears, and let them simmer until soft, then add six ounces of brown sugar, and a wineglassful of ginger wine; stir all together, simmer for a minute or two; when cool, turn out into a glass dish, and serve, after it has become quite cold, with glasses of custard as a dinner sweet.

In the late nineteenth century, however, most European-cultivated pear varieties were successfully introduced into Kashmir, the Kulu Valley and other parts of the Himalayas, usually near British hill stations.

Homesick Britons were delighted to find two varieties of strawberry growing wild in the Himalayas – the alpine strawberry (*Fragaria vesca*) and the Indian strawberry (*F.indica*). The latter yielded an abundance of insipid fruit which could be much improved by cultivation. The alpine strawberry is found wild in the temperate Himalayas; curiously, it was ignored by local inhabitants until its cultivation was begun in the gardens of the British. It is significant that in the *Ain-i-Akbari*, a work which treats in great detail the fruits cultivated during the reign of Akbar in India (1556–1605), Kashmir and Afghanistan, no mention is made of the strawberry.

With the introduction of cultivation, the strawberry plant spread rapidly to other hill stations where the temperature and natural conditions resembled those of Europe. At Mahabaleshwar, during the season, a strawberry tea would be held each Friday at the club, and indeed strawberies were still being served at the club when I visited it in 1988.

Later it was found the strawberry could be successfully cultivated on the plains also, and could even withstand the hot weather. By the late nineteenth century strawberries were being grown in the Punjab, the north-west provinces (modern Pakistan) and Behar. In many areas, cultivation was later abandoned for want of a market, but the strawberry found favour with Colonel Kenney-Herbert:

The association of spirits with fresh fruit is, to my mind, nearly as commendable as the use of cream. In handing round melons, mangoes, pineapple, strawberries &c., therefore, I would always let the brandy accompany the cream, so that those who prefer the former may have an opportunity of indulging their penchant.

As a dessert dish nothing is nicer for a change than a Strawberry Salad; it is singularly simple, and with the sterner sex always popular: Having obtained a nice dish of strawberries, pick off their stalks, casting each berry into a slop basin full of cold water: stir them gently round in the water to get rid of sand, earth, &c., &c., then set them on a clean sieve to drain: when thoroughly dry, arrange the fruit in a pyramid upon a dessert dish, using a dessert knife and fork to conduct the operation, and handling each berry with infinite tenderness. When you have arranged the bottom layer of your pyramid, dust over it a layer of pounded loaf sugar, continuing a similar process until you crown the pyramid with your choicest berry; now measure a liqueur glass of the best brandy you can command, and let the nutty spirit trickle lovingly in and over your layers of strawberries, do this very gently, drop by drop, until the sugar has absorbed the brandy then give the pyramid an external dusting of sugar, and put the dish in the ice box.

Mrs Temple-Wright also favoured cream and alcohol as accompaniments to strawberies, but with the emphasis on the former.

STRAWBERRY FOAM

Take one pound of fresh strawberries, three ounces of powdered sugar, the whites of three raw eggs, whipped to a very stiff froth, a teaspoon of any red wine, and a coffeecupful of cream. Put the strawberries into a bowl, and sprinkle the sugar on them, and with two forks crush the fruit lightly, add the wine, now whip the cream, and keep adding to it the whipped white of egg, then add by degrees the crushed fruit; serve on ice plates as a dinner sweet. (From *Baker and Cook*, by Mrs R. Temple-Wright)

The yellow raspberry (*Rubus ellipticus*), found in the Himalayas, was prized by both Indians and Europeans as one of the finest wild fruits of India. Similar in flavour to the European raspberry (*R. idaeus*), it was collected during May and June and sold at the bazaars of most hill stations along the Himalayas. At Simla it was regularly exhibited at the Horticultural Society's shows. The European raspberry was experimented with at several hill stations and while it did well in some places (such as the low hills of Madya Pradesh) it was later abandoned for lack of a market.

Other berries included a type of blackberry (mistakenly called a raspberry) found around Bangalore, and mulberries. Florence Marryat recalled in 1868:

I remember being particularly charmed with a thick hedge of bushes which divided our carriage drive from the flower-garden, and bore a plentiful crop of the tiniest and sweetest of mulberries, not much larger than English blackberries, and much the same in flavour. I used to be very greedy about those mulberries. The natives constantly brought baskets of them and other fruits to us for sale, but I never cared for any but as such I gathered from our own bushes.

The grapes of Kashmir were famous, but due to the period of harvest, the methods of packing and difficulties with transport, they lost much of their flavour by the time they reached the plains. In the seventeenth century the grapes had to be carried by the basket-load down to the plains, but by the nineteenth century much of this trade had been usurped by the merchants of Kabul who would send small circular boxes of high quality grapes to India, preserved in cotton wool.

In the hill stations there was brisk trade in small black grapes derived from wild or semi-cultivated forms, which had a peculiar flavour halfway between a blackcurrant and a grape. At some stations, such as Simla, high-quality grapes were grown from European stock planted in the late nineteenth century.

The Himalayan hills stations also produced the finest dessert plums; those grown on the plains were only suitable for preserving. There was a wild plum in the jungle, although Emma Roberts describes it as 'too resinous to be relished by unaccustomed palates'.

An Englishman arriving in India early in the nineteenth century would have regarded the banana as a great curiosity for, being so perishable, the fruit had to await the invention of steamships before it could be successfully transported to Europe. The British liked bananas mashed with milk and sugar, in which they fancied a resemblance to strawberries and cream.

While deep-fried vegetables in batter were well known to the Indian cook as pakora, it was apparently the British who introduced the idea of applying the same principle to fruit, particularly the banana. Banana fritters were a great favourite among the Anglo-Indian (mixed ancestry) community:

ANGLO-INDIAN BANANA FRITTERS

This is an unusual method, but mashing the bananas into the batter solves the problem of the latter slipping off during cooking.

4 oz (125 g) flour   milk
2 eggs   caster or icing sugar
2 large ripe bananas, well mashed

Make a thick batter with the flour, eggs and mashed bananas, adding a little milk if necessary. Mix well and drop by the spoonful into deep boiling oil. Fry until golden brown, drain on absorbent paper and dust with sugar.

POOTOO RICE FRITTERS

A variation of banana fritters created by the Anglo-Burmese community.

8 oz (250 g) rice flour   tinned or instant coconut cream
2 eggs   sugar, to taste
2 ripe bananas, well mashed

Combine rice flour, eggs and bananas, adding sufficient coconut cream to make a thick batter. Add sugar to taste. Cook as above.

Fritters were also made with mixtures of sweet potatoes and coconut cream, while in sophisticated households in the late Victorian era, fruit such as peaches, apricots, apples and pineapples would be marinated in brandy or rum before being turned into fritters.

As significant as any of the introductions of Latin American fruits was that of the cashew nut. In the latter half of the sixteenth century the Portuguese took the cashew tree to Goa, and on the west coast it was first used primarily to check erosion. The tree thrived there and today India is a world leader in cashew production, with exports outstripping even Brazil, the cashew's original home. The local name, *kaju*, is a Portuguese corruption of the Brazilian name *acajau*, and the antecedent of our 'cashew'.

The cashew nut dangles, almost as an afterthought, from the orange fruit of the tree. This fruit is highly astringent, but in Goa was soon being put to good use in distilling a spirit known as *feni*, a murky, rather evil-looking brew still popular there today. The nut became widely used in sweetmaking by professional Indian confectioners. It was cheaper than the traditional almond, for which it was often substituted. And in *Dainty Cooking for the Home*, Margaret Denning suggests cashew nuts as a substitute for chestnuts. This is an adaptation of her recipe for a popular sweetmeat:

CHESTNUT OR KAJU BALLS

25 chestnuts or 35 cashew nuts, white of 1 egg
  shelled 8 oz (250 g) icing sugar
½ oz (15 g) butter 2 tsp orange flower water
8 tbsp cream

Shell the nuts, boil or bake them for a few minutes, then clean off their inner skins. Dry thoroughly and grind as finely as possible. Mix the ground nuts together with the butter, cream and egg white, beating until smooth. Add the sugar and orange flower water. Roll the paste into small balls, place on buttered paper and bake in a hot oven (220°C/425°F/Gas Mark 7) until lightly browned. Sift more icing sugar over before serving.

The English never acquired much of a taste for Indian sweets: 'We found them altogether too sweet and rich', explains Lady Hay. In his *Second Book of Curries*, Harvey Day postulates another, rather novel reason: that the delicate flavour of Indian sweets was 'killed by the alcoholic beverages favoured by Europeans'.

One notable exception was halva. The art of halva-making came to India with the Moguls in the sixteenth century, and in Muslim shops a dozen or more different varieties might be on display. Being overly suspicious of the conditions of hygiene which prevailed at these shops, the British had their own cooks prepare halva at home.

The success of halva making depends on getting the right consistency before removing it from the heat. Generally, this is when the halva begins to leave the sides of the pan and forms a ball. Another sign is when a little of the halva, the size of a marble, can be rolled between the fingers without adhering and is very firm. Halvas require continual stirring to prevent lumps and to avoid the mixture catching. This basic recipe, and the pumpkin one which follows it, are both from E. A. M. Franklin's *The Wife's Cookery Book*. (*Rolong* is semolina.)

DHALL HULVA

REQUIRED:— 2 lbs of black dhall, 4 lbs of sugar, 2 lbs of ghee, 1 lb of rolong, 1 wineglassful of rose water, 2 cocoanuts, 1 lb shelled almonds, salt.

TO MAKE:— Soak the rolong over night in some water, which must be drained off carefully the next morning.

Put the dhall on a plate, and carefully pick out all stones etc., then put it into a bowl, and wash thoroughly; soak it in water for four or five hours, then rub it between the palms of the hands, picking off all the black skins from the dhall, use plenty of water to wash it.

Scrape the cocoanuts, and take out all the milk; dissolve the sugar in the first milk, add the rose water.

Put the dhall in an enamel saucepan with the second milk of the coconut and add two large tablespoonfuls of ghee, and allow the dhall to boil until it is quite soft and can be mashed with a wooden spoon; now remove from the fire.

Put another saucepan with the sugar, cocoanut milk and rolong on the fire, and keep stirring till half done; then add the dhall and ghee, and continue stirring until all is thoroughly mixed. Just before the hulva is done put in the cut almonds, and remove from the fire.

Omit the cocoanut milk if the hulva is to be kept long. Use cow's milk.

PUMPKIN HULVA

REQUIRED:— 1 ash coloured pumpkin, 6 lbs of sugar, 3 lbs of ghee, 6 cloves, 3 pieces of cinnamon, 6 cardamoms, 1 teaspoonful of rose water, 1 large cupful of milk.

TO MAKE:— Cut the pumpkin into small pieces, and scrape out the seeds and pulp; then skin each piece.

Steam over a deckchi till the pumpkin is quite soft; then place in a bowl and mash with a wooden spoon.

Boil the milk till it becomes a thick cream. Mix the sugar with the rose water, and boil to a thick syrup over a low fire, then add the mashed pumpkin, spices, and milk; keep stirring till the hulva thickens, and there is no fear of it catching; then add the ghee by degrees, and continue stirring till done.

Take from the fire, and pour into buttered dishes. Set aside to cool.

Beatrice Vieyra's banana halva (from her *Culinary Art Sparklets*) is quite different:

BANANA HULVA

REQUIRED:— 1 lb bananas, 12 oz sugar, 2 oz of ghee

METHOD:— mash very smooth, free from hard lumps and keep by.

Now make the sugar into a syrup and put in the mashed bananas, and keep stirring till the paste is well dissolved in the syrup and free of lumps of the paste.

Keep constantly stirring about till the hulva forms into a mass, then add the ghee by degrees, toss it about in the vessel till ready, then take and spread on a greased board. Use wooden ladle and a silver knife or spoon in the preparing of this hulva, as iron utensils effect a discoloration. If carefully made this hulva has a fine golden colour. For 8 large bananas, 1 lb of sugar could be used.

Lastly, an up-to-date recipe which can be flavoured in a variety of ways. If serving as a pudding, the proportion of sugar ought to be reduced.

SEMOLINA HALVA

8 oz (250 g) sugar
16 fl oz (475 ml) water
8 oz (250 g) semolina
4 oz (125 g) ghee or butter

seeds of 1 large cardamom pod, crushed
12 almonds, toasted and sliced lengthways
¼ tsp rose essence

Place the sugar and water in a saucepan and boil for a few minutes.

Meanwhile place the semolina in another, larger, saucepan over a low heat and stir for five minues or so until it begins to give off an appetizing smell. Add the ghee or butter and continue to stir for five minutes longer. Gradually add the syrup and stir for another 10 minutes, until the mixture leaves the side of the pan.

Finally, add the toasted sliced almonds and the rose essence. If serving cold, press into a greased tin and when cold turn out from mould and cut into diamond shapes.

As a variation, honey can be substituted for the sugar, and pistachios for the almonds. Some raisins can also be added.

15

Coffee and Afternoon Tea

———

Coffee is said to have been introduced to south India in the seventeenth century by Baba Budan, a pilgrim returning from Mecca, who brought seven seeds with him to Mysore. In about 1690, the Dutch began systematically to cultivate coffee in Sri Lanka, and these plantations were greatly expanded by the British after Holland was forced to renounce the wealthy island in 1803.

At first, the British had little interest in growing coffee in Sri Lanka, but during their brief occupation of Java during the Napoleonic wars, they noticed how well coffee grew there, and also how similar were the climates and soil conditions between the two islands. There was also a political motive for wishing to create a domestic Indian supply of coffee, as the British administration was anxious to promote a coffee trade between Arabia and the Muslims of India, and the closer ties with the Turkish caliphate which this implied. In 1812, the export of coffee from Sri Lanka totalled 330,000 lb, a figure which increased steadily throughout the century until it peaked at over 100 million lb in 1869.

India's first coffee house opened in Calcutta after the battle of Plassey in 1780. Soon after, John Jackson and Cottrell Barrett opened the original Madras Coffee House, which was followed in 1792 by the Exchange Coffee Tavern at the Madras Fort. The enterprising proprietor of the latter announced he was going to run his coffee house on the same lines as Lloyd's in London, by maintaining a register of the arrival and departure of ships, and offering Indian and European newspapers for his customers to read. Other houses also offered free use of billiard tables, recovering their costs with the high price of one rupee (then half a crown) for a single dish of coffee.

Since they were especially popular during the hottest part of the day, the Calcutta coffee houses were kept as cool as possible, the marble floors and tables, and steady breezes from the *punkah* offering a refreshing contrast to the intense heat and red brick dust outside.

The coffee houses were in direct competition with the taverns of the time, and it was with the express purpose of providing an alternative to alcohol that Henry Piddington opened coffee shops near the Calcutta wharves, where men could pass the time while awaiting the arrival of ships from England.

Calcutta businessmen would meet and discuss their affairs in their favourite coffee houses, and the young soldiers would also go to coffee houses near their barracks after the early morning parade and stay there until noon. During the cool weather they might sit out in the open air, reading newspapers and gossiping about newly arrived women, dances, and who had got drunk the night before. (As in London, these coffee houses were for men only, although the premises might from time to time be opened to women for public concerts and balls. On such occasions, hookahs were banned.)

At remote country stations before the days of the club, the coffee shop was especially important as a social centre, where the men would gather around bare deal tables after an early morning ride. These up-country places were considerably less elegant than their counterparts in Calcutta, as Lieutenant Majendie discovered when he visited the coffee room of Lewis' Hotel in Delhi and found

a dingy appearance of chaos, more singular than pleasing, furniture new and old and not a small quantity antediluvian; potted meats and treatises on astronomy; faded neckties and bloater paste; preserved soups and books without backs; glass lamp-shades and rusty knives; rakish old chairs on three legs, making love to young book-cases with no books in them.

However, it was the company rather than the decor that was important. With their servants in attendance and their dogs at their feet, the men would light up cheroots and tell each other, amidst great guffaws of laughter, that Nicaldo, the itinerant dentist, had arrived and that Mrs McGhee, whose teeth, numerically as well as positively, had dwindled to their shortest span, had had the balance summarily extracted, and that Nicaldo is engaged to supply new ones, which have already been designated 'Mother McGhee's new dinner-set' . . . that old McGhee had been seen that morning at the auction-sale of poor Sergeant Trail, and that he had purchased for the sum of two rupees eleven annas, three flannel waistcoats, five pair of socks, and an old toothbrush – all of which he carried home in his hat; and that he frowned so hard at the bugler boys that they were afraid to bid against him – sufficiently proving his character is favourable to economy . . . that the turkey ['at last night's feed at the Ganders"] was the leanest old bird in creation, and that its breast was puffed out by the ingenious introduction of a tough old fowl, but which the keen eye of Pullow detected. (From *Curry and Rice on Forty Plates*, by G. F. Atkinson.)

In the early years of the nineteenth century the habit of paying casual visits at all hours of the night and day died out, and about this time taverns and coffee houses became equally unfashionable. For a time after 1835, the advent of imported ice from American ships revived their flagging trade, and ices and sherry cobblers (a sweetened iced drink, flavoured with fruit) served at the coffee houses became all the rage. By this time, however, gentlemen's clubs were on the rise.

The Bengal Club, India's first, was established in Calcutta in 1827. The Byculla club opened at Bombay in 1833, and the Madras Club at the same time. It was not until the Indian Mutiny that clubs appeared in the remoter stations of the *mofussil*. Until 1857, for example, Cawnpore had a church, racecourse, theatre, Freemasons' lodge, tennis court, library, billiards rooms, and an assembly rooms where dinners were held for passing Governors-General, but no club.

Despite the fact that women had no official standing and did not appear on the official list of members, they benefitted most from the establishment of the clubs, as previously their only public meeting place had been the local band rotunda, where performances were given in the evening.

Afternoon tea parties became popular after the middle of the nineteenth century, by which time women had come to settle in India in large numbers. As far as entertaining went, such gatherings were seen as an economical alternative to lavish dinner parties, and there was keen rivalry among hostesses in their provision of biscuits and cakes.

At garden parties guests might play tennis or a leisurely game of croquet, or simply stroll around the grounds, quietly chatting, and then sit in garden seats in shaded nooks while the *khitmutgar* handed around drinks and cakes. In *A Bungalow in India* (1928) by Mildred Worth

Pinkham, we read of one such party, held under a mango tree on the front lawn; at which an uninvited guest eyes the delicacies:

Most tempting pastry appeared – concoctions which Joan had not had the imagination to order. Everything progressed serenely until something happened that the Boy had not anticipated. While the Memsahib and her guests were sipping tea, a huge vulture swung down upon the table, and grabbing an inviting cocoanut frosted tart, made off with it to a distant tree.

'Chota Sahib', in his *Camp Recipes for Camp People*, gives just such a vulture lure:

PRESIDENCY CAKES

Grate a fair sized cocoanut down to the rind and dissolve a cup of sugar in a little water; then add the cocoanut and keep on stirring till it boils; turn this out and let it cool; then add the yolks of 4 eggs well beaten up and place in the oven in small pans lined with a thin layer of good paste. These are good either hot or cold.

During the hot weather granitas and sorbets were popular, along with chilled cups made from wine and cider. In the cold weather ginger wine, cherry brandy and other liqueurs might be offered, but whatever the season the mainstays were always coffee and tea.

While tea drinking in British India never got under way in earnest until the planting of the Assam tea estates in the 1830s, the beverage had been known to them from the earliest days of their trading posts at Surat and Bombay, some twenty years or more before it reached England. In 1638 J. A. Mandelslo noted: 'At our ordinary meetings [at Surat] every day we took only The, which is commonly used all over the Indies as a drug that cleanses the stomach and digests the superfluous humours.'

China tea was first taken to Surat by the Dutch, who also introduced it to Europe. According to the Rev. F. Ovington, who wrote an account of his journey to India – *A Voyage to Suratt in the Year 1689* – the Dutch traders in India 'used it as such a standing entertainment, that the teapot's seldom off the Fire or unimploy'd.' The Surat traders did not add milk to their tea, although it was generally drunk with sugar, a variety of spices, 'or by the more curious, with small conserved lemons'. Citron leaves were also used, and the brew was drunk from tin 'tea-dishes'.

The cultivation of tea in India began only after the ailing East India Company, propped up by the British taxpayer, finally lost its monopoly over the China tea trade in 1833 and was forced to look elsewhere for a steady tea supply, preferably one under its control. As early as 1780 the Company, under pressure from the British government to diversify its source of supply, had sent experimental seed to Calcutta. A Colonel Kyd had planted it in his garden (which was later to become the Royal Botanic

Gardens, Seebpore), but nothing much more was heard of it, and even the discovery by British explorers between 1819 and 1821 that indigenous tea had been growing all along in Assam, went largely unnoticed.

In 1834 however, a Tea Committee was set up by the Governor-General of India to establish commercial tea plantations. The first tea gardens in Assam were thus government ones, but when the prices for the first shipment to London in 1839 showed that Indian tea would certainly pay, private enterprise nobly stepped forward and accepted the risk. Foremost was the Assam Company, formed in 1840, but many others followed.

Indian tea arrived on the British market at a convenient time, just as the public was becoming aware that China tea was being appallingly adulterated. Gunpowder tea, a fine variety of green China tea in which the leaf is rolled up into a tiny ball, was in some cases literally gunpowder mixed with gum, pale Prussian blue dye, turmeric and sulphate of lime. Other 'teas' were made from ash, elder and sloe leaves picked from English hedgerows and curled and coloured on copper plates.

Indian tea had the advantage from the outset of being easily recognizable as black rather than green in colour, and while its flavour was totally different from China tea, its more robust character appealed to the English palate, and India has benefitted ever since.

In the 1860s the Indian tea plantations extended into several other parts of India, notably Darjeeling, where the mists and high altitude slow down the growth of the leaf, concentrating the flavour, and producing some of the most prized tea in the world.

Sri Lanka entered into tea growing in the 1870s, after a killer fungus, *Hemileia vastatrix*, struck their coffee plants in 1869 and within ten years devastated the coffee industry. The climate and soil conditions proved ideal for tea, however, and by 1895 the island's tea plantations covered 300,000 acres.

Tea was drunk in Victorian India the way it still is today in Britain, with milk and sugar (which might mean jaggery or date palm sugar), although some British also enjoyed it Mogul-style, with spices. As this recipe from Beatrice Vieyra illustrates, tea itself was not always the prime ingredient:

CUTCHEE TEA
REQUIRED:— ¼ lb of sago, ¼ lb of almonds, 6 pods of cardamom, rosewater, milk and tea leaf, sugar to taste.
METHOD:— Shell, blanch and grind the almonds to a fine paste; wash the sago.
    Make a muslin bag, and put into it the ground almonds and sago, tie or stitch up the bag and throw it into the quantity of water required, and then boil.

Add the cardamom, powdered, and lastly the rosewater.

Have sufficient water to make about 12 cups of tea.

Use plenty of good thick milk.

Put just sufficient tea leaf into a teapot and pour over it the boiling water; when it has drawn, strain away into another vessel, add milk and sugar to taste, and serve.

If dried rose-buds or rose-petals are used, it gives a better and stronger flavour than rosewater.

The less tea leaf used the better.

Indeed the ginger tea from *The Original Madras Cookery Book* used no leaf tea in the brew at all:

GINGER TEA

Bruise two or three pieces of white dry ginger, put into a saucepan with a little more than half a pint of cold water and a dessert-spoonful of coriander seed; let the whole simmer until the tea tastes strong of ginger; strain through a muslin into a teacup; add milk and sugar. An excellent remedy for indigestion.

'In regard to eatables,' wrote Flora Annie Steel of afternoon teas, 'plain bread and butter should invariably be a standing dish. Many people do not care for cakes, and yet find a cup of tea or coffee better for something to eat with it.' Besides the inevitable cucumber, tomato or cress sandwiches, fresh strawberries and raspberries were used for fillings, along with concoctions of a more peculiarly Anglo-Indian nature.

DELHI SANDWICHES

12 fillets of anchovy	2 hard-boiled egg yolks
12 oz (350 g) sardines	1½ tsp curry powder
2 tsp mango chutney	

Pound all of the ingredients with a mortar and pestle or in a food processor/blender, and cook over a low heat until they amalgamate. Allow to cool before spreading into sandwiches.

Baking in British India presented a huge number of obstacles to the cook, not the least of which were the primitive ovens and the rarity of fine flour, properly washed butter which was free of buttermilk, and yeast. Cookery books of the Raj are filled with recipes for home-made yeast, using ingredients as diverse as potatoes, hops, bananas, barley, toddy (palm sap) and a fruit flower known as *mowha*. Often the memsahib had to send away to the Army and Navy Stores of the big towns in order to obtain quality tinned butter.

Since it was considered a refined and particularly dainty branch of the culinary art, cake-making was one kitchen task the memsahib might deign to undertake herself, although in the Calcutta and Simla of Edwardian times there was undoubtedly a great temptation to fall back on the products of Peliti, the famous European confectioners. As Mrs Isobel Abbott found, the memsahib's own Indian cook might also prove to be a dab hand:

Bashir was in his glory whenever we had a tea party and his variety of cakes, scones, buns, puffs and sweets were a revelation. His oven was a kerosene tin placed on an open wood fire, with a few of the burning embers on top of the tin to produce an even heat. One had to be a past master to keep the fire at just the right temperature. His kitchen, on party days, had to be seen to be believed. Dough, slowly rising, swelling and spilling over one corner of the rough table, fudge cooling on another, a mountainous pile of newspaper quills under the table and a blot of pink icing decorating the ceiling. But a beautifully iced and decorated layer cake always serenely reposed on the kitchen stool. Crushed egg shells lay, like the May petals, on the mud floor and it was a gymnastic feat to avoid the mixing bowls, the plates of washed, dried fruit, and the large hookah in the centre of the floor. At first I was appalled by the confusion, but I realized I could do no better with an open wood fire, a kitchen table and a stool. Indeed I could have done nothing at all, except mop my eyes and cough, for the wood was always new and damp.

Where they were baked by the memsahib's fair hands, cakes and biscuits in British India tended to become sternly practical affairs, with names like Tirhoot Tea Cake (flour, sugar, eggs and butter), Gymkhana Cake (the same, only with plums and currants added), Tiffin Cakes, Dholi Buns and Bombay Golden Cake. Nurmahal Cake was a wondrously ghastly multi-tiered creation stuck together with three different flavours of jam, with a custard-filled well in the centre and a frosting of egg white and sugar. The fearsome Flora Annie Steel sets the correct tone:

Cakes and bonbons suitable for tennis parties are legion, and, as a rule, the one thing to be observed in selecting them is to avoid stickiness or surprises. It is not pleasant to find the first bite of a firm-looking cake result in a dribble of liqueur or cream down your best dress.

Some of these Raj-era cakes are nevertheless interesting for their Indian influence, and use of local spices and ingredients. Mrs Bartley's 'Saucy Kate' is a typical adaptation:

SAUCER CAKE (SAUCY KATE)
Mix together a lb of fine flour, three ounces of powdered sugar, and three ounces of melted butter, make it into a dough with milk. Scrape the white part of two

cocoanuts into flakes, which mix with a tablespoon of sliced almonds, two tablespoons of white plums, the same amount of currants, half a lb of sugar, and the seeds of six cardamoms pounded. Roll your pastry very thin, put a layer in a tin plate, sprinkle some of the sweetmeat over the pastry, repeat the process, pastry and sweetmeat, alternately, until there are seven layers. With a knife cut the paste in cross lines, two inches apart, not quite through. Put lumps of butter all over the surface, using about four ounces more. Bake a light brown.

Memsahibs took advantage of local fruits and spices to make tea-time favourites, such as this fruit cake, based on a recipe from G. H. Cook's *The English-Indian Cookery Book*.

FRUIT CAKE

6 large eggs
1¼ lb (575 g) plain flour
2 oz (50 g) rice flour
3 tsp baking powder
15 oz (450 g) butter or 6 oz (175 g) ghee
1½ lb (750 g) sugar

1 lb (500 g) raisins
1 oz (25 g) crystallized citron or orange peel
½ tsp ground cloves
½ tsp ground cardamoms
Some milk or water

Beat the whites and yolks of eggs separately. Mix the flours with the baking powder by sieving three times. Then mix the butter or ghee and sugar together. Put all the ingredients into a large bowl and mix together with milk or water until you make a soft dough. If too much fluid is added and the dough gets too soft, the raisins will settle at the bottom in cooking. Grease four small tins and spoon the mixture into them till they are about half full. Bake for about an hour at 180°C/350°F/Gas Mark 4.

Remove from the oven when the tops are brown and test with a knife: if the blade comes out clean the cake is cooked, but if some of the mixture sticks to the blade, replace the cakes in the oven for a further quarter of an hour and test again as before. When cooked, remove from the oven and allow to cool for about half an hour.

PUMPKIN PIE (AN INDIAN RECIPE)

Despite the title of this recipe (which is based on one of Mrs A. K. Shelton's 'dainty confections') the shortcrust pastry reveals an obvious European influence.

shortcrust pastry	3–4 tbsp caster sugar
2–3 green mangoes	2 eggs
3 slices cooked pumpkin	scant 4 fl oz (100 ml) milk
2 oz (50 g) butter	

Line a pie dish with shortcrust pastry. Prick the base, line with aluminium foil and weigh down with dried beans. Bake for 15 minutes at 400°F/200°C/Gas Mark 6.

Finely slice the mangoes and pumpkin. Cream the butter and sugar, then mix in the mango and pumpkin. Separate the eggs and mix in the yolks, along with the milk. Beat the egg whites until stiff and fold into the mixture. Pour into pastry case and bake for 20 minutes at 400°F/200°C/Gas Mark 6.

'Notwithstanding the fact', wrote Colonel Kenney-Herbert in *Sweet Dishes*, 'that, thanks to Messrs. Peak, Frean and Co., Huntley and Palmer, &c, tinned biscuits of undeniable quality are to be got without difficulty, there are some varieties that are better made at home if possible.'

INDIAN GINGERBREAD

Take 12 oz sugar, ¼ lb butter, 1 lb flour, 2 oz pounded ginger, ¼ oz ea. of cloves and cinnamon. Mix ginger and spice with the flour; put the sugar and a small teacupful of water in a saucepan; when it is dissolved add the butter, and as soon as it is melted mix it with the flour and other things; work it up, form the paste into cakes or nuts, and bake them upon tins. (From *The Indian Cookery Book*, by a thirty-five years resident, 1869.)

G. L. Routleff, in *The Economical Cookery Book (for India)*, recommends Kul Kuls as 'an excellent old-fashioned recipe you are sure to be delighted with'. (*Soojee* is a type of semolina.)

KUL KULS

1 lb soojee, 1 tea-cup thick coconut milk, 3 eggs. Knead to a stiff dough, form into shapes with the back of a fork, greasing the fork occasionally with a little butter. The shapes should be in the form of little curls. Fry in boiling ghee. After they have cooled, weigh the kul kuls, and to every 2 lb allow 1 lb sugar, make it

into a syrup; when it thickens and gets stringy throw in the kul kuls, and mix them thoroughly till they are coated with sugar, and the syrup dries.

The following two recipes are from Mrs Bartley's *Indian Cookery 'General'*. The inelegantly named Mass Plow may be recognized as having close kinship with marzipan.

ALMOND ROCK OR CORDEAL

Blanch 1 lb almonds, and either slice fine or pound them coarsely. Melt 2 lb sugar in a little water over a slow fire, colour syrup pink with a few drops cochineal, and flavour it with a wineglass of rose water. When the syrup boils and feels sticky, add the almonds, stir the mixture til it thickens and, before it dries, remove and place the cordeal on a buttered board and over the mass place a piece of buttered paper, and with the bellen roll it out to the thickness of ⅓ in. Cut in diamonds when cool.

MASS PLOW

INGREDIENTS:— The kernels of a lb. of new almonds blanched and ground smooth with a little rose water, two lbs. of loaf sugar crushed and sifted through muslin, the whites of two eggs beaten to a firm froth, one wineglass of best rose water. Mix these well together, and simmer the mixture on a slow fire, stirring constantly till of the consistency of wax. Place the almond paste on a large dish and knead it well. Sprinkle the moulds with corn flour or powdered sugar, make a ball of paste, place it over the block, and roll the bellen over. Should the paste dry, moisten it with rose water.

Mass Plow Blocks or Moulds: A picture of an animal, fruit, flowers etc, is carved smoothly in wood, the blocks are about 3 ins square and kept to make Mass Plow. The pressed paste receives a beautiful raised impression, the surplus being used again. Cardamom seeds are used for the eyes of fish, etc, and gold leaf is often used in the decoration.

Finally, a splendid, if labour-intensive, confection from Beatrice Vieyra's *Culinary Art Sparklets*. The curious addition of pounded chicken breast to a sweet dish is by no means an Anglo-Indian invention, and a sweet chicken cream, flavoured with rose water, is popular in Turkey today. The 'broiled rolong' which thickens this dish is semolina which has been toasted or browned.

BAL DE RAM

REQUIRED:— 8 ozs. of rolong, 200 almonds, 2 lbs sugar, 1 full chest of a chicken, rosewater, 10 eggs, 1 lb sugar.

METHOD:— Broil the rolong well. Take 100 almonds, blanch and grind, or pound it to a paste; the remaining almonds blanch and chop up finely.

Boil the chicken chest till soft, then remove the skin from it and grind this also to a paste.

Now make the 2 lbs sugar into syrup, then put into it the ground almonds and chicken chest, stir well and add the chopped almonds and lastly, strew in the rolong. Keep stirring, take a little and roll it between the fingers, if it does not adhere, it is ready, take it off the fire, and spread it on buttered plates an inch thick, and keep in reserve. Next take the yolk of eggs, beat up well, and strain. Make the 1 lb of sugar into syrup. Take an empty egg shell, make an hole in the bottom of it, and pour the strained yolks into it; then drop it in the boiling syrup, placed on the fire. Spread in such a way as to form a net work; when done, take out with forks, being careful not to separate it, and place it on the prepared sweet, which was spread on a plate and reserved; sprinkle rosewater over and arrange it well on the plate of sweetmeat. Cut in slices when cold and serve. The top of the sweetmeat must be well covered with this net work.

As the sugar syrup in the oven gets thick, add a little rosewater to keep it up to the required consistency.

This is a very old family recipe and seldom used now. It makes a very tasty and delicious sweetmeat.

Instead of almonds, cashew-nuts could be substituted and would be found economical.

16
Drinks

___

In a society which offered few entertainments outside working hours, it is not surprising that during the first two centuries of British presence in India, a great deal of hard drinking took place. From the very earliest time of the English factory at Surat, drunkenness was rife; when the factory president set about controlling the amount of alcohol served in the communal dining hall, the individual ration was set at a quart of wine and half a pint of brandy per meal!

Officially, there were a number of punishments for being drunk 'and thereby prostituting the worthiness of our Nation and Religion to the calumnious Censure of the Heathen', but in fact the president himself would shout for mulled wine as soon as he awoke in the morning, which the Italian traveller Della Vallee tells us, 'he drank frequently to comfort the stomach'.

Over-indulgence in drink was equally typical of early Calcutta, as the Rev. Patrick Warner warned the directors of the East India Company in 1676:

There are also some of the writers who by their lives are not a little scandalous to the Christian religion, so sinful in their drunkenness that some of them play at cards and dice for wine which shall pay all, and sometimes who shall drink all, by which some are forced to drink till they be insensible and then strip them naked and in that posture (*horresco referens*) cause them to be carried through the streets to their dwelling place. Some of them with other persons whom they invited, once went abroad to a garden not far off, and there continued a whole day and night drinking most excessively, and in so much that one of the number died within a very few days after, and confessed he had contracted his sickness by that excess. A person worthy of credit having occasion to go next day into the same garden could number by the heads 36 bottles, and by the best of his judgment they were all bottles, for it is their frequent custom to break bottles as soon as they have drunk the wine and this they have done sometimes within the walls of the Fort, and withal, sing and carouse at very unseasonable hours.

At this time it was not uncommon for a man to lay in a full stock of wine and invite his friends to dinner, and in the process of their giving their judgement of its quality, finish off the whole chest at one sitting.

At the beginning of the nineteenth century, according to a Miss Goldbourne, wine was still 'the heaviest family article, for whether it is taken fashionably or medicinally, everybody, even to your humble servant, drinks at least a bottle *per diem*, and the gentlemen four times that quantity.' (Quoted in *British Social Life in India*, by Dennis Kincaid, 1938.) She added that the men would demonstrate their prowess by piling the empty bottles on the table, like trophies. If there was to be a ball or reception, people generally had a drinking session in their houses first, arriving in loud and dishevelled groups.

Not even the clergy could be relied upon to set an example of sobriety. The diarist William Hickey tells of the army chaplain Mr Blunt:

This incomprehensible young man got abominably drunk and in that disgraceful condition exposed himself to both soldiers and sailors, talking all sorts of bawdy and ribaldry, and singing scraps of the most blackguard and indecent songs, so as to render himself a common laughing stock.

Nor were Islamic strictures against alcohol sufficient to deter certain Muslims when they dined with the British. Indeed, John Fryer reports in *A New Account of East India and Persia*, that they were not content with little English wine glasses, preferring to swig brandy and sack directly from the bottle. The more cunning Koranic scholars argued that as the Prophet's ban applied only to wine, any other form of alcohol was permissable. This explains the popularity of brandy, particularly cherry brandy, which was also a favourite among Hindus who enjoyed getting *burra coosee* (very happy).

The military very early gained the reputation as the hardest drinkers of them all. The Mogul emperor Akbar is said to have condoned the sale of wine to his English gunners because 'the Europeans must have been created at the same time as spirits and if deprived of them, were like fish out of their element, and unless they had drink, they would not see plain.'

In a nineteenth-century officers' mess a typical evening would begin with sherry or Madeira before dinner. Claret would accompany the meal, after which the tablecloth would be removed (presumably in anticipation of spills) and toasts drunk, each honoured by a tune from the regimental band. After the commanding officer left the room there would be a course of savouries and then the serious drinking would begin. Anybody who left early would be shouted down as a 'milk sop', 'shabby fellow' or 'cock tail'.

Until the nineteenth century the enlisted men mainly drank the indigenous arrack, a cheap, strong spirit distilled most commonly from the fermented sap of palm trees, but also from rice and sometimes even dates or seaweed. The most common brands came from Bengal (the most potent), and from Goa, which was of better quality. The method of tapping palm sap for arrack, which remains unchanged today, was to cut off the thick flowering stalk and bind the stump tightly with rope, then hang a pot underneath to catch the sap. When first drawn, the sap tastes like a sweet, aromatic coconut milk, but if the pots are left during the day the heat of the sun will ferment the sap into toddy. This cost only a pice or two per quart and was also drunk by British soldiers.

A daily ration of arrack was issued to the East India Company's soldiers in the field, who, despite being ordered to drink up on the spot, often saved their drams in order to have one good bout of drunkenness. When Clive captured Chandernagore in 1757, he was so worried about the effect of the arrack there on his troops that he ordered them to encamp a mile north of the city.

The French traveller Bernier was disgusted that the English had developed a taste for such a crude liquor, which he described as 'a drink very hot and penetrating like the brandy made of corn in Poland. It so falls upon the nerves that it often causeth shaking hands in those that drink a little too much of it.'

In 1760 measures were taken to limit the distillation and sale of arrack in Calcutta, but fifteen years later Alexander Mackrabie, puritanical secretary to an early Governor of Calcutta, found the city still swarming with arrack sellers 'to the ruin and ill-health of the lower class of people'.

The upper classes found arrack acceptable only as an ingredient of punch. Indeed, seventeenth-century India was the great age of punch, drunk by every European and to excess by many of them. Punch is an Indian drink some 2000 years old, its name derived from the Hindi word for five, the number of its ingredients: arrack (or some other spirit), sugar, citrus juice, water and spices (or other aromatic flavourings such as rose water). It was generally served in bowls with toast, or with toasted biscuits floating on top.

Punch was also a favourite drink of the Portuguese at Goa, who established special punch houses there in the early seventeenth century. This idea eventually spread to Calcutta and Madras, where a distinction was made between the common punch houses, and 'houses of entertainment'. The latter were permitted by their licence to admit only 'officers and gentlemen' and most had nostalgic English names such as the King's Arms or the Old London Tavern. The charge for lodging was a pagoda (8 shillings), but the publican could be assured of his guests spending this much again on his highly priced alcohol.

East India Company merchants introduced punch to England where, early in the eighteenth century, milk punch became all the rage. This was the successor to the old English posset, and a verse-recipe for 'East-Indian style posset' is attributed to Alexander Pope:

> From far Barbadoes on the Western main
> Fetch sugar, ounces four, fetch sac from Spain,
> One pint, and from the East Indian coast,
> Nutmeg; the glory of the Northern Toast,
> On flaming coals let them together heat,
> Till the all-conquering sac dissolve the sweet,
> On such another fire put eggs, just ten,
> (New-born, from tread of cock and rump of hen),
> Stir them with steady hand, and conscience pricking
> To see the end of ten fine chicken,
> From shining shelf, take down the brazen skillet,
> A quart of milk from gentle cow and fill it
> When boiled and cold, put milk to sac and eggs,
> Unite them firmly, like the triple league,
> And on the fire let them together dwell.

Punch went out of fashion in India in about the middle of the eighteenth century but remained in favour in Britain for another 50 years. According to Mrs Beeton it had been superseded by wine, but she nevertheless gives a recipe for it:

EAST INDIA PUNCH

½ a pint of brandy, 1 pint of port wine, 1 pint boiled sugar and water syrup (sweeten to taste), ½ a pint of lime juice syrup, 1 bottle of seltzer or soda water iced, ⅛ pint arrack, the thinly pared rinds of 2 lemons, 2 or 3 sprigs syringa,

1¼ cups crushed ice. Soak the lemon-rind in the brandy for 3 hours, then strain, add the rest of the ingredients, and serve.

The punch habit never died out completely in India, however, even if the beverage was given new names. From C. C. Kohlhoff's *Indian Cookery and Domestic Recipes*:

THE COMMANDER-IN-CHIEF

Pour 1 bottle of good claret, 1 bottle of soda-water, 1 wine glass of curaçao, with sugar to taste, in a large bowl. Throw in 1 lb of broken ice half an hour before the drink is needed. When about to serve, add l bottle of champagne, stir briskly, and put into a glass jug and serve.

And from Margaret Denning's *Dainty Cookery for the Home*:

EYE OPENER À LA DURBAR

To a pint of champagne well iced, add in a jug a few sprigs of mint, a liqueur glass of curaçao, a liqueur glass of vermouth, a few cloves and the rind of half a lemon cut into strips. When fizzing, drink.

(But please, if trying out either of these, use a cheap champagne-method white wine, not vintage Krug!)

European wines were imported from Germany, Italy and France. Inferior wine was known as 'Danish' (sometimes 'Dutch') wine, while 'English' was good French claret to which some brandy had been added in England to enable it to withstand the Indian climate.

The early British in India sometimes drank their wine out of rhinoceros horns, believing them to be an antidote to poison, and their rather coarse palates favoured mixing their wine with heavy doses of spices. In Bombay and Calcutta a popular beverage was mulled or 'burnt' wine (claret boiled with cinnamon, cloves and other spices) while in Madras the favoured drink was mug – a mixture of Madeira, porter, spices and sugar.

In the era of the early merchants Shiraz wines from Persia had been so popular that the English had their own wine-maker there, but the trade fell off abruptly after political troubles broke out in Persia in the mid-eighteenth century. Their place was taken by Madeira. One of the East India Company ships would call into Madeira annually to take aboard a supply for the Company employees in India. William Hickey was aboard one such ship and reported that the pipes (huge barrels, each holding 105 gallons) 'not only impeded the ship's progress by making her too deep in the water but greatly increased her motion; at times we rolled so dreadfully deep it was with utmost difficulty we preserved our seats at meal-time.' In one storm which Hickey experienced, some of the crew were crushed to death by the rolling pipes.

Curiously, the tossing of the sea voyage was thought to be particularly good for the wine; a certain Colonel Martinz of Madras went so far as to hang his pipes from his cellar roof and from time to time set them spinning or, as he put it, 'give them a voyage around the Cape'.

Madeira was also the only wine that was thought actually to improve in the Indian climate, and Calcutta firms would send pipes up-country to Cawnpore to season. So popular was Madeira that 150 to 200 pipes were sent annually to Madras alone, on the Company's account, and even these were supplemented by a good deal more which came in privately.

With a ration that amounted to 4200 bottles for the Governor and 130 for even the lowliest Company clerk, one might wonder that extra supplies had to be imported – that is, until one considers the 268 bottles drunk in one month in the household of a Mr Francis. His 'wine book' for 1774 shows that in one month he and his guests drank 75 bottles of Madeira, 99 bottles of claret, 74 bottles of porter, 16 bottles of rum, 3 bottles of brandy and 1 bottle of cherry brandy. Clearly the habit of heavy drinking was as strong as ever, even if the cost had risen as arrack was replaced with imported wines, beer and spirits.

Madeira was drunk not only as a dessert wine but was also watered down for consumption throughout the main meal, and at other times as a thirst quencher. A measure of Madeira was commonly diluted with three of water, and special 'wine and water' glasses were often seen at table. Returning back to London after a long residence in India, a Captain Eastwick horrified a merchant friend by mixing his prime London Particular with water.

Indeed, for all their massive consumption, few English settlers seem to have been connoisseurs of wine. William Hickey tells of a party to which he invited certain local notables 'and others of equal fame in the bottle way', and, being anxious to impress, had obtained three dozen very expensive bottles of English claret. These were ordered to be served at lunch, but unknown to Hickey, the *khansamah* instead served some cheap Danish claret. When the mistake was discovered the quality claret was produced; however, the party unanimously decided that the first batch had been 'infinitely the best, it being uncommonly highly flavoured, whereas the other was abominable, not fit to be drunk.' Hickey was amused:

I told them I rejoiced to find they had such correct taste, especially as I could indulge them upon very easy terms, the wine they had admired having cost me no more than eighteen rupees a dozen, while that they abused and rejected was at the enormous price of sixty-five rupees a dozen. To show how little real judgment operates, and how few men are capable of deciding from their own palate, the moment I noted the vast difference in prices several of the party began to change their tone, some of them observing 'there certainly is a delicacy and a flavour in the English wine which the other wants' and they stuck to it the remainder of the day, merely, as I firmly believe, because it cost sixty-five sicca rupees a dozen instead of eighteen.

Port sometimes partnered Madeira and sherry at dessert, although it was considered a little too rich and heavy for the climate. Champagne, though it was to enjoy a brief flourish of popularity during the Edwardian era, was too expensive to be drunk at any other than a special occasion. Indian servants called it 'Simpkin' which was either a corruption of the name itself, or a reference to an early importer named Simpson.

From about 1820 beer began to displace wine as the favoured drink. Imported English beer had been available from the earliest days of the Company, but had always been expensive and was considered too 'liverish' for India. Consequently it was often watered down with a mixture of toddy, brown sugar, ginger and lime peel. In 1821, however, Hodgson and Co. began to brew a light ale especially for India, and by offering generous discounts to East Indiamen captains, soon created a fashion for it. After it became popular the firm abolished these discounts in 1825, paving the way for rival English breweries to cut into the market, among them Charrington, Ind, Tennent, Bass and Allsopp, the latter two producing their own brands of East India Pale Ale.

While some maintained that imported beer tasted better, and that beer that had not made a voyage was 'a barbarous beverage fit only for coal heavers', the consensus was that English beer which had been too long in the bottle was apt to become somewhat sharp and bitter. Accordingly, locally brewed beer began to appear. The pioneer brewer was Mr Henry Bohle, who began business at Meerut and Mussourie in 1825. His initial product was disappointing, and it was not until 1870 that the brewery was truly successful. Many of the breweries which began in the hill stations went bankrupt between 1850 and 1860, but a second wave appeared after 1870 and by 1890 25 breweries were at work. Some of the best beer was brewed in the Himalayas, mainly by the family firm of Dyer, (a name later to gain infamy when a member of the family, Brigadier Dyer, gave the order to shoot in the Amritsar Massacre).

Despite its popularity, beer was not quite the drink for a lady of refinement. Mrs Major Clemons, after noting that a certain Mrs Colonel Woodcroft had, before her marriage, been a cook to the Colonel's father in England, takes obvious relish in reporting that, upon being asked to take wine with a young officer, the woman replied: 'No thank you, I don't care a rush for wine; but I am a very tiger for beer.'

Among the enlisted men, beer replaced the toddy and arrack of earlier centuries, and was available cheaply from 'wet' canteens.

The age of brandy succeeded that of beer, accounting for the introduction of soda water to India. First manufactured in Futtyghur about 1835, by the mid-1840s soda water was to be found in every British household. Servants knew it as *billayati-pani* or English water.

Brandy and soda ruled supreme until the 1870s, when the devastation of France's vineyards by phylloxera resulted in a scarcity of brandy. This coincided with the mass-marketing of blended Scotch whiskies, and so whisky supplanted brandy as the favourite drink of the Raj.

Contrary to the English practice of adding just a dash of soda to whisky, in India the whisky was well diluted. Spirits were dispensed in pau-pegs (quarter tots – a single-finger measure), chota-pegs (a two-finger measure) or burra-pegs (a three-finger measure, or about 3 fl oz). At the Calcutta Club, if one ordered a whisky soda, the whole bottle was placed on the table. The member then helped himself to as much whisky as he liked, for a flat rate of only 15 annas (then 1s 6d), a practice which persisted as late as the 1920s.

The invention of tonic water in the 1860s lent a new respectability to gin, the poor man's spirit of preceding centuries. Tonic water was first marketed in India and Africa by the firm of Schweppe as an anti-malarial remedy. To make this quinine-based medicine more palatable, people began mixing in a little gin, and very soon a drink of gin and tonic became a pleasure rather than a chore.

Gin also forms the basis of British India's most famous cocktail, the Gimlet. Exactly what this drink shares in common with the carpenter's tool of the same name, beyond a penetrating sharpness, has never been explained. An early recipe for 'a Bengal Gimlet' calls for one part each of Cockran's lime juice and milk punch to two of dry gin, with a dash of soda water, but here is the more usual recipe:

GIMLET

3 parts dry gin	1 part Rose's lime juice (or other lime juice cordial)

Shake with ice and strain into large cocktail glasses. A dash of soda water may be added if desired.

This was the drink which, according to popular imagination, the British sipped on the verandah while watching the sun sink behind the banyan groves.

Cocktails reached the height of popularity during the interwar era. This one, found in *Things for the Cook* (1914) by 'Shalot', was invented at the Simla Club:

RUM COCKTAIL
1½ large whisky measures rum; the juice of ½ a lemon; a dash of Angostura bitters; a liqueur glass full of red or white curaçao; 2 liqueur glassfuls of water. Mix and shake up with crushed ice: then strain. Sufficient for two cocktails.

EAST INDIA COCKTAIL

1½ fl oz (45 ml) brandy   1 tsp curaçao, preferably red
1 tsp pineapple juice   3 dashes Angostura bitters

Shake with crushed ice, strain into a glass. Now add:

1 tsp curaçao   1½ fl oz (45 ml) brandy
1 tsp pineapple syrup

Stir with a spoon and serve with a cherry in a cocktail glass.

A John Collins is described by Alys Firth as 'the famous American drink and nearly everyone who has been to the Bombay Yacht Club knows it. To a bottle of lemonade or tonic add a wineglass of gin – add crushed ice at discretion and suck out of straws. An ideal drink after tennis.' A hot and thirsty game of tennis, indeed, appears to have provided many a justification for a drink:

TENNIS CUP
Into a big jug pour 1 wineglassful of gin and bitters, ¼ gill of ginger syrup, a slice of cucumber and a block of ice. Then pour in simultaneously 2 bottles of fresh lemonade that have been iced in a ice box, and a quart of lager beer.

If the proper ingredients have been used this is an excellent drink. (*Things For The Cook*, by 'Shalot')

From the beginning of the nineteenth century, and particularly with the onset of the Victorian era, hard drinking began to wane. The prevailing morality which now condemned the keeping of Indian mistresses began to level its sights at drunkards as well. 'How many of us are as fit for work, as clear-headed, as even-tempered, as fit for meditation and prayer, after dinner as before?' thundered a Mrs Colonel MacKenzie. 'I have long thought we should abstain from wine and beer (for many ladies in India drink both) in order to redeem the time, to keep our bodies in subjection, and . . . be more able to minister more largely to the wants of others.' Sidney Blanchard writes in 1867 of

the new fashion, introduced of late years with considerable success – of leaving off drinking beer and brandy-panee before a point at which the consequences become disgraceful. Anglo-Indians in the present day are almost as sober as any class of persons I know.

A Victorian army chaplain refused to visit soldiers in hospital whose diseases had been aggravated by alcohol, claiming that these were evidence of God's displeasure at their conduct. Lord Dalhousie was full of consternation at the English soldier's taste for beer, and another Governor-General, Lord Auckland, visited a group of sailors and lectured them on drinking no more than was good for them. In 1868, as a measure to curtail the production of arrack, the Bombay administration ordered the destruction of large numbers of palmyra and date palms at Surat.

While a short drink before lunch was still tolerated in the cities, out in the *mofussil* drinking before sunset and after dinner became frowned upon. Hard drinking at the local club was equally unacceptable. Any member who showed signs of drunkenness would be quickly shunted out, either by friends or by the club secretary, often an ex-army man who stood for no nonsense.

In the army, any private who staggered out of the wet canteen was now likely to be arrested and thrown in the guard house for being drunk. Nevertheless, it would have been impossible to eradicate alcohol in the army, of all places, and some regiments, especially the Scottish and Irish, continued to pride themselves on their drinking prowess. There is a story of an entire regiment getting drunk on the eve of their departure for the First World War. The following morning only the Colonel, his adjutant and 30-odd privates managed to make the march to the railway station. The rest were left drunk on the parade ground or bundled into carts and then loaded aboard the train.

Nor was there any lessening of the social acceptability of alcohol, and indeed there was a distinct peer pressure to partake of a social drink in British India. This is amply illustrated by Isobel Abbott who, recalling a Sunday morning band concert she attended in the 1930s, was asked by the commandant what she would like to drink. She replied that she would like a cup of tea.

For a moment I thought he had not heard me, then I heard him murmur 'Cup of tea? – well I never.' He cleared his throat and shouted 'Bearer, bearer. Memsahib would like a cup of tea.' Everyone stopped talking. They all looked towards us.

After the cup of tea was produced Mrs Abbott was playfully chided for being the first person who had asked for a cup of tea at a Sunday band concert since the mess was created.

At least part of the reason for the massive consumption of alcohol during the first 200 years of British presence in India was that little else was fit to drink. In the early settlements the source of drinking water was often as not badly polluted. In Calcutta, for instance, residents were content to drink from the vast tank of putrid green water still to be seen today near BBD Bag (formerly Dalhousie Square). Both humans and mange-ridden dogs bathed in it, and during the monsoon, from July to September, it would be further contaminated by sewage and seepage from the Portuguese cemetery in the centre of the city.

In Benares an engineer reports in 1790 that one of the main drinking tanks was the receptacle of all the drains and filth of adjacent high grounds, and that people would crowd its banks all day long, 'and the stench occasioned by it is hardly to be described'. Water from the nearby River Ganges, which for thousands of years has been the cremation place for orthodox Hindus, was equally suspect, as was that of the River Hooghly in Calcutta. A ship's captain reported in 1802 that every morning while his ship was at anchor he had to detail a man to free the bodies which had accumulated among the ship's cables overnight.

Rather than purify their water, the early European settlers preferred to disguise its rank flavour with alcohol. The totally erroneous notion that alcohol could somehow counteract the ill-effects of polluted water was being perpetuated as late as the 1840s, by writers such as Mrs Major Clemons, who advised soldiers to drink a mixture of brandy and water while on a march through areas where well water was doubtful.

Eventually the high mortality rate in the larger towns from cholera, typhoid and other waterborne diseases forced the abandonment of public supplies in favour of rain water. Huge earthenware jars were used to collect the rain water as it drained off the roof, and the filled jars were then stored in a godown (storeroom). Captain Williamson states in his *East India Vade Mecum* (1810) that the average family of Calcutta used to set aside sixty or seventy hogsheads (over 3000 gallons) of rain water during the year.

Even rain water had to be purified, a process which in the early days involved plunging in a red-hot iron and then adding a solution of alum to the water. Some people also had a small quantity of very fine sand sprinkled over the surface of the water in the belief that this would precipitate any impurities that remained. Only in Victorian times did people begin boiling the water for 10 to 15 minutes, the only sure way of killing all harmful bacteria. The water then had to be filtered, first through a bowl of sand and then through another of charcoal. By the early part of the twentieth century some residents of Calcutta considered the municipal water sufficiently pure as to drink straight from the tap, although they were careful to draw it off at a point of high pressure, where it was thought less likely to harbour germs.

The other great problem was keeping their drinking water cool, for when, about May, the hot weather reached its peak, cracking lamps and wine glasses and warping furniture at the joints, nobody found the heat more intolerable than the British – whatever Noël Coward might have sung.

It was during these months that the *aubdar* came into his own. His job was to cool not only water and drinks, but also perishable food such as butter and jellies, and, from the eighteenth century, to supervise the making of ice. Later, with the advent of refrigeration, the *aubdar* became an unnecessary retainer in private families, although he was still to be found well into the twentieth century in clubs and messes which kept large wine cellars.

In the seventeenth century drinks were kept cool by immersing the bottle or flask in a solution of saltpetre. The cooling vessel, or *taus*, was shaped like a cylinder, with rounded edges and a round opening in the top. About a gallon of water was poured into this receptacle, a couple of handfuls of saltpetre were thrown in, and then spherical pewter flasks of fresh water were half-immersed in the *taus* for several minutes until the saltpetre dissolved. The long necks of the flasks, projecting up through the opening of the *taus*, were covered with a damp cloth. In about five minutes the water inside them would be quite cool. Later salmoniac was used, as well as saltpetre, and in the nineteenth century, a large variety of sophisticated chemicals, such as nitrates of potash and ammonia, were employed.

Since decanters were liable to crack with the sudden change of temperature, wine was always cooled in the bottle. The bottles thus appeared at the table with silver mounted corks and wrapped in 'petticoats' of wetted cloth. 'Their ugliness', wrote Emma Roberts, 'is compensated by their utility, as the wine is kept cool by the wetted cloths which are somewhat fancifully arranged around the necks of the bottles: port, claret, and Burgundy are characteristically attired in crimson, with white flounces; while sherry and Madeira appear in bridal costume.' To prevent the petticoated bottles wetting the tablecloth, a turned wooden stand was devised.

It was, of course, the host's responsibility to have the wine cooled for the table, but in the Company days a noted *aubdar*, brought along by a guest to cool his master's water, might also be given the honour of cooling the host's wine.

Although effective, cooling by saltpetre was expensive and trouble-some. Gradually it was replaced by a simpler arrangement whereby bottles were put outside in a cage or cradle which was covered by a wet cloth. This was hung from a wooden frame, and allowed to swing in the hot winds, the evaporation from the cloth having the effect of cooling the bottles of drink inside the cage. To keep the cloth wet, its hem rested in a trough of water at the bottom of the cage, and so the water slowly siphoned through the cloth like oil through a lamp wick. Sometimes khus-khus grass was used instead of cloth. In the remoter parts of the *mofussil* the gadget was still in use as late as the 1920s.

At the large British stations in the colder northern regions of India, crude ice-making operations were established in the eighteenth century. The method was very laborious. A flat area of ground was covered with beds of straw, on which were placed shallow saucer-shaped pans filled with water. If the night was frosty and windless, a layer of ice would form on each pan, and early the next morning a team of hundreds of coolies would arrive to gather it. The ice was knocked out of the pans and carried by the basket load to the ice house, where it was tipped into a deep pit lined with matting or reeds. When the night's ice had been dumped, a group of workers descended into the pit and hammered at the ice with mallets in order to let it weld into a solid block. Protecting the pit at ground level was a low circular hut with massive mud walls and a thick thatched roof.

The costs of running these operations were met by subscription to an ice club, a co-operative run along the same lines as a mutton club (see page 144), with a voluntary secretary who ran the accounts and supervised the rationing of the ice. Each member got a daily (or sometimes weekly) ration, which was collected by servants who would put their lump in a canvas bag, wrap it in a thick blanket, and hurry home with it. Once home, the lump of ice would be deposited in a basket containing beer, water, butter and fruit. Later these baskets were replaced by zinc-lined tundices (ice-boxes), with a hole in the bottom to allow the water to drain out.

Although the supplies laid down in the ice house would ideally last the whole of the hot season, in warmer areas such as Allahabad the ice would have run out by August, and people then had to put up with tepid drinks or resort to the old method of cooling with saltpetre.

The solution to the ice problem was found in 1833, when a trial shipment of American apples arrived in Calcutta. Much to the surprise of the ship's owners it was not the apples which caused the sensation, but the ice which had been used to cool them. This fetched a higher price than the apples, and henceforth special American cargo ships kept up a constant supply of ice from Wenham Lake. The first shipment to Bombay landed in 1836, where the coolies who carried it ashore complained it 'scalded' their backs. Later Madras got a regular supply, and when the railway system was introduced, those settlements close to one of the coastal ports could send for the American ice without going to the expense of making their own.

'Artificial ice, made by the assistance of an air pump and other machinery, has been found too expensive, and is seldom or never resorted to in India,' remarked Emma Roberts in 1835, but by the 1870s technology had improved and Carres ice machines, costing £25 each, began to appear at stations all over the interior. They could make about 4 lb of ice in five hours, although they required careful working and might merely produce cold water instead of ice. The process was one of very rapid evaporation, a cylinder charged with ammonia being heated and then plunged into water. 'The natives of Mymensingh had never seen ice before, and when they saw that this very cold stuff was produced from heat, their wonder was very great indeed,' wrote 'Ex-civilian' in 1878.

During the latter part of the nineteenth century ice factories were also established with great enthusiasm, although many of those in more remote areas were later to close down.

Although refrigerators as we know them had been developed in the 1890s, it was not until the 1920s and 30s that they reached Indian homes, and even then only in the larger cities and towns with an electricity supply.

Even the introduction of refrigerators did not totally alleviate the problem of keeping milk, and all milk was boiled before use, not only to prevent it going sour but to kill bacteria.

Milk was supplied by the *gow-wallah*, or cow-keeper. Because the yield of milk of an ordinary Bengali cow was only a pint or even half a pint, in some parts of India the herds numbered into the hundreds. A great deal of the milk supplied by dairies came from buffaloes and, if we are to believe Florence Marryat, writing in 1868, sheep, ponies and even pigs! Buffaloes were used because their output is greater than that of cows and their yielding life longer. For the milk-drinker, buffalo milk had the added advantage of not being a carrier of tuberculosis.

Frequently the milk was diluted with water, although this practice was brought under control in the latter part of the nineteenth century with the growth of regulated jail and regimental dairies. Flora Annie Steel, however, distrusted even these:

She [the author] has seen the demand for butter, cream and milk at some of these institutions treble in a week, and yet be satisfied by a guaranteed supply. How was this done? In England such fluctuating demand can be met without much risk to impurity by tapping other sources. In India there is nothing to fall back on save the bazaar.

In order to guarantee a supply of unadulterated milk in country areas, many English residents kept their own cows. This was an expensive business, however, and most impractical in the cities. In any case, by the early part of the twentieth century pasteurized milk was available from some commercial dairies, such as the English-established firm of Keventas in Calcutta.

Anglo-Indian cookery books were full of advice on how to detect diluted milk. One suggestion was to dip the blade of a perfectly clean knife into the milk: if it was pure, a thickish film would cling to the blade; if it had been adulterated, it would run off the knife in separate waves. Another alternative was to have the cow brought to the house and milked in one's presence, which afforded the memsahib the added advantage of ensuring the health and cleanliness of both cow-keeper and cow. Even then a wily *gow-wallah* was known to resort to tricks, such as partially filling the pail with water before milking began. There is even a case on record of a *gow-wallah* who had a goatskin bag full of water up his arm, which he squeezed into the pail as he milked.

The surest test of the purity of milk was to use a lactometer, as this showed not only if the milk had been diluted, but also if it had been artificially thickened. *Congee* or rice water, being white in colour and very cheap, was often added.

Despite its role as a milk adulterater, the British enjoyed *congee* as a drink in itself, as *The Original Madras Cookery Book* advises:

CONGEE WATER
Wash well a quarter of a pound of broken rice, put into a saucepan with two pints of water and let it simmer until reduced to one pint, strain the quantity required through a piece of muslin; flavour with either salt or sugar and lemon juice; drink when perfectly cold; it will be found most refreshing in fever cases.

17

Chutneys, Pickles and Preserves

—

Rank Injustice
All things chickeney and mutt'ny
Taste better far when served with chutney
This is the mystery eternal:
Why didn't Major Grey make Colonel?
　　　　　　　　　John F. Mackay

Chutneys and Pickles

Derived from the Hindi *chatni*, a chutney differs from a pickle in that sweeteners such as treacle, palm sugar and raisins are used, and that the main ingredients are finely chopped or pulverized rather than kept more or less whole.

Even though the British had been pickling fruit and vegetables in vinegar and brine since Roman times, the sophisticated chutneys they encountered in India came as something of a revelation. To the provisioners of the East India Company ships, these chutneys were the perfect answer to the requirement for foods which could withstand a long sea journey and add variety to the diet of both passengers and crew.

With the increased trade of the late seventeenth century, Indian chutneys and pickles began to reach Britain and became so fashionable that they spawned a host of imitations. From about 1700 onwards in country houses of the southern gentry (for the vogue never penetrated far from the great southern sea ports), cooks were busy turning out imitations of pickled mangoes using marrows, cucumbers, melons, lemons and peaches. Such 'mangoes', as they were called, were made by hollowing out the fruit or vegetable and filling the centre with onions, horseradish, ginger and spices. Marrows were also boiled in spiced syrup to imitate preserved ginger, great stoneware jars of which had also come to England in the East India Company ships. Previously ginger had been brought overland on the backs of camels, and had only been available dried. To those who were acquainted with the flavour of the real thing, it must have taken a fertile imagination to see any resemblance in the 'English bamboo' given in Mrs Rundell's *A New System of Domestic Cookery* (1806) consisting of elder shoots preserved in spiced vinegar.

English imitations of the Indian chutney known as piccalilli were more successful. A recipe of 1694 entitled 'To pickle lila, an Indian pickle' describes a sauce of brine and vinegar, flavoured with ginger, garlic, bruised mustard seed and pepper, with turmeric to turn it the now-familiar yellow, in which were pickled pieces of cabbage, cauliflower, celery and plums. At one time it was also known as Indian pickle, and by the nineteenth century, when Eliza Acton and Mrs Beeton gave recipes for it, the recipe included the pickled pods of radishes which had been allowed to flower and go to seed.

PICCALILLI

1 lb (500 g) pickling onions	4 oz (125 g) sugar
1 small cauliflower	2 oz (50 g) flour
1 small cucumber	2 oz (50 g) dry mustard
8 oz (250 g) green tomatoes	1 oz (25 g) turmeric
8 oz (250 g) French beans	½ oz (15 g) ground ginger
2 green capsicums	2 pt (1.2 l) vinegar, white or malt
4 oz (125 g) salt	1 tsp celery seed

Leave any very small onions whole but chop the rest of the vegetables into small pieces. Sprinkle with the salt, let them stand overnight, then wash and drain well.

In a saucepan, mix together the sugar, flour, mustard, turmeric and ground ginger, then blend to a paste with a little of the vinegar. Stir in the remaining vinegar and the celery seeds, bring the mixture to the boil, stirring constantly, then boil for about 10 minutes, until the sauce is thick.

Pack the vegetables into jars, pour over the hot mustard sauce to cover them completely, and seal.

While obviously deriving their inspiration from Indian recipes, most Anglo-Indian chutneys contain considerably less heating ingredients to suit the tastes of Europeans. More than any other, it was mango chutney which captured the imagination of the British, both in India and 'back home', and it has been one of the most enduring culinary inheritances of the Raj.

Recipes for the chutney are many and diverse, but these two methods from Lucy Carne's *Simple Menus and Recipes for Camp, Home and Nursery* (1919) are typical: the second is probably more familiar to us.

MANGO CHUTNEY
One pound green mangoes, peeled and minced; 2 oz. green ginger peeled and minced; ¼ oz. garlic; 2 oz. dried red chillies ground; ½ lb sugar; 3 oz. salt.

Mix all together and add sufficient vinegar; cork down firmly and put in the sun daily [or put in a low oven for half an hour, then in a warm dry place such as near a hot water cylinder] for a fortnight.

Another way:– Two pounds mangoes; 1½ lb sugar; 2 oz. ginger; 1 oz. garlic; 2 oz. chillies, without seeds; ½ lb raisins; 3 oz. salt; one bottle vinegar.

Peel and slice the mangoes; make a thick syrup with the sugar and a little water; pound half the green ginger and thinly slice the rest; pick, wash and dry the raisins; pound the garlic with vinegar; break up half the chillies into little bits and grind the rest in vinegar. Boil the mangoes in the syrup until thick, mix all the other ingredients with the mangoes (except the raisins) and boil for quarter of an hour; add the raisins and stand to cool.

In Delhi, far from the prime mango-growing regions of the south, the chutney was often made with expensive dried mango eked out with raisins, while in Bengal plums and tamarind were popular additions. Indeed, the sweet-sour flavour of tamarind proved so suitable for chutney that it dominated some recipes, such as this from *The Englishwoman in India* by 'A Lady Resident' (1865):

BOLARUM CHUTNEE
3 lbs kismis [raisins], 3 lbs tamarinds, 3 lbs green ginger, 3 lbs brown sugar, 1 lb onions, 15 ounces green chillies, 4 or 5 green mangoes, 3 dessertspoons salt.

Beat each to a pulp and clean from stones and fibres: then weigh and mix. Strain through a mosquito net, and use three pints of vinegar in pounding it: it will be ready in a fortnight, and is by far the best chutnee I know.

The very blandness of green papaya, on the other hand, was seen as a convenient vehicle for fiery flavourings, such as Beatrice Vieyra's Pachad Pickle:

PAPAYA PACHAD PICKLE

REQUIRED:— One green papaiya fruit, a heaped tablespoon each of finely chopped green chillies, garlic, dried chillies, ginger, a dessertspoon cleaned mustard, 1 stick saffron, 1 tablespoon sugar, 1½ coffee cups vinegar, salt.

METHOD:— Skin fruit and wash it, hold the papaiya in the hand and with a fine knife chop it well. Discard inside portion. Take 3½ large coffee cupsful papaiya, boil 10 minutes in water, drain (to remove stain in fruit). Dry in sun a day. Next day prepare pickle. Place vinegar on fire and mix in ground saffron. When it boils, throw in the chopped ingredients and papaiya. Keep on the fire 5 minutes only. Remove and cool. Mix in mustard and sugar. Add salt, place in jars. Vinegar should just soak the ingredients, no gravy.

Apart from mango, the most popular pickle in India was (and still is) that made of lemons or limes. These lemon or lime pickles are associated especially with the cooking of Gujarat. A similar method of salting and preserving lemons exists in North African cookery. The fruit may either be served whole, or quartered.

LEMON PICKLE

Cut thirty lemons or fine skinned limes (kagzi neemboo) with two cuts, so that each lemon should be cut only half-way down; remove as many seeds as you can without bruising the pulp of the lemon. Rub each lemon with salt, using six or seven ounces for this purpose; put the salted lemons in a large jar, and keep the jar in the sunshine for three days. Now pour off the juice and fill each lemon with some powder made as follows:— A quarter of a pound of mustard seed, one ounce of fenugreek (maithee) and one ounce of turmeric, each finely pounded separately, then mixed together. Pack your lemons closely together in a large stoppered jar, then pour back the salt juice, and if this is not enough to cover the lemons, squeeze the juice from some more lemons to make up the deficiency.

This recipe was given me by a Brahmin lady who was considered an excellent cook. Very good with cold meat, curry and rice, etc. (From *Baker and Cook: A Domestic Manual for India*, by Mrs R. Temple-Wright.)

Beatrice Vieyra suggests preparing limes in a similar fashion:

REQUIRED:— 35 limes fresh and ripe, 5 tablespoons white salt, 40 dried chillies, 1 heaped tablespoon of coriander, 1 bit saffron, 2 teaspoons each of cummin-seed, mustard and sufficient vinegar.

METHOD:— Wash and wipe the limes and then cut each lime into four parts, but do not break the parts; stuff them with the currystuff broiled and pounded and mixed with the salt. Arrange the limes in a jar and pour in sufficient vinegar to cover the limes.

The pickle will be ready for use within a fortnight.

And *The Original Madras Cookery Book* includes a very hot version:

LUCKNOW CHUTNEY

Limes 2 seers; sugar ½ seer; raisins or plums ½ seer; chillies, ginger, garlic, salt, each ¼ seer; vinegar ¾ of a bottle.

Quarter the limes and soak them in the salt for three days, putting them daily in the sun and mixing; on the second day soak the raisins, chillies, ginger, and garlic in a little vinegar; the next day grind to a paste, remove the seeds, and pound the limes in a marble mortar to a pulp, mix well with the ground stuff and sugar, adding just enough vinegar to make it into a thick chatney.

Care should be taken not to touch with the hand when grinding, &c., use wooden spoons as pickles touched spoil soon.

The introduction of European fruits opened up possibilities for a whole new range of chutneys. Sweet and hot apple chutney, such as this one from Alys Firth's *Dainty Cookery for Camp*, has in particular remained an integral part of Indian cuisine.

BENGAL CLUB CHUTNEY

Four a half pounds large apples, ½ lb sugar, ½ lb small raisins, ¼ lb green ginger (pounded), ¼ lb ground salt, ½ lb mustard seed (bruised), ¼ lb garlic, chopped, and ½ chittack cayenne. Split the apples, take out the core and pare them very carefully. Put them into a pan with ¼ lb sugar and a little water. Boil till quite tender, then with a wooden spoon beat it to a pulp. Add all the ingredients to the pulp, mix well, adding a little boiled vinegar to make it nice and thick. This chutney will keep for 2 or 3 years if cooked and prepared according to directions.

In *'What' and 'How'*, E. S. Poynter uses gooseberries in a chutney called 'Tippari', in which turmeric (*huldy*) joins the usual flavourings of ginger and chilli.

TIPPARI CHUTNEE

One seer gooseberries, 5 chittacks raisins, ½ do. garlic, all chopped, 2½ chittacks sugar, 1½ [oz] green ginger, ½ [oz] red chillies, all ground, 1½ [oz] salt, 1 bottle vinegar, 8 knots huldy ground. Mix all together and boil 15 minutes. Cool and bottle.

Tomato chutney, like mango, has become an established 'English' recipe. This sweet and spicy version is a speciality of the Anglo-Indian community of Calcutta:

TOMATUR CHUTNEY

2–2½ lb (1 kg) tomatoes
6 fl oz (175 ml) cider vinegar
3 tbsp dried tamarind paste,
  broken into small pieces
1 tbsp root ginger, finely chopped
4 cloves garlic, crushed

1–2 fresh green chillies, minced
4 cardamom pods
4 cloves
2 tsp ground cinnamon
8 oz (250 g) sugar

Cover the tomatoes with boiling water, leave for several minutes, then peel off the skins. Chop the tomato flesh roughly.

Bring half the vinegar to the boil and add the tamarind paste. Leave for five minutes, then press through a sieve to remove pith and stones. Place the other half of the vinegar in a large pot and add the tomatoes. Cook over a medium heat for 5 minutes, then add ginger, garlic, chilli, cardamoms, cloves and cinnamon. Stir well, then add the strained tamarind liquid and the sugar.

Keep stirring over a low heat for another 5–10 minutes, until the chutney thickens. Allow to cool, then bottle. It will keep under refrigeration for several months.

Vegetables never remained fresh for long in the heat of India, and in many areas it was impractical to preserve them by drying, due to the humidity. The solution was to pickle them, an old and familiar English technique which also made for variety.

RED CABBAGE PICKLE

Clean, quarter and slice thin, sprinkle well with salt and set away for 48 hours. Pour off all water. Then pour over the cabbage hot vinegar in which has been boiled 1 ounce salt, ¼ ounce whole black peeper, 2 sticks mace or five pieces jaipatti, 2 sticks of cinnamon and 1 tea-spoon of cloves. Very sour and appetising. (From *Dainty Cookery for the Home*, by Margaret Denning, 1911.)

A recipe for the chilli vinegar called for 'to impart a warm flavour' to Dr Riddell's pickled onions is given on page 224.

ONION PICKLE

Take any quantity of small white onions, lay them on a sieve or basket and sprinkle them well with salt; let them remain for 24 hours to drain; put them into wide mouthed bottles with a few slices of green ginger and a blade or two of mace; fill up with good vinegar; and if you desire to impart a warm flavour add either green chillies or chilli vinegar.

They may or may not be put in the sun for a day or two.

' "Try a chili with it, Miss Sharp," ' said Joseph Sedley in *Vanity Fair*.
' "A chily?" said Rebecca gasping. "Oh, yes! . . . How fresh and green
they look," she said and put one into her mouth. It was hotter than the
curry; flesh and blood could bear it no longer.'

Pickling chillies is a good way to remove some of their fire while
retaining their flavour.

CHILLI PICKLE

Fifty fresh green chillies, slit them a little at the points and soak for three days in a
strong brine of salt and water; drain well and place in a dry stone jar with three
dozen cloves of garlic peeled; pour over the whole a pint of the best boiled
vinegar which has been thoroughly cooled; cover close. This pickle will be ready
for use in a week. (From *The Original Madras Cookery Book*.)

'Bombay chillies have a better flavour than up-country chillies, so get
them if you can,' advised Mrs Temple-Wright in *Baker and Cook*:

CHILLI VINEGAR

Cut four ounces of green chillies in two, lengthwise, put them into a bowl, and
add one glass of sherry, and a teaspoonful of sugar. Boil a quart of English
vinegar, and pour it boiling hot on the chillies; let it stand for three days, then
strain and bottle it. In decanting for the cruet, don't disturb the sediment.

Make more than one bottle at a time, for you will require it for very many
purposes.

Enormously popular in Victorian times, mushroom ketchup was more
extravagant than chilli vinegar, in that the mushrooms had to provide
liquid as well as flavour. (The leftover mushrooms from this recipe can,
however, be baked into a loaf with beaten eggs and chopped fresh herbs.)

MUSHROOM KETCHUP

4–4½ lb (2 kg) mushrooms	1 tsp allspice
8 oz (250 g) salt	1 tsp cloves
2 tsp black peppercorns	brandy if wished
2 tsp nutmeg or mace	

Wipe but do not wash or peel the mushrooms, chop and place in an
earthenware jar or bowl with salt sprinkled between the layers. Leave
for two days, stirring from time to time after the first 12 hours.

Cook them, still in the jar or bowl, for 30 minutes in a cool oven
(140°C/275°F/Gas Mark 1).

Strain off the liquid without mashing the mushrooms, add the
spices, and boil to reduce to half its original quantity.

Allow the sediment to settle, then strain off into 2 small bottles. Top them up with a dash of brandy if desired, and cork or seal.

In direct contrast to the store-cupboard chutneys which need substantial quantities of salt, sugar, vinegar and oil to preserve them, are chutneys made fresh each day. While the British ate them, they do not ever seem to have enjoyed the same popularity outside India. They are eaten as an accompaniment to rice and some not overly spicy meat or vegetable dishes.

MRS TEMPLE-WRIGHT'S FRESH CHUTNEYS

FRESH MANGO CHUTNEY is made thus:— Pare and mince very finely as much green mango as will fill a large tablespoon; then pound to a paste a piece of fresh cocoanut about two inches square, with one green chilli, a little salt, a bit of ginger the size of an eight-anna piece, and a squeeze of onion juice; mix together and serve.

TOMATO CHUTNEY:— Mince up two ripe tomatoes, and keep them for fifteen minutes in a small plate tilted so as to let the juice run off; then mince finely one very small young onion, a tiny bit of ginger, and two green chillies; add these to the minced tomato, with a little salt and a teaspoonful of lemon juice, and serve.

MINT CHUTNEY:— One tablespoonful of mint pounded to a paste, with lemon juice and a little salt, is very nice with cold meat.

GREEN CHUTNEY:— Pound to a paste a quarter of a fresh cocoanut with a little lemon juice, and two or three green chillies; grind separately some leaves of the coriander plant (dhunnia), squeeze away the juice in a piece of muslin, and put the green curds that remain into the cocoanut paste; add a little salt, mix well together, and serve with kitchcree, or with rice and fried fish.

FRESH APPLE CHUTNEY

Mince two large green apples. Throw them into salted water for a few minutes. Then drain carefully, add two tablespoonsful sliced young onions, four green chillies sliced, one small cupful minced cocoanut, the juice of a small lemon. Mix well and serve in a glass dish with curry and rice. (From *Indian Chutneys, Pickles and Preserves*, by L.V., 1914.)

Preserved Eggs, Fish and Meat

The preoccupation of British India with the pickling, salting and drying of eggs and meat is understandable. In remote areas of the country slaughter of animals tended to be sporadic, and provided more meat than could be used immediately. In the absence of refrigeration, armies of bacteria would begin work in the tropical heat, spoiling fresh meat in just a few days, and fish in a matter of hours. Preservation was thus the only way to ensure an even supply. In time, a virtue was made of necessity and spices were added to the vinegar or salt, in order to improve the flavour.

From E. S. Poynter's *'What' and 'How'* we have an example of another store-cupboard standby for when the hens were off laying:

PICKLED EGGS

Boil 1 oz. ginger, 1 teaspoonful cloves, a blade of mace, 1 teaspoonful peppercorns in 1 quart vinegar. Leave it to steep for 3 days, strain, and add the eggs hard boiled and shelled.

Calcutta's status as an international port probably accounts for the adoption by the Anglo-Indian community there of Indonesian *belachan*, or shrimp paste, popularized as ballychow. Here is Henrietta Hervey's version:

BALLACHOW

Wash, head, tail and shell a pound of small sized prawns (if possible, not larger than those we get out yonder) and pound or grind them to a paste. Take six dry chillies or capsicums, a tablespoonful of salt, one whole garlic, two ounces of green ginger, and a pint of tamarind water. Mix these ingredients with half a pound butter; add the prawn paste, and amalgamate the whole mass. Keep in glass bottles. When required for use, fry the paste with chopped onion and a little lemon peel. To be eaten as a zest with curry, or with bread and butter.

The pungent paste, sometimes referred to as 'nappey' goes into one of Calcutta's most famous specialities:

TOMATO BALLYCHOW

2–2½ lb (1 kg) ripe tomatoes	¼ pt (150 ml) cider vinegar
8 cloves garlic, crushed	4 fl oz (125 ml) peanut oil
2 in (5 cm) piece fresh ginger root, finely chopped	1 tsp salt
	1 tbsp shrimp paste
1 tbsp dried chilli flakes	

Cover the tomatoes with boiling water, leave several minutes, then remove and peel the skins. Chop roughly and set aside.

Steep the garlic, ginger root and chilli flakes in half the vinegar for 15 minutes. Process to a purée in a blender/food processor or with a mortar and pestle.

Over a low heat, heat the oil in a pan and add the puréed condiments, the remaining vinegar and the salt. Fry for one minute, stirring constantly, then add the tomatoes and shrimp paste. Simmer, uncovered, over a low heat for about 20 minutes, or until the mixture is reduced to a thick paste.

Cool before bottling. This will keep for eight or nine months under refrigeration.

PRAWN PADDA

Based on the vindaloo spice mixture, this recipe from the Anglo-Indian community of Goa is for preserving prawns rather than converting them to paste.

2½ fl oz (70 ml) peanut oil
2 tsp turmeric
1 tsp chilli powder
1 tsp ground cumin
½ tsp fenugreek seeds
8 fl oz (250 ml) malt vinegar

5 cloves garlic, crushed
2 in (5 cm) piece root ginger, finely chopped
8 red chillies, finely chopped
1 lb (500 g) dried salted prawns, shrimp or fish

Heat the oil in a large saucepan or frying pan and add the turmeric, chilli powder, cumin and fenugreek seeds. Cook for five minutes, stirring frequently, then add the vinegar, garlic, ginger and chillies. Bring to the boil, add the prawns and simmer for 4–5 minutes only. Bottle when cool. The padda will keep for many months under refrigeration.

The padda spice mixture could also be adapted to pork or beef, but another popular method for preserving pork was widespread in Goa, where the 400-year rule of the Portuguese had established a large Christian – and therefore pork-eating – community. There are many variations on Vinde Auly or Vinde Aulx, but this is the recipe to be found in *The Original Madras Cookery Book by An Old Lady Resident*.

VINDE AULX

Six pounds of the belly part of pork (not too young), cut into pieces four inches square; rub on all sides well with salt and put into an earthenware pan for twelve hours; then set the pieces to dry on a tray covered with a towel for six or eight hours; then make a pickle as follows: take a quarter of a pound of red chillies, quarter of a pound of cumin seed, two ounces of turmeric, quarter of a pound of garlic, quarter of a pound of green ginger; grind all these ingredients to a paste with vinegar; then dilute with more vinegar until of a liquid consistence; dip each piece in the mixture and pack closely in a stone jar; pour over the whole the remainder of the pickle; it will be ready for use in three weeks, when two or three pieces can be taken (according to the quantity required) and cooked in a frying pan with some water until the curry stuff begins to look curdled, when it is ready to serve.

Especially favoured by travellers was Ding Ding – slices of beef rubbed with salt and cayenne and hung up to dry, rather like the South African biltong or the beef jerky of the American West. (Mrs Franklin, in her recipe below, warns against attracting the attention of scavenging birds . . .) An elaboration of this method, known as Ding Dong, involved rubbing the beef with a mixture of saffron, garlic and sugar prior to salting.

DING-DING
REQUIRED:– 1 lb of beef, 1 oz of dry chillies, ½ oz of turmeric, 4 oz of salt.
TO MAKE:– Cut the beef into steaks; grind the dry chillies, and turmeric, pound the salt.

Put the steaks in a bowl, and with a steel fork and wooden spoon rub the mussala and salt well into them, turning each steak repeatedly, then allow all to stand for three hours.

Now cut a small hole with the point of the knife through the centre of each steak, and thread each steak on some strong crochet cotton, and hang them out to dry in the sun, taking care, however, that the crows do not get at the steaks. Bring the ding-ding in at night, but repeat the drying for three days, when it can be put away for use. If kept long it should be occasionally hung out in the sun to dry.

Ding-ding should be slightly roasted on hot coals, pounded on a curry stone, roasted again, pounded again, and served crisp.

Bibliography

A. C. S. *see* Spry

Acton, Eliza, *Modern Cookery for Private Families*, London, 1845

Abbott, Mrs Isobel [Babbott], *Indian Interval*, London, 1960

Alicia *see* Shelton

Anglo-Indian, An *see* Bartley

Anon, *The East India Sketch Book*, 1832

Anon, *Dainty Dishes for Indian Tables*, Calcutta, 1879

Anon, *Sleepy Sketches from Bombay*, London, 1877

Atkinson, George Franklin, *Curry and Rice on Forty Plates*, London, 1859

Babbott *see* Abbott

Baldwin, Capt. J. H., *Large and Small Game of Bengal and the N. W. Provinces of India*, 1876

Balfour, Dr E., *Cyclopaedia of India*, London, 3rd ed., 1885

Bartley, Mrs J. [An Anglo-Indian], *Indian Cookery 'General' for Young Housekeepers*, Bombay, 4th ed., 1901

Beeton, Mrs Isabella, *The Book of Household Management*, London, 1861, 1888, 1910

Bemister, Clara Louise, *Vegetarian Menus*, Madras, 1917

Bengalee, A *see* Fenton

Blanchard, Sidney, *Yesterday and To-Day in India*, London, 1867

Bobb, Eleanor, *The Raj Cook Book*, New Delhi, 1981

Braddon, Edward, *Life in India*, London, 1872

Bradley, E. G., *A Household Book for Tropical Colonies*, Oxford, 1948

Brooks, T., *Weights, Measures, Exchanges &c., in East India*, 1752

Brown, Hilton (ed.), *The Sahibs: The Life and Ways of the British in India*, London, 1948

Browne, Capt. C. M., *Bombay Ducks*, Bombay, 1876

Bunyard, Edward and Lorna *et al*, *The Epicure's Companion*, London, 1937

Burke, W. S., *Every-day Menus for Indian Housekeepers*, Calcutta, 3rd ed., 1909

Burton, R. F., *Goa and the Blue Mountains*, 1851

Busteed, H. E., *Echoes of Old Calcutta*, Calcutta, 1882

Buyers, Rev. W., *Recollections of Northern India*, London, 1848

Carey, W. H., *The Good Old Days of Honble. John Company*, Simla, 1882

Carne, Lucy, *Simple Menus and Recipes for Camp, Home and Nursery*, Calcutta, 1919

C. C. K. *see* Kohlhoff

Chakravarty, Indira, *Saga of Indian Food: A Historical and Cultural Survey*, New Delhi, 1972

Chota Sahib, *Camp Recipes for Camp People*, Madras, 1890

Civilian, A *see* D'Oyly

Clemons, Mrs Major, *The Manners and Customs of Society in India*, London, 1841

Colchester-Wemyss, Sir Francis, *The Pleasures of the Table*, London, 1931

Cook, G. H., *The English-Indian Cookery Book*, Agra, c. 1904

Crawford Wilkin, Elizabeth, *Dekho! The Indian That Was*, New Hampshire, 1958

David, Elizabeth, *Spices, Salt and Aromatics in the English Kitchen*, London, 1970

Day, Harvey, *Curries of India*, Bombay, 1963

Denning, Mrs Margaret B., *Dainty Cookery for the Home*, Madras, 3rd ed., 1911

Dewar, Douglas, *In the Days of the Company*, London, 1926

Dias, P. D., *The Goan Cook's Guide*, Bangalore, 1926

Dodwell, Henry, *The Nabobs of Madras*, London, 1926

D'Oyly, Charles, *The Costumes and Customs of Modern India*, London, n.d.

—— [A Civilian] *Tom Raw, the Griffin*, London, 1846

E. A. M. F. *see* Franklin

Eden, Emily, *Up the Country*, London, 1866

Edwardes, Michael, *Bound to Exile*, London, 1969

Edwards, Marie, *Delicious Food for India*, Calcutta, 1935

E. S. P. *see* Poynter

Ex-civilian, *Life in the Mofussil*, London, 1878

Falkland, Viscountess, *Chow Chow, being Selections from a Journal kept in India, &c.*, 1857

Fay, Mrs Eliza, *The Original Letters from India*, Calcutta, 1866

Fenton, A. [A Bengali], *Memoirs of a Cadet*, London, 1839

Firth, Alys, *Dainty Cookery for Camp and Other Recipes*, Benares, 1905

Framji, Navroji, *Indian Cookery 'Local' for Young Housekeepers*, Bombay 1883

Franklin, E. A. M. [E. A. M. F.], *The Wife's Cookery Book*, Madras, 1906

Fryer, John, *A New Account of East India and Persia*, London, 2nd ed., 1698

Ghosh, Suresh Chandra, *The Social Condition of the British Community in Bengal 1757–1800*, Leiden, 1970

G. L. R. *see* Routleff

Gordon, Constance E., *Anglo-Indian Cuisine (Khana Kitab)*, Calcutta, 1913

Greenberg, Sheldon and Lambert Ortiz, Elizabeth, *The Spice of Life*, London 1983

Haldar, Mrs J., *Bengal Sweets*, Calcutta, 1921

Hare, R. A. P., *Tasty Dishes of India*, Bombay, 4th reprint, 1980

Heber, Bishop Reginald, *Narrative of a Journey through the Upper Provinces of India*, 3rd ed., 1878

Hervey, Henrietta A., *Anglo-Indian Cookery at Home: A Short Treatise for Returned Exiles by the wife of a retired Indian Officer*, London, 1895

Hickey, William, *see* Spencer

Hull, C. P. (Edmund), *The European in India, or Anglo-Indian's Vade Mecum*, London, 1871

Indian Military Manual of Cookery and Dietry, Simla, 1940

Indian Officer, An, *Society in India*, London, 1841

Jerdon, T. C., *Jerdon's Birds: The Birds of India*, London, 1874

—— *Jerdon's Mammals: The Mammals of India*, London, 1874

Kenney-Herbert, Col. [Wyvern], *Culinary Jottings for Madras*, Madras, 1878

—— *Sweet Dishes*, Madras, 1881

Khan, S. N. M., *The Finest Indian Muslim Cooking*, London, 1934

Kincaid, Dennis, *British Social Life in India*, London, 1938

Kinney, T., *Old Times in Assam*, Calcutta, 1896

Kohlhoff, C. C. [C. C. K.], *Indian Cookery and Domestic Recipes*, Madras, 2nd ed., 1906

Lady, A *see* Maitland

Lady Resident, A, *The Englishwoman in India*, London, 2nd ed., 1865

Lang, Monica, *Invitation to Tea*, London, 1953

Lawrance, Harriet, *Cookery for the Million, being 333 practical, ecconomical recipes in Indian cookery*, Madras, 1904

Lodwick, R. W., *Humorous Sketches of the World We Live In*, Bombay, 1851

L. V., Indian *Chutneys, Pickles and Preserves*, Calcutta, 1914

Maitland, Julia Charlotte [A Lady], *Letters from Madras during the Years 1836, 1839, 1843*

Mandelslo, J. A., *Voyages and Travels of J. A. Mandelslo into the East Indies*, 1669

Markham, Gervase, *The English Hus-wife*, 1615; 4th ed., 1631

Marryat, Florence, *'Gup': Sketches of Anglo-Indian Life and Character*, London, 1868

Menkel, H. Carlson, *Healthful Diet for India*, Lahore, 1927

Old Lady Resident, An, *The Original Madras Cookery Book*, Madras, 1874

Oman, C. P. A., *Eastwards, or Realities of Indian Life*, London, 1864

Ovington, Rev. F., *A Voyage to Suratt in the Year 1689*, London, 1696

Parkes, Fanny, *Wanderings of a Pilgrim in Search of the Picturesque*, 1850

Pinkham, Mildred Worth, *A Bungalow in India*, New York, 1928

Poynter, E. S. [E. S. P.], *'What' and 'How' or What shall we have and How shall we have it?*, Calcutta, 1904

Pringle, A. T., *Selections from the Consultations of the Agent, Governor and Council of Fort St George, 1681*, Madras, 1893

Quiz, *The Grand Master of Adventures of Qui Hi? in Hindustan*, London, 1816

Rawlinson, H. G., *Life in English Factory in India in the Seventeenth Century*, Calcutta, 1921

Richards, Philip, *Indian Dust*, London, 1932

Riddell, Dr. R., *Indian Domestic Economy and Receipt Book*, Madras, 1850, 7th ed., 1870

Roberts, Emma, *Scenes and Characteristics of Hindostan*, London, 1835

Roe, Sir Thomas, *Embassy to the Court of the Great Mogul, 1615–19*, ed. W. Foster, 1899

Routleff, G. L. [G. L. R.], *The Economical Cookery Book (for India)*, Calcutta, 1926

Rundell, E., *A New System of Domestic Cookery*, 1806

'Shalot', *Things for the Cook*, Calcutta, 2nd ed., 1914

Shelton, Mrs A. K. [Alicia], *Dainty Confections: 400 Splendid Recipes for Puddings, Bread, Cakes and Sweets*, Calcutta, 1918

Spear, Percival, *The Nabobs. A Study of the Social Life of the English in Eighteenth Century India*, Curzon Press, 1932

Spencer, Alfred, (ed.), *Memoirs of William Hickey*, London, 1913–25

Spry, Angela C. [A. C. S.], *The Mem Sahibs Book of Cookery*, Allahabad, 2nd ed., 1894

Stanford, J. K. (ed.), *Ladies in the Sun: The Memsahib's India 1790–1860*, London, 1962

Steel, F. A. and Gardiner, G., *The Complete Indian Housekeeper and Cook*, 1898

Stewart, J. L., *Punjab Plants*, Lahore, 1869

Subaltern, A, *Recollections of the East*, n.d.

Swayne, Thomas, *Indian Summer*, London, 1981

Tayler, William, *Thirty-eight Years in India*, London, 1881

Temple-Wright, Mrs R., *Baker and Cook: A Domestic Manual for India*, 2nd ed., 1894

Terry, Edward, *A Voyage to East India*, reprint 1777

Thirty-five Years Resident, A, *The Indian Cookery Book*, Calcutta, 6th ed., 1944

Vieyra, Beatrice, *Culinary Art Sparklets*, Madras, 1904

Watt, G., *A Dictionary of the Economic Products of India*, Calcutta, 1889–93

Williamson, Capt. Thomas, *The East India Vade Mecum*, 1810

Wilson, Emma, *Gone with the Raj*, London, 1974

Woodford, Peggy, *Rise of the Raj*, London, 1978

Woodruff, Philip, *The Men Who Ruled India*, London, 1953

Wyvern, *see* Kenney-Herbert

Yule, Sir Henry, and Burnell, A. C., *Hobson-Jobson, A Glossary of Colloquial Anglo-Indian Words and Phrases*, London, 1903

Index

——